Trivial Pursuit™

TV

TV EDITION
Quiz book
‖ ·PARRAGON· ‖

TV EDITION

First published in Great Britain in 1993 by Boxtree Limited.
Questions © 1993 Horn Abbot International Ltd.
Trivial Pursuit is a Registered Trademark of
Horn Abbot International Ltd.

Horn Abbot International Ltd., Villa Franca,
Hastings, Christchurch, Barbados, West Indies.

1 3 5 7 9 10 8 6 4 2

Designed and typeset by Swann, Pearce, Jeanes Ltd.
Printed and bound in Portugal, by Printer Portuguesa for
Parragon Book Services Limited.

A CIP catalogue entry for this book is available from
the British Library.

ISBN 0-75251-182-3

Photographs courtesy of the
Hulton Deutsch Picture Library,
Syndication International,
Scope Features, NME and Channel 4.

Trivial Pursuit™

· C O N T E N T S ·

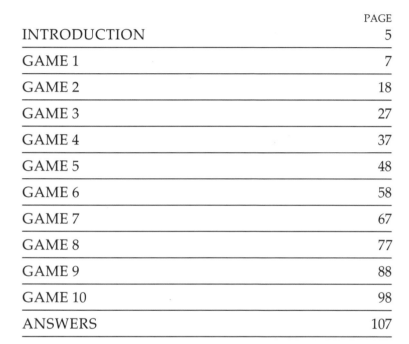

Trivial Pursuit™

· I N T R O D U C T I O N ·

I became obsessed by Muffin the Mule at the age of five. We didn't have a television and my parents couldn't quite understand why Sunday afternoon visits to previously avoided TV-owning aunts suddenly became so attractive to me.

■ The Coronation brought TV to the nation but in the 1980s it suddenly became fashionable to turn off the set and bring out the latest edition of **Trivial Pursuit**. I write the questions so you will understand that I don't spend my evenings playing the game. While you've been sticking your wedges into your cheeses I've been watching the TV and this book is the result of my tele-viewing.

■ I find it amazing how many people accept a fact as being carved in stone if they've seen or heard it on television. Even soap characters have become part of real life in many households, which is why I like to dig just a little deeper in the hope that I can make you think, make you smile and, hopefully, keep you just as entertained as the box in the corner.

■ I once noticed that the Rovers Return in **Coronation Street** shared a wall with Albert Tatlock's house. However, when the cameras showed the inside of the pub (a studio set) this was the wall in which the door to the gents toilet was situated. In other words, the male drinkers in the Rovers Return were "going" in poor old Albert's kitchen. This was encapsulated in a **Trivial Pursuit** question and three months later the Rovers was burnt down to be rebuilt along slightly different architectural lines.

■ I'm not saying that I was to blame for the **Coronation Street** fire, but I am warning that TV faces and places come and go, and this book contains many ghosts who will still be with us when the little dot of light disappears at the end of the day. I hope you enjoy meeting them all again.

Brian Highley.
U.K. Trivial Pursuit compiler.

1

SD Which actor died in *Coronation Street* and turned up in *Brookside* with a drug problem?

SS Which product's name was written in a trail of salt in a TV commercial?

FG Which *Russ Abbot Madhouse* regular was a *Hi De Hi* entertainer?

FF Which Welsh actor narrated the ITV coverage of the Prince of Wales' investiture?

IP Which TV brothers were black and white?

EH Which cartoon character has an anchor tattooed on his arm?

2

SD Whose hit *The Sideboard Song* was used for a beer commercial?

SS Who were sharp enough to become the world's first sponsors of a televised sporting event?

FG What was Mrs Miggins's job in *Black Adder the Third*?

FF Which acting superstar was made-up to play a Red Indian on *Gunsmoke*?

IP Which TV title character went on the run from his job as a Sandman and tried to find Sanctuary?

EH What subject was Del Boy's brother Rodney studying?

3

SD Which comedy duo's show included a dance group called *Foxy Feeling*?

SS Where did Joe Sugden and Kate go for their honeymoon?

FG What are these two comic's first names?

FF Which famous funnyman's TV parents were played by Twiggy and Ian McShane?

IP Who rode an elephant called Bimbo?

EH What was the subject of the 1960s TV series *Gallery*?

4

SD Which TV clean-up campaigners had a hit with *Minuetto Allegretto*?

SS Who was kidnapped from *The Colbys* by a UFO and turned up on *Dynasty*?

FG Which series features a painter and decorator called Jacko?

FF Which of the *Monty Python* team played an art critic in *Dr. Who*?

IP Which Alan Bleasdale offering won the BAFTA Drama award in 1982?

EH Which comedy series starred Dave King and Joe Marcell wandering through life as two fanciful tramps?

Photo: Syndication International Ltd

Photo: Hulton Deutsch

5

SD Which pop group was Anita Pallenberg associated with in TV news broadcasts of the '60s?

SS Which soap is based on a book by Richard and Esther Shapiro?

FG Which Welsh comedian provided some of the voices for *The Tellygoons*?

FF Which '60s star always ended his show in a white E-type?

IP Which Alan Plater adaptation for television starred Kenneth Branagh as Guy Pringle?

EH What was the title of *Bonanza* changed to?

6

SD What five syllables does Fred Flintstone yell when elated?

SS Which *Dallas* actor's feet filled the flippers of *The Man from Atlantis*?

FG What is the name of Del Boy's local pub in *Only Fools and Horses*?

FF Whose most famous role was Amos Burke?

IP Which TV title character was a stunt man with pals called Jody and Howie?

EH Who parked the horses when Maverick visited a stable called *77 Cherokee Strip*?

7

SD How many children were there in *The Partridge Family*?

SS Which city's detention centre was Alexis Colby held in whilst awaiting trial for murder?

FG Who drove the bus if Bob Grant was the conductor?

FF Which conjurer launched this furry fellow's career?

IP Why was Juliet Bravo so called?

EH Which series had Nick Anderson chasing crooks in the first half of each episode and John Egan defending them in the second half?

8

SD Who were the very last band to perform on *Thank Your Lucky Stars*?

SS Where did Ken Barlow's father get the money from that enabled him to move out of *Coronation Street*?

FG Which Saturday afternoon quiz show was hosted by Dickie Davies?

FF Which *Wind in the Willows* narrator played Lord Peter Wimsey?

IP How many years had the Majestics been together at the start of *Tutti Frutti*?

EH What did Bill Anderson change his name to prior to pulling on his underpants over his tights?

SD Which Paul McCartney composition did Cilla Black sing as the theme for her 1968 series?

SS Which chocolate bar commercial featured a race between a red car and a blue car?

FG What is the *Munsters'* pet dragon called?

FF What is Terry Wogan's first name?

IP Which TV detective was played by one-armed actor Donald Gray?

EH Who once said on television: "And I hope your doughnuts turn out like Fanny's"?

SD Which trumpeter sang *This Guy's In Love With You* on the *Beat of the Brass* TV special?

SS Which soap saw Jason Gioberti die in its first episode?

FG Who played Josephine opposite Ernie Wise's Napoleon?

FF Who played the English 'Maverick'?

IP Which light-hearted series saw Frank Windsor as the owner of a Rolls-Royce?

EH Who supposedly owned the car that *Starsky and Hutch* travelled in?

SD What was the first *Top of the Pops* number one to be credited just to Paul McCartney?

SS What claimed to make you feel better "When you wished you hadn't eaten the whole thing"?

FG What was Marty Feldman's first BBC series called?

FF Which American cop actor was said to be television's highest paid actor at the end of the 1970s?

IP Which young superhero is played by John Haymes Newton?

EH Which title character wrote for a women's magazine in a series starring Phyllis Calvert and Penelope Keith?

SD Which Berlin hit featured in the *Top Gun* video?

SS What eight words ended the commercials in which chocolates were delivered by a man in black?

FG What was the family relationship between Reginald Perrin and Jimmy?

FF Which boxer handed Princess Anne her BBC Sports Personality of the Year trophy?

IP What does I.M.F. stand for on *Mission Impossible*?

EH What ended with the words: "so it's goodnight from me, and it's goodnight from him"?

SD Who is the richest person to have accepted a bit-part on *Bread*?

SS What was Miles's favourite sport in *The Colbys*?

FG Who was the investigative reporter in *A Kick Up the Eighties*?

FF Which *Moody and Pegg* actress played Mrs Christmas in *Santa Claus, The Movie*?

IP What item of jewellery did Robbie Box often have to pawn to finance his gambling?

EH Which English county was the setting for *The Farming Week*?

SD Which eastern city did Mick Jagger and David Bowie shout "Hello" to at the start of their *Live Aid* video?

SS Which soap did TVam astrologer Russel Grant make an appearance in?

FG Which fictional English village was the setting for *Dear Ladies*?

FF Which famous actress played Mary in *Dixon of Dock Green*?

IP What type of building was home to Mary in *The Life and Loves of a She Devil*?

EH Which river saw Ralph Waite plying his trade as a boat-owning lawyer?

SD Which TV channel broadcasts the *Saturday Chart Show*?

SS Which *Crossroads* character was the first person on a UK soap to have a test tube baby?

FG What is the name of the act that sees Ian Tough threatening to spank his wife Janet on children's television?

FF Who played the role of Baretta?

IP Which TV cops raced from crime to crime in a Ford Torino?

EH What was the first team game to be publicly televised?

SD What began: "Like a streak of lightning flashing 'cross the sky"?

SS What is the name of the closest children's playground to *Coronation Street*?

FG Who has a friend called Spotty?

FF Who was the first person to host *Wogan* other than Wogan himself?

IP Which US detective's first name has never been revealed?

EH Which prime minister brought in a 10.30pm TV curfew in 1973?

Photo: Scope Features

17

SD Who presents *America's Top Ten*?

SS Which city did *Brookside's* Sheila take a bar job to help pay for a ticket to?

FG Which puppet ape says: "I hate that duck"?

FF Which '50s TV role did Conrad Philips become type-cast in?

IP Who set up shop as a general practitioner in Santa Monica, California?

EH What was Queen Mary seen to do to her son in *Edward and Mrs Simpson* that censors cut from the version shown in Islamic countries?

18

SD What is the better-known name of Nick Perido who had his own very popular TV series in the '50s and '60s?

SS Which *Coronation Street* character kidnapped his own son and headed for Ireland?

FG What is it if "It's Friday...It's Five O'clock..."?

FF Which pop singer took a role that Paul Nicholas had turned down in *The River*?

IP What did *77 Sunset Strip's* Cookie want delivering when he said: "Play like a pigeon"?

EH How many times has the Queen rounded off her Christmas message by pulling a cracker and reading the joke?

19

SD Who presented *They Sold a Million*?

SS Who was best man when Alf Roberts married Audrey?

FG Whose show featured Yakky Doodly Duck?

FF Who provided the voices for the Dynamic Duo in the cartoon version of *Batman*?

IP Which other soap is Jodie named after in *Soap*?

EH Who was the first reigning sovereign to visit a TV studio?

20

SD What religion are the Osmonds?

SS What does the N.Y. of *Emmerdale's* N.Y. Estates stand for?

FG What was the name of Sid's next door neighbour in *Bless This House*?

FF Which comedy actor made his final TV appearance in *Bloomers*?

IP Which series features a sleuth with the middle name Beatrice?

EH Where does the father of this family work his three-day week?

21

SD Whose TV theme was *Happy Trails to You*?

SS Which soap's legal wrangles are dealt with by Smithfield and Bennet?

FG What was the *Take Your Pick* big money prize kept in?

FF Which factual programme does Geoff Hamilton introduce from Barnsdale?

IP Which resort did Mr Roarke become the owner of?

EH Which series featuring a comedy trio was originally going to be called *Narrow Your Mind*?

22

SD Who was working as an apprentice hairdresser until someone introduced her to Johnny Dankworth?

SS Which Ramsay gave his name to Ramsay Street?

FG Which American comedienne made little impact with her British *Can We Talk* series?

FF Who created *The Baron* under the pen name Anthony Morton?

IP Which island does Chief Inspector Crozier police?

EH Which *Adrian Mole* actress was nominated for an Oscar for *Educating Rita*?

23

SD Which *London Palladium* compere released *Swinging In The Rain* in 1962?

SS Which *EastEnder* thought that Pete Beale was his father when it was actually Kenny Beale?

FG Which member of the Boswell family wrote poems about his girlfriend Carmen?

FF Which Western series starred David Carradine before he got into *Kung Fu*?

IP Which publishing company do Caroline and Donald own in *Executive Stress*?

EH Which *Dr. Who* died at a *Dr. Who* convention in 1987?

24

SD Who was "feared by the bad, loved by the good"?

SS What is this landlady's middle name?

FG What is Scooby Doo's favourite food?

FF What was Keith Floyd's first cookery series called?

IP Which cop series features a friendship between a judge and a convict?

EH Which cop series starred Mike Connors as an agent whose name changed each week?

25

SD Which show's theme song included: "A horse is a horse, of course of course"?

SS Which soap was based on a best-selling steamy novel by Grace Metalious?

FG Which comedy series saw Bob marry Thelma?

FF Which *Batman* role was played by Alan Napier?

IP What was the name of the dog in *The Thin Man*?

EH What was *Amos Burke, Secret Agent* the follow-up series to?

26

SD Whose TV show did Petula Clarke make her US TV debut on?

SS Who used his job as a window cleaner as a cover to case houses for burglar Monkey Gibbons of *Coronation Street*?

FG What are you watching if Brenda Wilson lives with her sister Pamela?

FF Which Nazi's boots were filled by Ian Holm in *Holocaust*?

IP What was Robin Tripp studying when he lived upstairs from the Ropers?

EH Who was the TV investigator for Scotland Yard's Department of Queer Complaints?

27

SD Who did Joan Rivers describe on TV as "The only man with child-bearing lips"?

SS Which TV company said they would consider selling *Coronation Street* to the BBC if they didn't retain their franchise in 1991?

FG What was Ronnie Corbett's industry in *Now Look Here*?

FF Which *EastEnder* went on to present *Daytime Live*?

IP What was Hilary's minor bird called?

EH What job did Dickens and Fenster do?

28

SD Which singing star was featured in *Set 'Em Up Joe*?

SS Why did Noelle Gordon leave *Crossroads*?

FG Which radio series did Hancock send up in *The Bowmans*?

FF Which award-winning actress plays Edie on *Last of the Summer Wine*?

IP Which Western series featured the Western Stagecoach Service?

EH Which sci-fi series did Rob Sering host in addition to *The Twilight Zone*?

29

SD Which TV personality and pianist once said: "I think if you swing with the chickens, that is your perfect right"?

SS What should you buy, according to the commercials, if you want to 'lift and separate'?

FG What is this comedian's catchphrase?

FF Which actress appeared in *Smiley's People* and *Telecom* commercials?

IP Which city did Marcus Welby work in?

EH Which horror actor hosted the *Out of This World* sci-fi series?

30

SD Which *Coronation Street* star once played the piano to silent movies?

SS What were "made to make your mouth water"?

FG What are Cannon and Ball's real first names?

FF Which former controller of BBC2 is said to have originally missed out on a knighthood that went to his actor brother by mistake?

IP What colour was Captain Kirk's seat on the Starship Enterprise?

EH What did Robert Modini change his surname to before becoming one of TV's most famous cops?

31

SD Which production was given a big "Yes, Yes" by the critics when it became the first post-war musical comedy on television?

SS Who owns the launderette that Dot Cotton works in?

FG Who is the captain of the *Trumpton* fire brigade?

FF Which British soap star did Alan Whicker interview in *Living With Uncle Sam*?

IP What was Keith Barron's job in *Take Me Home*?

EH Which series was set in the Shiloh Ranch before *The Men From Shiloh* moved in?

32

SD Which Gracie Fields hit did the wonderful Hilda Ogden sing at her Rover's Return farewell do?

SS What percentage of the *Coronation Street* cafe did Gail buy from Alma for nine thousand pounds?

FG Which show sees teenagers asking Bob if they can have a 'P'?

FF Who had *A Bit of a Do* in the role of Rita Simcock?

IP Which Western saw Buck and Manolito living at the Cannon ranch?

EH Which team gave Mike Post a 1984 hit?

33

SD Which British-based romp was the first musical production to be televised in America?

SS Which *Coronation Street* role is filled by Kevin Kennedy?

FG Which mouse had a friend called Joe Melia?

FF Which *Blue Peter* presenter hosted *Kick Start*?

IP Which series starred David McCallum suffering the effects of an accident at the KLAE Corporation?

EH What did Commissioner Gordon's daughter do for a living when she wasn't being the caped crusaderess?

34

SD Who composed Britain's first ever TV theme *Television March* to re-open the BBC after the war?

SS Which of the principal *EastEnder* characters spent some time counselling for the Samaritans?

FG Which broadcasting company has a tea lady called Betty?

FF Who played TV's Mayor of Casterbridge?

IP What was the original American title of the *Just Dennis* TV series?

EH What was the setting for *Harpers West One*?

35

SD What did Liberace have on top of his grand piano when he made his first appearance on ITV in 1955?

SS Which market was inspected by Derek Owen?

FG Which series saw millionaire Phillip Drummond adopt two boys?

FF Which of *The Railway Children* joined in *Logan's Run*?

IP What is Red Indian for "Faithful friend"?

EH Which city houses the headquarters of Granada TV?

36

SD What decade saw television's first dance band take to the air?

SS Which *Emmerdale* character found Jackie Merrick's body?

FG What is Del Boy's actual first name?

FF Which *Magpie* presenter was the daughter of a star of the *ITMA* radio series?

IP What were the Lone Ranger's final words each week?

EH What kind of creature was 'Gentle Ben'?

37

SD Who made TV history in 1953 by becoming the first group of dancers to be given individual contracts by the BBC?

SS Who owned the car that Pat Sugden was killed in?

FG Which comedian's catchphrase was "Settle down now"?

FF Which famous funnyman was played on TV as a young man by Joe Geary?

IP Which US state was the setting for *Flipper*?

EH Which 1979 mini-series was based in Hawaii at the time of the attack on Pearl Harbor?

38

SD Which Queen track is credited as being the first single sold on TV by its video?

SS Who did Malcolm Ryder try to poison so as to claim insurance?

FG Who claims to come from Ballgobackwards?

FF Which half of a double-act had his football career with Manchester City ended by a road accident?

IP What was Uncas the next to the last of?

EH Which Scottish comedian's first TV series was *On The Bright Side*?

(39)

SD What is the time of day when Postman Pat loads up his van, according to his theme song?

SS Who was advertised as being the patron saint of pipe smokers?

FG Which actor's letters began "Dear Mother" and ended "Love Albert"?

FF Who wrote *This One's On Me* after kicking a drink problem?

IP What is Dr Rudy Wells's most famous reconstruction?

EH What did *OSS* stand for in the series of that name?

(40)

SD Which John Leyton hit shot up the charts after he'd performed it in *Harpers West One*?

SS Which *Dynasty* role was played by both Al Corley and Jack Coleman?

FG What name did Miss Wilma Flaghoople take on the occasion of her marriage?

FF Who played Candice in *Girls on Top*?

IP What was 'Rover', the outside perimeter patroller in *The Prisoner*?

EH Which TV epic based on an Anthony Trollope work starred Susan Hampshire as Lady Glencora?

(41)

SD Which member of the Goons had a regular comedy spot on *Six Five Special*?

SS Which *Emmerdale* resident was accused of killing Harry Mowlam?

FG What is this character's first name in *'Allo' Allo* ?

FF Which artist starred in *Vision On* for nearly 15 years?

IP How many main stories were followed in each episode of *Doctor Kildare*?

EH Which TV comedy duo starred in *The Picnic*?

(42)

SD Which 1961 dance craze gave David Frost the subject for his first TV shows?

SS Which *Coronation Street* actor was voted the Male Televison Personality of the Year in 1983?

FG What was pictured on the partitions between the *Take Your Pick* numbered boxes?

FF Which *Dr Who* appeared in the film *Clockwork Orange*?

IP Which duo had the call-sign 'Zebra 3'?

EH What kind of creature is Snagglepuss?

43

SD Which Bellamy Brothers hit resurfaced on a *Levi's* commercial?

SS Who tried to give Bobby Ewing a lethal injection while he was recovering from being shot?

FG Who appeared on TV with his wife, Grace Allen?

FF Which comedy duo starred in *Plaza Patrol*?

IP Which London street was the setting for *Inside Story*?

EH Which 33-part TV cop series ended up with its hero, played by Alfred Burke, in jail?

44

SD Which phrase from a bread commercial led to a hit title for Cockerel Chorus?

SS Who wore an anorak to stand on station platforms advertising cheap Awayday Returns?

FG What was the name of the tortoise in *The Flowerpot Men*?

FF Whose 60th birthday was celebrated with a live TV special in 1986?

IP Which programme features Luke and Bo Duke?

EH What is Britain's longest-running children's TV show?

45

SD Which major '50s TV star had his first hit with *Don't Let the Stars Get In Your Eyes* and his last with *I Want to Give*?

SS What was the *Shangri-la* that Jerry Booth built in Len Fairclough's yard?

FG Where do the *Brush Strokes* characters sip their wine?

FF What are the first names of scriptwriters, Galton and Simpson?

IP Which service is featured in *Piece of Cake*?

EH Which TV sci-fi series featured Cally, Jenna and Vila?

46

SD Which TV cop series theme provided a modest hit for Norris Paramour in 1962?

SS Who was the first member of the *Coronation Street* cast to be awarded an OBE?

FG Which Tom O'Connor game show was a follow-up to *Top Secret*?

FF Who went from being Circus Boy's Uncle Joey to become Jim Rockford's dad?

IP Where did John and Maureen Robinson get 'Lost'?

EH Which famous case was reconstructed on British TV in 1981, twenty years after it had taken place, complete with four-letter words?

47

SD Which '50s singing TV star claimed to be a descendant of American frontiersman, Daniel Boone?

SS Which street is *Neighbours* centred around?

FG Which *Soap* character was abducted by aliens?

FF Who returned to the small screen to play the title role in *Smiley's People*?

IP What did this character overdose on that started all his problems?

EH Which programme always includes the line: "So who would live in a house like this?"?

48

SD Who is known for his singing but played the chairman of the National Coal Board in the kid's drama *How To Be Cool*?

SS Which early soap was recreated in 1991 with *EastEnder's* Leslie Grantham as Dad and Nick Berry as Jack?

FG What colour was the cover of *Monty Python's Big Red Book*?

FF Which comedian played the father in *How's Your Father*?

IP Why was no-one allowed to cough and only the good guys allowed to smoke in the US *The Man Against Crime* series?

EH Who starred as *The Texan*?

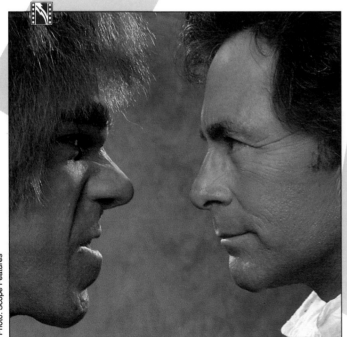

Photo: Scope Features

15

SD Which actress joined Ed Byrnes on his *Kookie Kookie* hit from the series *77 Sunset Strip*?

SS What is the name of Jane Harris' grandmother on *Neighbours*?

FG Which day of the week provided a name for one of the Addams' children?

FF Which BBC newsreader presented *Treasure Hunt*?

IP Which lawyer's receptionist answered to the name of Gertie?

EH What is the British equivalent of America's *College Bowl*?

SD Who wore the *Levis* on the commercial that featured Percy Sledge's *When a Man Loves a Woman*?

SS Which soap's first death came when May Hardman passed away on New Year's Eve, 1960?

FG What is Casper

FF Which television reporter put in appearances on *Yes Minister*?

IP Which city's police department does Columbo don his tatty mac for?

EH What was the sensitive title of the first TV programme for children with impaired hearing?

(51)

SD What nationality was Nicole who had a Eurovision winner with *A Little Peace*?

SS What happened to the baby that *Neighbours'* Zoe Davis was due to have after an affair with Jim Robinson?

FG Which series saw a wife split up the house by building a wall through it?

FF Who must have had his thoughts in the stars when he became the first person to swallow a fly in mid-sentence on TV?

IP What two words began the title of every *Burke's Law*?

EH What medical condition did Marcus Welby MD suffer from?

SD Which Elvis hit did Roland Rat perform a cover version of?

SS What accusation did Carole Burns make about Alan Bradley in *Coronation Street*?

FG Which comedy series featured a couple with deck chairs for furniture in their lounge?

FF Who was the subject of *A Prince for Our Time*?

IP What was the name of *The Virginian*?

EH Which series won Emmys that hopefully didn't self-destruct when it became best TV drama in 1966 and 1967?

(53)

SD Which TV western hero gave Quantum Jump their only hit single title?

SS Which *Coronation Street* character had a taste of the high-life as a cleaner on a cruise liner?

FG Who, other than Bruce Forsyth and Larry Grayson, has presented *The Generation Game*?

FF Who commented on the first televised State Opening of Parliament?

IP What had *A Man Called Shenandoah* lost?

EH Who called New Zealand "Zoo Nealand"?

SD Which TV comedian had a top-100 hit with *A Day In the Life of Vince Prince*?

SS How many J.Rs are there in *Dallas*?

FG What is the name of Rhoda's sister?

FF Who is the more famous brother of the actor who played Detective Stavros in *Kojak*?

IP Which cop series' characters include Davenport and Furillo?

EH Which TV series starred Margaret Lockwood as a lady barrister?

SD Which was the only top ten hit for the Wombles that didn't include any mention of Wombles or Wombling in its title?

SS Which soap did Eamonn Walker turn up in after suffering at the hands of Alf Garnett?

FG Which *M*A*S*H* character stayed on in Korea to marry Soon-Lee?

FF Which former northern policeman turned up as a presenter of *Beat the Cheat*?

IP Which city was Joe Friday's *Dragnet* dragged through?

EH What was the minimum age an artist had to be to appear on *The Old Boy Network*?

SD Which ventriloquist and dummy had a 1985 top-50 hit with *White Christmas*?

SS What was the name of the pianist at *Coronation Street*'s Gatsby Club who died in a shooting incident?

FG Which cartoon character has a teddy bear called Pooky?

FF Which children's comedy performer was the first person to have his own British TV programme?

IP Which TV series involved Jeremy Brett in a sequence filmed at the Reichenbach Falls in Switzerland?

EH Which *That Was The Week That Was* songstress had her own series called *From A Bird's Eye View*?

57

SD Which children's comedy performer was the first person to have his own British television signature tune?

SS What yellow liquid did you get if you "followed the bear"?

FG Which comedian gave David Hamilton the nickname 'Diddy'?

FF Who presented *When In Spain* after rising to fame thanks to his Spanish accent?

IP How did *The Fall Guy* earn extra cash on the side?

EH Which series' title character read a newspaper called *The Village*?

58

SD How many times has the Queen included a song in her Christmas Day message?

SS How many people died in the *Crossroads* motel fire?

FG Which comedian hosted the British version of *The Gong Show*?

FF Which actress's TV roles have included Queen Victoria and Catherine of Aragon?

IP Which 1986 political drama saw Granada TV build a realistic replica of the House of Commons?

EH What kind of car could be won in *Top of the World*?

59

SD Which early TV pop show gave Squeeze their first top-5 hit title?

SS Which *EastEnder* has a tatooed neck?

FG Who live at Mockingbird Heights, 1313 Mockingbird Lane?

FF Whose chat show was first transmitted in the UK in October 1981 and began with the words "Heeeeeeeeere's Johnny"?

IP Why did James Bellamy commit suicide in *Upstairs Downstairs*?

EH Which comedy actor performed *A Hard Day's Night* during the 1965 *Music of Lennon and McCartney* spectacular?

60

SD Which TV theme floated the Vienna Philharmonic Omnibus into the top-20?

SS Which soap star never speaks on a Sunday?

FG Who was the I in *Hugh and I*?

FF What did Sir Robin Day do for a living before he became a full-time TV presenter?

IP Which team is regularly on the opposite side to Lieutenant Decker?

EH Which film critic became the presenter of *Omnibus* in 1982?

61

SD Which TV cast had a hit with *Hi-Fidelity*?

SS Which detergent commercial asked: "Where do they go at playtime"?

FG Which lodge did Howard Cunningham belong to in *Happy Days*?

FF Which quiz and chat show host devised *Whose Baby*?

IP What is the maximum number of people that can be beamed up into the *Starship Enterprise* by Scotty in one go?

EH Which city had a new TV station built to make the 1970s *Donny and Marie* series?

62

SD What name did Matt Frewer find on a bridge that he adopted when introducing a TV video series?

SS Which soap is set in the Wandin Valley?

FG Which show's prisoner-of-war camp boasted a barber's shop, French chef and a steam room?

FF Whose tight jeans appear to have been the main attraction to females when he went 'In search of the Trojan Wars'?

IP Which *Dukes of Hazzard* character boasts the first names Jefferson Davies?

EH Which TV show was based on a northern working men's club and had Colin Crompton as its entertainment committee chairman?

63

SD Which TV comedian had a hit about a party with *Atmosphere*?

SS Which soap saw actress Teri Lally padded up to play the pregnant Carol McKay?

FG Which Muppet was referred to as the 'Thing' and the 'Whatever'?

FF Which television newsreader boosted his career as an entertainer by interviewing the Miss World finalists?

IP What colour was the chess knight on Paladin's business card?

EH Which annually televised event was the subject of a book written in 1967 by Eric Morley?

64

SD Who stood between Kim Carnes and Diana Ross on the USA for Africa video?

SS Who married his boss, Jackie Ingram?

FG Which southern state is patrolled by Deputy Dawg?

FF Which private eye was co-created by footballer Terry Venables?

IP Which show managed to smash up dozens of identical *Dodge Chargers* during filming?

EH Who appeared on worldwide television as she held up a bank in San Francisco in 1974?

65

SD What event gave Helmut Zacharias and his German band a 1964 hit with *Tokyo Melody*?

SS Which soap shares its name with a 1976 TV movie starring Sarah Miles and Stacy Keach?

FG What was the name of *The Muppet Show* eagle?

FF Which sports reporter received his first show-biz break as entertainment director on a cruise liner?

IP Who was 'The Last of the Mohicans'?

EH What was the drug that had deformed the child who featured in *On Giant's Shoulders*?

66

SD Which TV theme was the first UK single to sell a million without reaching number 1 in the charts?

SS Who bought The Kabin in Rosamund Street and signed up Rita to work there?

FG Who was the first real black to appear on *The Black and White Minstrel Show*?

FF Which racing commentator's father was a judge at the Nurnberg Trials?

IP Who was in charge of the servants at 165 Eaton Place?

EH What was being smuggled into the country in *A Passage to England*?

67

SD Name this Irish group's second hit TV theme?

SS Which *EastEnder* received a proposal of marriage from Benny Bloom?

FG What is Freddie Starr's real name?

FF Which quiz show host and comedian's daughter has one of the main roles in *Watching*?

IP Which *Avengers* girl drove a *Lotus Elan*?

EH Which British *My Fair Lady* actor starred in the American *Our Man Higgins* series?

68

SD Who had a hit with her 1971 TV theme *Something Tells Me (Something's Gonna Happen Tonight)*?

SS Whose wall was covered by a 'murial' when Eddie Yates ran out of wallpaper in 1976?

FG What is the main colour of the K in *Krypton Factor*?

FF What did Jimmy Tarbuck do for a living before becoming a stage and television entertainer?

IP Which rags-to-riches serial about a little girl was based on a book by Frances Hodgson-Burnett?

EH What did an Amercian suburban family inherit in *Our Man Higgins*?

69

SD Which Kenny Rogers hit was the inspiration for a 1985 mini-series?

SS Which Australian soap toured Britain as a musical stage show in 1991?

FG Which Popeye character lives off burgers?

FF Which TV detective actor's father is a minister with the name Richard Soulberg?

IP What was papa's job in *Black Beauty*?

EH Which poet was the subject of *Paradise Restored*?

70

SD Which TV series starred Bob Hoskins and featured '30s music from Al Bowlly and Harry Roy?

SS What is "Your flexible friend"?

FG What was the name of the *It Ain't Half Hot Mum* pianist?

FF Who played Alex in *Family Ties*?

IP Which drama series centred around the activities of Sir John Wilder?

EH What kind of animal is Bullwinkle?

71

SD Which is Paul McCartney's favourite TV bear?

SS Why didn't the management sue her when *Brookside's* Petra Taylor failed to pay her North Wales hotel bill?

FG What is Alan B'Stard's wife called?

FF What is the better-known name of female impersonator George Logan?

IP Which Yorkshire-based series stars Christopher Timothy without a trace of a Yorkshire accent?

EH Who pursues Roadrunner?

72

SD Which soap star had a hit with *Benny's Theme*?

SS What is Curly Watts's first name in *Coronation Street*?

FG Which comedy series began each week with the title character taking off his clothes and wading out to sea?

FF Which actor devised and produced *Dragnet*?

IP What could Princess Diana of Paradise Island become?

EH What sport was the subject of *Jack Solomon's Scrapbook*?

73

SD Which *Top of the Pops* presenter sang with the Ian Ralfini Orchestra?

SS Which soap building had three white feathers as its logo?

FG Which sophisticated actor played the doctor in Hancock's classic *The Blood Donor*?

FF Which country was Nerys Hughes born in?

IP Which sci-fi series saw Marc Singer leading the 'rebel' forces against an alien invasion?

EH Which sci-fi series should have seen everyone terminated at the age of thirty?

74

SD Which show-biz anniversary did Cliff Richard celebrate with a 1982 TV special?

SS Which *Crossroads* character spent a week in Winston Green Prison on dangerous driving charges?

FG Which Radio 4 show came to television with Clive Anderson in the chair?

FF Who originally presented *Wish You Were Here* with Chris Kelly?

IP What relation to *The Brothers* was the man who died at the start of *The Brothers*?

EH What did Hugh Krampke change his surname to before donning his six-shooter?

75

SD Which children's TV signature tune was a hit for Mike Oldfield?

SS What brand of cider was advertised as having "Cum oop vrom Zumerzet"?

FG What is Kathy Staff's *Last of the Summer Wine* role?

FF What nationality was bandleader Desi Arnaz who married Lucille Ball?

IP What crime series asks viewers to solve the crimes?

EH What was the better-known name of AIDS victim Roy Scherer?

76

SD Which TV comedy show spawned the hit record *Nappy Love*?

SS Which department at the *Crossroads* Motel was run by Vera Downend?

FG What is Rodney's wife called in *Only Fools and Horses*?

FF What country is home to camp TV cooks Hudson and Halls?

IP Which TV series is set in the northern village of Dereby?

EH Which sci-fi series won the 1967 Hugo Award for a two-part episode called *The Menagerie*?

77

SD Which Saturday night pop show saw the first national TV appearance of the Rolling Stones?

SS What product was said to lift you when you were "one degree under"?

FG Who stars in *And There's More*?

FF What is David Frost's middle name?

IP Which city does Ironside trundle around in?

EH Which all-action series featured America's Special Weapons and Tactics unit?

78

SD Which Beatles song was used as the theme for *Read All About It*?

SS What did the *Bleedooler* sell?

FG Which member of the *Monty Python* team was the naked organist in the *Blackmail* game show sketch?

FF Which actress was having the baby in *Late Expectations*?

IP What was the name of Mary's boss in *The Mary Tyler Moore Show*?

EH Who called his first car *The Love Bandit*?

79

SD Which TV theme gave Elmer Bernstein his only hit?

SS Which soap features Tom and his children, Lynne and Leo?

FG Which of the *Monty Python* crew was a doctor?

FF Which senior ITN newscaster retired in 1976 to take up writing?

IP Whose archenemies included a Penguin?

EH Why were the series of plays gathered together as *The Scorpion Tales* so called?

80

SD What two letters gave the *Rock Follies* girls a hit title?

SS How long did Cecil Colby's marriage to Alexis last?

FG How many buttons are there on Popeye's jacket?

FF Which TV comedian's autobiography is called *On The Way I Lost It*?

IP What is the secret identity of Babs Gordon, daughter of Gotham City police Commissioner?

EH Which war was the subject of *The Secret War*?

81

SD Which Queen video saw Freddie Mercury in black stockings and a tight leather mini-skirt?

SS Which *EastEnders* bar burnt down in 1988?

FG Which show's catchphrases included "You bet your bippy"?

FF Who left *Tomorrow's World* soon after newspapers reported that he'd sacked his gardener?

IP Which 1988 drama series saw actor Ron Perlman with a furry face?

EH What colour was the book when Eamonn Andrews was the subject of *This Is Your Life*?

82

SD What is the only hit to have been simultaneously at 1 and 3 in the UK charts on different labels whilst banned on TV?

SS What did Gail Tilsley name her daughter?

FG What do Top Cat's close friends get to call him?

FF Who reduced grown men to tears on *Face to Face*?

IP Which TV drama series starred a hairy baby?

EH How many days of commercials were dropped from US TV as a mark of respect on the death of President Kennedy?

83

SD Which former member of Harold Melvyn and the Bluenotes is the inspiration for Lenny Henry's Theophilus T.Wildebeest?

SS What was the name of the *Coronation Street* greyhound that had to pull out of a race when it became pregnant?

FG Which show had an American spin-off called *Joanie and Chachi*?

FF What nationality were deep-sea explorers Hans and Lottie Hass?

IP Which BBC drama series featured lawyers played by Jack Sheppard, Jane Lapotaire and Julian Wadham?

EH What appeared out of Steve and Diane Freeling's TV set?

84

SD Which 1984 chart-toppers' promotional video showed an apparent fight between Reagan and Brezhnev?

SS What does Dot Cotton drink in the Queen Vic, other than at Christmas when she has a small sherry?

FG What do the Munsters keep their telephone in?

FF Who played Debussy in the Ken Russell TV film?

IP Which malignant disease did *St. Elsewhere's* Dr Auschlander discover that he had?

EH What was Channel 4's first colourful Afro-Caribbean magazine called?

85

SD Which TV show claimed an eighteen months waiting list for tickets in 1988?

SS Which part of his body did Neighbour Des injure during his honeymoon?

FG Who named his son Mearth?

FF Who kept up Britain's corner in the 1969 four-way Eurovision Song Contest tie?

IP Who has a built-in grid screen in one of his eyes?

EH What did Howard Hughes buy so that he could watch late-night movies on television?

86

SD Which rock'n'rolling leather wearer did TV producer, Jack Good, advise to "limp you bugger, limp"?

SS Who rescued Bet when the Rovers Return caught fire?

FG What was Jed Clampett doing when "up through the ground came a bubblin' crude"?

FF Which playwright had acting roles in *Fortunes of War* and *Selling Hitler*?

IP Which *Star Trek* character lists botany and fencing among his hobbies?

EH What name was given to the very first television set?

87

SD Which 1970s Strawbs hit was sung on TV in the '80s by striking miners?

SS What does Pete Beale sell from his Albert Square stall?

FG Which *Taxi* character shakes hands by bumping bums?

FF What is the family relationship between these two actors who were both in the Forsyte Saga?

IP Whose parents were Bunta and Omoro?

EH Which popular character usually has Annie and Clarabel in tow?

88

SD Which hit was promoted by a video showing Paul McCartney as two-soldiers on opposite sides in a war?

SS What was Carney's job at the *Crossroads* Motel?

FG What do Lenny and Squiggy deliver in *Laverne and Shirley*?

FF Which actor played Regan's boss in *The Sweeney*?

IP Who adopted an orphan named Danny in the final episode of *Happy Days*?

EH What language was the Greek tragedy *Electra* presented in on British television in 1962?

Photo: Hulton Deutsch

89

SD Which 1985 number 1 hit group included TV presenters Bruce Forsyth and Keith Chegwin singing *You'll Never Walk Alone*?

SS What did Dirty Den serve to Angie just before he served the Christmas Turkey?

FG Who was sent to earth as punishment for drawing a moustache on a picture of the Solar Leader?

FF Which singing cowboy ran the Double R Bar Ranch?

IP What was the full title of the series in which David Suchet played Hercule Poirot?

EH What is the childrens' version of *TV Times* called?

90

SD Who won the Eurovision Song Contest singing *Hold Me Now*?

SS What did Vera find in Jack's pocket that proved he must have been taking another woman out?

FG Which member of the *I Love Lucy* cast was 41 years-old when the first episode was shown?

FF Which crime show with plenty of stories to tell, provided Jon Voight and Dustin Hoffman with their first major TV roles?

IP Which Dickens work did the BBC dramatize to celebrate the 200th anniversary of the French Revolution?

EH Which city was the city in *Second City Firsts*?

91

SD Which star was the subject of a Jonathan Ross 'special' in 1991, on the 14th anniversary of his death?

SS What is Gary Ewing's first name short for?

FG Which historical event was re-created by the Townswomen's Guild in *Monty Python*?

FF Who habitually ended his show with the words: "Say goodnight Gracie"?

IP Which city was *The Naked City*?

EH Who makes tea for T-Bags?

92

SD Who was the star of Michael Aspel's chat show on the day that New Zealand model, Rachel Hunter, was in the audience?

SS Who did Connie Hall stab in 1988?

FG What was the first *Monty Python* big screen effort which was almost the same as the TV show?

FF Which TV side-kick was played by the somewhat rotund Leo Carillo?

IP What did the *M* in *M Squad* stand for?

EH Where was *Stingray* based

93

SD Who had her own UK TV show after topping the US charts with *To Sir With Love*?

SS Which *Howard's Way* sex bomb turned up in *Dynasty*?

FG What was the name of Popeye's enemy Bluto changed to, when the cartoons were made specially for television?

FF Which member of *The Good Life* team played the lodger in *Goodbye Mr. Kent*?

IP What kind of expert was Marius Goring in the TV series *The Experts*?

EH Which sitcom series saw Diane Keen and Martin Jarvis decide to get married after living together for several years?

94

SD Which top-ten singer of a TV sporting event theme described opera as "howling in a trained manner"?

SS Which soap saw Blake and Sophie being dared to spend a night together in a cemetary?

FG What feature was dropped from *The Great Egg Race* in 1981?

FF Which deceased comedy actress was the first wife of 'Minder' barman Glynn Edwards?

IP Who was the only character apart from Doc to last right through the *Gunsmoke* series?

EH Which ancient London prison was the setting for *Rogues' Gallery*?

95

SD Which Maplins maid sang in an all-girl band called Midnight News?

SS Which *Coronation Street* actress is the sister of comedian Duggie Brown?

FG Who was the *I* in *Hugh and I*?

FF Which TV newsreader was married to cartoonist Mark Boxer?

IP Which ordinary copper got his sergeant's stripes on 19th September 1964?

EH What was the follow-up to *Roots*?

96

SD Who sang the theme from *Going Straight*?

SS Who took few business chances as the manager of the *Crossroads* health-centre?

FG What are the first three words spoken by contestants on *Tell the Truth*?

FF Which *Man from UNCLE* was married to Jill Ireland?

IP Which of Dr. Who's enemies had pipes running down their arms and down the front of their silver legs?

EH Whose initials were the S.M. part of the TV *S.M.S.* story series?

97

SD Who were given the best *Live Aid* seats for free and then seen on TV to sneak out after hearing only two bands?

SS Which *Coronation Street* character was stopped by the police on suspicion of stealing a car, during her driving test?

FG What sport does *Taxi's* Tony Bants want to make it big in?

FF What 1991 occasion brought the unlikely pairing of Raquel Welch and Freddie Truman to our TV screens?

IP What affliction forced Dr. Robert Caldwell to leave *St. Elsewhere*?

EH Which bird was seen twice a week for 12 years on children's television?

98

SD Whose final hours were the subject of the drama-documentary *Words of Love*?

SS Which former *EastEnder* actor is married to actress Jane Laurie?

FG Which show did Henry Gibson and Joanne Worley regularly appear in?

FF Which comedy actor played a straight role as the father of a condemned drug offender in *Amongst Barbarians*?

IP Which '60s spoof spy series featured Captain Robert Virgin?

EH How many episodes were there in the 1971 drama series *The Ten Commandments*?

99

SD Which animated TV character gave Jackie Lee a hit?

SS What is the exact relationship between Pauline Fowler and Pete Beale in *EastEnders*?

FG Which actress fluttered into the starring role in *Laura and Disorder*?

FF Who sat on a protesting lesbian when the Six O'Clock News studio was invaded in 1988?

IP Which northern city was the setting for *Brick is Beautiful*?

EH How did camerawoman Lee Lyon die whilst filming an edition of *Survival*?

100

SD Which hit found snooker stars appearing on TV alongside Chas and Dave?

SS Which soap did this gangster move into?

FG Which *Comic Strip* presentation saw the genes of a video director mixed with those of a hooligan in a plot based on *The Fly*?

FF Which former editor of *The New Statesman* and future ambassador to Washington presented *Face to Face*?

IP Which superhero has been played by George Reeves on TV and Christopher Reeves on film?

EH Who created *Till Death Us Do Part*?

Photo: Channel 4

101

SD Which detective theme gave Joe Loss a 1962 hit with French connections?

SS Who was the owner of the kidnapped horse called Allegree?

FG Who was the headmaster in *Please Sir*?

FF Which *Crossroads* star was used by John Logie Baird in his early colour television experiments?

IP Why did a fully-costumed Batman refuse a front row seat in a dance hall?

EH How many 26-part series of *The Flowerpot Men* were made?

102

SD Who had their 1990 Best New Artist Grammy Award taken away when they admitted to not performing on any of their number 1 hits?

SS Which of the *Neighbours* crashed a car whilst taking it for a test drive?

FG Which British comedian had a role in *Chitty Chitty Bang Bang*?

FF Which artist/naturalist presented the first British TV programme of birds in their natural habitat?

IP What is the series if the enemies are the Cylons?

EH In which city was *The Man From UNCLE's* headquarters?

103

SD What provided actor Keith Michell with a double A-side hit along with *Wilfred the Weazel*?

SS What did Lou Beale catch to make herself less than popular when Pauline Fowler was pregnant?

FG What is the comedy series if Vera is Eleanor's friend and Clare is Sarah's daughter?

FF Which British personality was Australia's first female newsreader?

IP What first name did *Hot Metal's* Rathbone share with a model?

EH Which British series about two girls and a guy was called *Three's Company* in its American version?

104

SD Which city 'became a hit' for Freddie Mercury and opera singer Montserrat Caballe?

SS How did Ralph Hardwick of *Brookside* get to know Madge Richmond after his wife had died?

FG Which comedian wrote the book *Trumps*?

FF Who did a 1978 poll of 250,000 deaf and hard of hearing viewers vote as being the most easy to understand TV newsreader?

IP What was Olive's job in *That's Love*?

EH Which British school comedy was the basis for America's *Making the Grade*?

105

SD What job did Bert Hayes do on *Hopscotch* in 1956 through to *Top of the Pops* in 1980 to gain a world record?

SS Which soap featured the Castlehulme Health Centre?

FG Which Irishman hosts *Password*?

FF Which *Private Schultz* star had a role in the film *The Elephant Man*?

IP What does the programme title *CHiPS* stand for?

EH Which Dickens title was borrowed for a 1970s documentary series about school-leavers?

106

SD What was Tommy Steele's backing group called on the first edition of *Six-Five Special*?

SS What was the name of Maureen Lipman's Jewish *British Telecom* character?

FG What is the name of Rene's wife in *'Allo 'Allo*?

FF Which star of *Falcon Crest* is a former Mrs. Ronald Reagan?

IP Which city did Yosser live in?

EH Which children's programme was created by Frenchman, Serge Danot?

107

SD How many years old will *Top of the Pops* be if it survives to 1994?

SS How many years probation did Blake Carrington get for manslaughter?

FG Who hosted *Every Second Counts*?

FF Who fell over on the first of his own chat shows?

IP Which Carla Lane series saw Felicity Kendal having an affair with Jack Galloway?

EH What name is given to the programme that features the BBC International Sheepdog Championships?

108

SD Who took over the compilation of the BBC record charts in 1983?

SS Whose 18th birthday party was taking place when Alan Bradley beat up Rita Fairclough?

FG What was the name of Felix Unger's former wife?

FF What name did Terence Nelhams use when he sang on TV and acted in *Budgie*?

IP What is the name of test pilot Peter Peel's wealthy widow?

EH Which show was presented by Barry Sheene, Kenny Lynch and Suzanne Danielle?

SD Who became a sports reporter after presenting *Cool for Cats*?

SS What had you got a lot of if the commercial selling the product ended with "Wotalot-I-got"?

FG What did *TW3* stand for in 1962?

FF Which tiny comedian starred in *Bingo Madness*?

IP Which major series ended when Tara King accidentally blasted the main character into space?

EH Who was the first member of the Royal Family to be interviewed on television?

SD Which TV bandleader bought *Bluebird* from Sir Malcolm Campbell?

SS What wasn't mum using if her little girl's dress was grey and her friend's identical garment was white?

FG Which TV newsreader made the news when pictures of her legs were leaked to the press?

FF Which very famous comedian changed his name from Eric Bartholomew?

IP Which TV sci-fi monsters are said to have been named after the letters on an encyclopaedia spine?

EH Who was the sheriff of *Four Feather Falls*?

SD Which Liverpool football pools company provided the all-female resident singing group on *Oh Boy!*?

SS Whose boss was Dr. Gillespie?

FG Who had his hand up Lennie the Lion?

FF What kind of programmes were made by Hans and Lotte Hass?

IP What was the name of the dolphin in *Marine Boy*?

EH What was launched in 1956 as ITV's answer to *Panorama*?

SD Who formed the panel on the only occasion that the *Juke Box Jury* had five members?

SS Which year saw the introduction of *Steptoe and Son, The Saint* and *Z Cars*?

FG What was Sgt. Bilko's first name?

FF Who said on approximately 1800 occasions "The next *Tonight* will be tomorrow night"?

IP Which futuristic vehicle was driven by Mike Mercury?

EH Which science programme was introduced to TV in 1957 and is still going strong?

SD What instrument did Shirley Abicair plink her way to fame with?

SS Which *Emmerdale* role is filled by Richard Thorp who was *Emergency Ward 10's* Dr. Rennie?

FG Which was the first ventriloquist's dummy to have his own TV series?

FF What was Bill Fraser's *Army Game* role?

IP What was the name of Steptoe's horse?

EH What was Britain's first regular Saturday afternoon sports programme?

SD Who compered the first *Sunday Night at the London Palladium*?

SS Which sign meant "Happy motoring"?

FG What stood between David Jacobs and the jury on *Juke Box Jury*?

FF Who broadcast his first D.I.Y. programme in 1957?

IP What was Bernard Breslaw's *Army Game* catchphrase?

EH Which sports commentator was Cheshire's champion miler at the age of twenty-three?

SD Which long-running series was introduced by the music *An Ordinary Copper*?

SS Which ward have Ian Hendry, Albert Finney and Joanna Lumley all been patients in?

FG Which TV show has been hosted by David Jacobs, Noel Edmonds and Jools Holland?

FF Which TV Western series starred John Hart and Lon Chaney Jr.?

IP Which cop series regularly heard Broderick Crawford snapping "Ten-Four" into his radio-mike?

EH What job did Australian Len Martin do from the very first edition of *Grandstand*?

SD What became TV's longest-running musical show after first being suggested in 1953 by Mr. Mecca, Eric Morley?

SS Which was ITV's first twice-weekly soap?

FG Which TV quiz show was based on noughts and crosses?

FF Who got a job teaching at Fenn Street when his only qualification appeared to be as a nurse on *Emergency Ward 10*?

IP Whose secretary was Della Street?

EH Which scientist claims to be the first person to swallow a fly accidentally on live television?

117

SD Which TV 'talent' show presented Bonnie Langford, Bobby Crush and Lena Zavaroni to an ever-grateful public?

SS What was described in the words "Looks good, tastes good, and by-golly it does you good"?

FG Which surburb of Liverpool does Ken Dodd live in?

FF Which member of the Royal Family took part in the 1971 *Blue Peter Safari*?

IP What is the name of this hazzardous looking car?

EH Which *Blue Peter* pet died after her debut programme and was substituted without the audience being told?

118

SD What is the name of Ray Allan's aristocratic drunken dummy?

SS Who went from being the youngest male in *The Grove Family* to become the under-butler in *Upstairs Downstairs*?

FG Which character's unkempt clothes were filled by Richard Hearne?

FF What was explorer Armand Denis's wife called?

IP Whose 'Experiment' starred Reginald Tate in the title role?

EH Which children's programme featured Mr. Turnip and Hank?

119

SD Who had a major hit with *The Last Waltz* after failing his audition for *Opportunity Knocks*?

SS What was *Oxo* Katie's husband called?

FG Whose catchphrase was "I hate those meeces to pieces"?

FF Which father of a famous son starred in *Sea Hunt*?

IP Which mountain range provided the setting for most of the location shots in the 1950s *William Tell* series?

EH Which TV Western did the Labour Party think would damage its election chances by keeping voters away from the 1959 poll?

120

SD Which Labour MP's housekeeper appeared on *Opportunity Knocks* as 'Bristol's phenomenal lady tenor'?

SS What is "Full of eastern promise"?

FG Whose catchphrase was "Heavens to Murgatroyd"?

FF Which member of the *Blue Peter* team was once knocked out by a flying marrow?

IP Which TV detective was played by J.Carrol Naish?

EH What kind of creature was Fred, the first *Blue Peter* pet, that later turned out to be female?

Photo: Hulton Deutsch

(121)

SD Which British band was too anti-establishment to go on the *London Palladium's* finale roundabout?

SS What was advertised as "A great little cigarette"?

FG Which TV comedian's teeth are said to be insured for over ten thousand pounds?

FF Which programme's many presenters have included Christopher Wenner, Janet Ellis and Tina Heath?

IP Which detective went from *Murder Bag* to *Crime Sheet* to *No Hiding Place*?

EH What did *Blue Peter* viewers collect 7.5 tons of in 1971?

(122)

SD Which dart player's picture was mistakenly displayed behind Dexy's Midnight Runners when they sang *Jackie Wilson Said* on *Top of the Pops*?

SS Which '60s series saw Barry Bucknell renovate a derelict Victorian building?

FG Which quiz show's questions were in a locked safe guarded by former Detective Fabian of the Yard?

FF What do these two Doctor's share, as well as the same role?

IP Which TV star slept on the floor at Fort Apache?

EH Which invention from the *Ampex* Company became popular in 1956 and almost killed live television?

(123)

SD What label did *EastEnder* Nick Berry record his number 1 hit on?

SS Which soap family had a butler called Raul?

FG What is the show if Dorien is Sharon and Tracey's neighbour?

FF What is the relationship between Moira and Pamela Armstrong?

IP Which series features a spaceship called *Jupiter 11*?

EH What event in San Francisco on 10th March 1933 was the first major disaster to be seen on television?

(124)

SD How many times was Irene Cara's number 1 hit from *Fame* sung during the TV series?

SS Who played Carla, the Dutch girl, on *The Sullivans*?

FG What was the title of the spin-off series about the *Flintstone* children?

FF Which 1950s all-action role was played by Ron Ely?

IP Which city had Matt Dillion and Wyatt Earp as its marshalls?

EH What was the subject of the British and Russian co-production *Ten Days That Shook the World*?

125

SD What is the only number one hit to have been played on *Top of the Pops* that has no letters in its title?

SS What unwelcome problem did Frank and Chrissy Rogers find when they moved in to the Grant's *Brookside* house?

FG Who must have had a brainstorm to accept the job of hosting *Brainstorm*?

FF Who starred in the winning series *Big Deal*?

IP Which drama series told the story of Margaret Kelly who set up a team of dancing girls in Paris?

EH Which TV series has been presented by Bamber Gascoigne, Clive James and Mike Parkinson?

126

SD Which *Crossroads* character had a hit with *More Than In Love*?

SS What was Lou's husband called in *EastEnders*?

FG Which puppet is terrorised by a green witch called Grotbags?

FF Which TV hero's wish when he dies is to be stuffed and sat up on Trigger?

IP Which member of the *A-Team's* favourite warning is: "You better watch out, sucker"?

EH What on-going tragedy has been the subject of more British current affairs programmes and documentaries than any other?

127

SD Which TV pop presenter made a guest appearance on *Brookside*?

SS Who was the cleaner at the Rovers Return when *Coronation Street* first started?

FG Which puppet lives in a pink windmill?

FF Who shared the screen with a puppet dog in *The Storyteller*?

IP Which marshall's deputies included Bat Masterson, Ed Masterton and Hal Norton?

EH What, in 1973, became the most expensive war documentary ever made?

128

SD Who played Holly Brown and sang *Born With A Smile On My Face* on *Crossroads*?

SS Which soap star played Katrina in *Monte Carlo*?

FG Which kid's show includes a race in go-carts?

FF Which famous TV heavy played *Just William* as a child?

IP Which prison did Jim Rockford serve time in?

EH Which nightly magazine programme won the 1958 BAFTA award for factual programmes?

129

SD Which hit was played throughout Scott and Charlene's wedding in *Neighbours*?

SS What was Jack Howarth's *Coronation Street* role for over 20 years?

FG What farmyard animal's noise indicated that *Fun House* contestants have found the star prize tag?

FF Who was the star of *Wizbit*?

IP Which futuristic adventurer takes his orders from Wilma Deering?

EH Which *Sesame Street* character was the star of the first Chinese-American co-production?

130

SD Whose *I Want Your Sex* wasn't played on BBC TV in 1987?

SS Which soap saw Dan Fixx charged with murder?

FG Who plays Dr. Cliff Huxtable in a show named after himself?

FF Which female continued reading the news when Nicholas Witchell was sitting on a demonstrator?

IP Which sci-fi show features the beautiful but evil Princess Ardala?

EH Which famous Lord received the Queen's Award to Industry as the leading exporter of British TV programmes to the USA?

131

SD Which was the first American variety show hosted by a brother and sister?

SS Which product's commercials warned us to "Watch out — there's a Humphrey about"?

FG Who claimed to have a friend called Slack Alice?

FF Which famous horror actor played Sherlock Holmes in the 1968 TV series?

IP Which 52-part drama series was set in the 1940s and featured the Ashton family of Liverpool?

EH Which southern town was the home of the Wilkins family who starred in the real-life documentary *The Family*?

132

SD Which TV family were managed by Reuben Kincaid?

SS Which company counted the little perforations in its tea bags, according to Brian Glover?

FG Which quiz show shared top ratings with *The Generation Game* in 1974?

FF Which member of the Royal Family chose a television documentary instead of a written biography?

IP Which Yorkshire actress played a Yorkshire lass's role in *Queenie's Castle*?

EH Which programme began in the 1970s in an attempt to encourage non-reading adults to seek education?

(133)

SD Which sitcom has *Thank You for Being A Friend* as its theme song?

SS Which *Coronation Street* character wrote the steamy novel *Song of a Scarlet Summer*?

FG Which comedy follow-up starring James Bolam won the 1973 Best Situation Comedy Award?

FF Who won the 1970 Best Television Actor award for his role in *The Six Wives of Henry VIII*?

IP Which country's censors turned down several episodes of *Upstairs, Downstairs* which couldn't be shown there until 1988?

EH Which prime minister's wife denied, in a David Frost interview, that she ever drank *Wincarnis* tonic wine?

(134)

SD Which member of The Who stripped down to his briefs on *Russell Harty Plus*?

SS Which actor once claimed that he had voiced 25% of all the TV commercials on air at one point in the 1960s?

FG Which puppet has his own museum in Shipley, Yorkshire?

FF Which of the *Monty Python* team went *Around the World in 80 Days*?

IP Which swinging sixties trend-setter series first saw the screen as *Police Surgeon*?

EH Who co-founded the Clean-up TV campaign in 1964 with Norah Buckland?

(135)

SD Which TV show used Phil Lynott's *Yellow Peril* as its theme?

SS What was the job of the man who raped *Brookside's* Sheila Grant?

FG Who has friends called Henry, Gordon and Bertie the Bus?

FF Which chat show host presented *One to One*?

IP What colour shirts do the *Hill Street Blues* cops wear?

EH Which DJ starred in the West End version of *The Hunting of the Snark*?

(136)

SD Which pop singer was the first person to appear on Australian television?

SS Who had a bet in the Rovers Return that he could have an affair with the next girl to walk through the door?

FG Which sitcom features the widowed Southern belle, Blanche Devereaux?

FF Which *Minder* actor tangled with the She Devil in his role as Bobbo?

IP What was Petrocelli's first name?

EH What anniversary did *The Sky at Night* celebrate in 1987?

(137)

SD What was the main event of the ITV programme shown on 20th July 1969 which featured Cliff Richard, Cilla Black and Lulu?

SS Which character left *Emmerdale* in 1991 to live in Norfolk with her son Sam?

FG Which teddy celebrated his 40th TV anniversary in 1992?

FF Who went on to star in *Star Wars* after playing roles in *General Hospital* and *The FBI*?

IP What colour is Mr Spock's skin when seen on a colour television?

EH Which children's fairy tale was re-told on television with Mia Farrow and Danny Kaye in starring roles?

(138)

SD Which *Top of the Pops* presenter joined DJ Paul Burnett to become Laurie Lingo and the Dipsticks?

SS Which *Coronation Street* actress appeared in *Another Sunday* and *Sweet FA*?

FG Who shared a flat with Chrissy and Jo in *Man About the House*?

FF Who was the first winner of the *Pot Black* trophy?

IP What military rank did B.A. Baracus reach?

EH Which long-running soap began its run in 1964?

(139)

SD Which former member of a British singing duo was offered $8 million to record *Diet Coke* commercials in 1988?

SS Which *Dynasty* character's dead sister was named Iris?

FG Which actor became a game show host on *Pass the Buck*?

FF Which chat show host is said to have a fat and a thin wardrobe to suit his fluctuating weight?

IP Which 'Affair' involved James Bolan and Barbara Flynn?

EH How many times was Jim Turner, star of the 1950s *Invisible Man* series, mentioned in the credits?

(140)

SD Which member of the Shadows appeared to have white hair when they first appeared on black and white television?

SS Which *EastEnders* character had a cellmate called Barnsie?

FG Which comedy series married David Jason to Gwen Taylor?

FF Who won the 1987 Richard Dimbleby Award for her campaigning work on televison?

IP What did Vaseline and Sicknote do for a living in *London's Burning*?

EH Which TV company's logo is like that of *MGM* but with a kitten instead of a lion?

141

SD Which TV singing sibling trio had the first names Tony, Mike and Denis?

SS Who did *EastEnders* gay resident Colin leave the Square to live with?

FG Which former *EastEnder* took a comedy role in *Split Ends*?

FF What was the name of Dame Edna's husband?

IP Which country was the setting for *Heimat*?

EH Which fashion craze did David McCallum start in *The Man From UNCLE*?

142

SD Which film was shown on TV in December 1967 that included an appearance by the Bonzo Dog Doo-Dah Band?

SS Which *Coronation Street* character suffered a broken ankle in a banger racing accident?

FG Which year first saw cars with red noses in support of *Comic Relief*?

FF Who produced the four-hour Joan Collins vehicle *Monte Carlo*?

IP Which industry featured in *Hot Metal*?

EH Who was known only as 'The Foreman of the Shiloh Ranch'?

143

SD Who sounded like a TV puppet duo when they went to number 4 with *Let's Go To San Francisco*?

SS In which country did Jenny Bradley spend an overseas holiday with Martin Platt?

FG Which son of a famous conjuror hosted *Lingo*?

FF Which titled actor guided viewers on a tour of *The English Garden*?

IP Which year provided the setting for the futuristic '60s series *Voyage to the Bottom of the Sea*?

EH What killed Danny Kendall of *Grange Hill*?

144

SD What brand of perfume is mentioned in the *Watching* theme song?

SS Which soap disaster saw the death of a cook called Mrs. Cornet?

FG What was the first quiz to be seen on Channel 4?

FF What colour were Big Ears' ears?

IP What did The Baron's shop sell?

EH Who had sabotaged the *Jupiter II* to cause it to be *Lost in Space*?

Photo: Scope Features

145

SD Which comedy's second series had Joe Fagin's *Back With the Boys Again* as its theme?

SS What had Hilda Ogden's lodger Henry Wakefield done to deserve the wrath of his union?

FG What did Neville take home as a permanent reminder of his visit to Germany in *Auf Wiedersehen Pet*?

FF Which commentator had to take over as linesman when the linesman took over as referee in a 1972 Arsenal-Liverpool match?

IP Which series featured a barrister called Erskine-Brown?

EH Which street gang did this tough-guy fly around with?

146

SD Who had a 1990 hit with *The Prisoner*?

SS Which *Coronation Street* character married Marion Willis because she was pregnant?

FG Which TV panel game rewards it guests with a golden key?

FF What imaginative name did Desi Arnaz give to his actor son?

IP What was the sequel to *A Woman of Substance*?

EH Which 'Goodie' starred in *The Bubblegum Brigade*?

147

SD Which DJ joined Mike Vickers on the hit *Captain Kremmen (Retribution)*?

SS Who got almost as fat as the man in the famous tyre commercial when pregnant with Mike Baldwin's child in 1982?

FG Who sometimes had trouble controlling Musky and Vince?

FF Which male presenter co-conducted Andrew and Fergie's pre-wedding interview?

IP Which TV series starring Roddy McDowell was set in the year 3085?

EH Which ex-footballer and TV presenter cannot read an autocue due to his being dyslexic?

148

SD Was Benny Hill, hit recorder of *Ernie the Fastest Milkman In The West*, ever actually a milkman?

SS Which EastEnder bought this character's drugs for him in 1991?

FG What was Shari Lewis's best known puppet called?

FF Who became Dr Who when Jon Pertwee went off to become a scarecrow?

IP Which *Secret Army* Nazi had his own spin-off series?

EH Which TV series was based on the life of John Adams who left his family to live alone in the mountains?

Photo: Scope Features

149

SD Which member of the *That's Life* team recorded with Blue Mink in 1976 (three years after their last hit!)?

SS What kind of cakes did Ena Sharples insist must be left out of the selection she purchased in episode 1 of *Coronation Street*?

FG What kind of creature was Dinsdale in *Monty Python's Flying Circus*?

FF Who did Margaret Thatcher think did the best impersonation of her?

IP What began: "There is nothing wrong with your television set, we are controlling the transmission"?

EH Which '50s comedy series returned in the '70s with Christopher Beeny replacing Reg Varney?

150

SD Which TV wrestler recorded *We Shall Not Be Moved*?

SS Who returned to work on *Emmerdale Farm* after writing a best-selling novel?

FG Which horse is the marshall of a town in New Mexico?

FF Which *Miami Vice* role was turned down by *Midnight Caller* star Gary Cole?

IP Which murderer's centenary was celebrated by a 1988 drama series?

EH How many people usually sit at the *Question Time* debate?

151

SD Which TV acting duo obviously didn't mind having a hit with *What Are We Gonna Get 'Er Indoors'*?

SS What did Adam show to Alexis to prove that he was her son?

FG What is the link between Huckleberry Hound, Yogi Bear and Daws Butler?

FF Which comedy actor played the part of Skullion?

IP Which TV vehicle has *NCC 1701* painted along its side?

EH Which Irish novelist had an acting role in *The Hard Man*?

152

SD Which TV hero was "born on a mountain top in Tennessee"?

SS What was *Coronation Street* intellectual Curly Watts's first job?

FG Which hound is "the biggest clown in town"?

FF Which French detective did Richard Harris portray in a 1988 TV series?

IP Which country was the setting for the hospital series *The Houseman's Tale*?

EH What is S4C?

153

SD Which talent show's contestants were always introduced by their sponsor?

SS Which soap character noted: "Once you give up integrity, the rest is a piece of cake"?

FG What was the name of the cleaning lady, as played by Julie Waters, at *Acorn Antiques*?

FF Who played Tony Britton's doctor son in *Don't Wait Up*?

IP Which drama series introduced Richard Chamberlain as a priest and Rachel Ward as a young girl called Meggie?

EH Which Channel 4 programme called itself "TV's first electronic weekly"?

154

SD Which programme gave Highly Likely a hit called *Whatever Happened to You*?

SS Who, in *Emmerdale Farm*, married Pat Merrick and then discovered that her son was actually his?

FG How many contestants line up at the start of *Strike It Lucky*?

FF Which TV star split with his brother Mike and played Bud Flanagan in a West End show?

IP What was Colonel Hall's fruity nickname in *The Phil Silvers Show*?

EH What was Hopkirk's first name in *Randall and Hopkirk Deceased*?

155

SD Which programme is introduced by *Non-Stop*, British television's longest-running theme tune?

SS What was Dot Cotton's maiden name?

FG Which quiz show host presents Cilla Black's *Searchlines*?

FF Who was *Blue Peter's* first Peter?

IP Which member of the *A-Team* is 'Howling Mad'?

EH What name was given to the small animal that turned up in *Lost In Space*?

156

SD What is Britain's longest-running theme tune for a drama series, which was written by Eric Spear who died in 1966?

SS Which soap character appeared on a fictional TV quiz show wearing a tie borrowed from Ian Beale?

FG Which TV series was created by Charles Schultz?

FF Which member of the *Alien* crew starred in *I Claudius*?

IP Which '50s TV hero had a sidekick called Bear?

EH Whose novel was the basis for *Wheels*?

157

SD Which spy series had the theme *Nunc Dimitis* sung by a choirboy against a background of Oxford church spires?

SS How much money did Arthur Fowler win on a TV quiz show to spend on his prize holiday?

FG How many teams took part in each edition of *Sporting Triangles*?

FF Which *Blue Peter* presenter is the daughter of the presenter of *That's Show Business*?

IP What did Zaphod Beeblebrox have three of dangling down that most men only have two of?

EH Which TV detective kept his gun in a biscuit jar?

158

SD Which Hollies hit was adapted for a double-glazing commercial?

SS Which mini-series, produced by Lorimar Studios, was first shown in April 1978 and then became a full-blown soap?

FG Which school do Pebbles and Bam Bam go to?

FF What is Dorian Williams most famous for commentating on?

IP Which regiment did Ben Cross's character belong to in *The Far Pavilions*?

EH Which black TV humorist's autobiography is called *Fatherhood*?

159

SD What uniform did the Joy Strings usually wear when singing on TV?

SS Who changed Sue Ellen's life after she first met him at the Miss Texas Beauty Pageant?

FG Who was the first presenter of *Chain Letters*?

FF What is one of Joan Collins's real names and a TV character for Yootha Joyce?

IP What was the name of the sister that Richard Kimble kept in contact with whilst on the run in *The Fugitive*?

EH Which TV captain lives in the Zee Zone?

160

SD Which TV dance team were featured in the film *Can't Stop the Music*?

SS What was Jamie Ewing-Barnes doing when he was killed?

FG Which TV comedian presented Bill Wyman with a walking frame when he married 19-year-old Mandy Smith?

FF Which former *Highway Patrolman* received a speeding ticket when he made a cameo appearance in *CHiPS*?

IP Which TV adventure character had a young orphaned pal called Jai?

EH Which actor links *My Favourite Martian*, *The Incredible Hulk* and *That Magician*?

SD Which musical gave Jason Donovan his first starring West End role?

SS Who died, but then returned to reclaim his 7000-acre ranch called Cedar Ridge?

FG How many legs does the *Mastermind* chair have?

FF Who played the part of Alf's son-in-law in *Till Death Us Do Part*?

IP Why, according to the each week's closing speech, were the names of the characters in *Dragnet* changed?

EH What kind of creature was Oink in *Stingray*?

SD Who has presented *Top of the Pops* and then an ITV game show on the same evening?

SS Which town's most prestigious residential street is Seaview Circle?

FG Which legendary Arthur Askey TV stooge appeared in *Blue Murder at St. Trinians* as a (VERY) large schoolgirl?

FF Who introduced *Panorama* from 1967 to 1972?

IP Which early cop series blew up Lieutenant Muldoon and replaced him with Mike Parker?

EH Which midland comedian's autobiography is called *Sweet and Sour Labrador*?

SD Which *EastEnder* had a hit with *The Ugly Duckling*?

SS Who left Lofty waiting at the altar?

FG What crime was Jessica Tate charged with in the very first year of *Soap*?

FF Who fills the role of Lovejoy?

IP What rank did the leader of *The A-Team* reach in the army?

EH What was the first occasion upon which a British TV audience outnumbered that for radio?

SD Which Australian singing soap star is nicknamed Bruiser?

SS Who couldn't eat the celebration dinner his wife had made because he was dining with Wendy Crozier?

FG Which famous marksman has the same theme-tune as this loner?

FF Who played Goldberg in the 1987 TV version of Pinter's *The Birthday Party*?

IP What began with the words: "Once upon a time there were three girls who went to the police academy..."?

EH From the top of which landmark was the world's second TV service beamed?

165

SD Who made a habit of singing *Dominique* on TV in 1963?

SS What are the first three digits of your postcode if you live in Albert Square?

FG Which *Soap* character had a fling with a South American revolutionary called El Puerco?

FF Which comedian played Bottom in the 1964 TV production of *A Midsummer Night's Dream*?

IP Which is female Dempsey or Makepeace?

EH Which TV company has a thistle as its logo?

166

SD Whose best-selling albums were advertised like washing powder on TV with the piano tune *Ballad for Adeline* as a jingle?

SS Why didn't Reg Cox appear in the second episode of *EastEnders* after he'd been the main feature of episode one?

FG Which cartoon characters should never be blue thanks to their law which says "Everything that can go right will go right"?

FF Which radio DJ starred in a TV programme about Broadmoor?

IP Which colour is the light that flashes on the front of *Knight Rider's* car?

EH Which kid's show featured Zelda, Imperial Queen of Planet Guk?

167

SD Which romantic ballad was a hit for TV tough guy Jimmy Nail?

SS Which *Coronation Street* resident won a car?

FG Who asked for his stall to be furnished in *Chinese Modern*?

FF Which show did Lloyd Bridges say provided him with a sure-fire way to escape Los Angeles smog?

IP What is Eddie Capstick's job in *Capstick's Law*?

EH Who was the bride at the first wedding ever to be watched by over 750 million people?

168

SD Which British TV hero was in the charts for Gary Miller at the same time that US hero Davy Crockett was there for Bill Hayes?

SS Which newspaper used Amos Brearly as a freelance reporter?

FG Who is the only cartoon canine to have an Antarctic island named after him?

FF What was Angela Lansbury's first TV series?

IP Which club was run by a former *EastEnder* and a de-frocked priest?

EH What is the background colour of a standard *Blue Peter* badge?

169

SD Who were the two blind people in the front row of the *USA for Africa* video?

SS Which *EastEnder* has a son called Nick?

FG Which animated couple had their second honeymoon in Las Venus?

FF Who played Gideon in *Gideon's Way*?

IP Which member of *The A-Team* is most regularly seen wearing a tie?

EH Why is *The South Bank Show* so called?

170

SD Which pop star appeared on TV singing *Barcelona* with Spanish opera singer Montserrat Caballe?

SS What was Gail Tilsley's former surname?

FG What colour socks does Cliff usually wear on *Cheers*?

FF Which country did Pete Beale visit to see his brother?

IP How much does Louis charge his drivers for taking their phone messages in *Taxi*?

EH Which two words appeared in brackets after *Softly Softly*?

171

SD Whose 1988 Rio concert attracted a world record solo performance crowd of 180,200 and was filmed for TV?

SS Whose was the first house in *Coronation Street* to boast an inside toilet?

FG How many guns does Deputy Dawg strap on?

FF Which series saw a gang of brickies constructing a swimming pool for Ally Fraser?

IP Which state is the setting for *Little House on The Prairie*?

EH Which children's TV show is based on *The Guinness Book of Records*?

172

SD Which TV cowboy breezed up the charts with *Wayward Wind*?

SS How does Rita Firclough spell the name of her shop?

FG What is Norm's favourite drink in *Cheers*?

FF Which film private eye was brought to TV by Richard Rowntree?

IP What was Smith called before he adopted his alias in *Alias Smith and Jones*?

EH What was the world's first Teletext service called?

173

SD Which record producer and *New Faces* panellist has changed his name from Michael Hayes?

SS Who bought, and then sold, the *Weatherfield Recorder*?

FG What colour is Mork's spacesuit?

FF Who played *The Charmer*?

IP How many guns did Tonto have on his belt?

EH Which programme's Sight Saver Appeal raised over a million pounds?

174

SD What was the title of the 1986 ITV World Cup theme which was performed by Rod Argent working under the name Silsoe?

SS What was Ken Barlow's occupation in the first episode of *Coronation Street*?

FG What kind of creature is ace reporter Huxley?

FF Who played his first sit-com role as the star of *Shelley*?

IP Which detective had a name that sounded like an electric razor and was played by Pierce Brosnan?

EH Which comedian played a property director in *Muck and Brass*?

175

SD Which Byrds song was banned by BBC TV because someone thought it was drug influenced?

SS Who won his seat back on the Wetherfield Council in a 1991 election?

FG What is the British equivalent of America's *Newlywed Game*?

FF Who straightened out her wrinkly stockings to star in *No Frills*?

IP With what did the women from the pub across the road fill the bath containing Magnus Pym's dead father, in *A Perfect Spy*?

EH What was the title of *Gun Law* changed to for most of its British run?

176

SD Which dance troupe made their name on *The Kenny Everett Video Show*?

SS Who did John Ross Ewing's camp counsellor have a hankering for?

FG Which Channel 4 comedy series saw Tony Robinson daring to appear in the nude?

FF Which former pop singer married Jan Francis in *Just Good Friends*?

IP Which spy was *An Englishman Abroad*?

EH Which bear has a friend called Edward Trunk?

177

SD Who wrote the *Coronation Street* theme tune?

SS What was Walter Lankersheim waving in his hand when he burst in on Blake and Krystle Carrington's wedding?

FG On which Gloria Hunniford game show did the BBC refuse to allow clips of their programmes to be shown?

FF Who played *The A-Team's* Hannibal Smith?

IP Which 'Team' were once recorded as having an average of 39 violent acts in each of their programmes?

EH Which film studio was the main focus of *Tales From Hollywood*?

178

SD Which singer fills the *Dallas* role of Clayton Farlow?

SS Whose car carries the number plate EWING 3?

FG Which TV quiz show saw Bob Monkhouse working with bingo cards?

FF Which member of the *Rock Follies* cast won ten thousand pounds in damages after the *Sunday People* said she had a big bum?

IP Which TV detective series starred Patricia Hodge in the title role?

EH What was the sporting subject of *Cudmore's Call*?

179

SD What was the first British TV programme to highlight the recording industry?

SS What did *EastEnders'* gay resident Colin Russel discover he was suffering from when he thought he had AIDS?

FG Which comedy series was a send-up of *Secret Army*?

FF Which actress starred in three episodes of *Dynasty* because her film director husband wanted to see her play a baddie?

IP Which John Wyndham novel was the subject of a drama series starring John Duttine?

EH Which *Daytime Live* presenter also pops up on *Crimewatch UK*?

180

SD What was the first name of the guy who played the keyboards in *Fame*?

SS How did Dirty Den apparently die?

FG Which American character was *Spitting Image* banned from portraying?

FF Which Canadian became an election-broadcast fixture with his Swingometer?

IP Which Stan Bristow film hit was adapted for TV in 1982?

EH What was Robin Day's usual four-word ending to *Question Time*?

181

SD Which camp comic's game show theme was *The Man Who Got Away*?

SS Which former champion advertised *Champion* bread with his daughter Nicola?

FG Which politician wanted to buy his *Spitting Image* puppet but refused to make the cheque out to The Labour Party?

FF Who played herself in Alan Bennett's play, *An Englishman Abroad?*

IP Which 1980s series starred Kenneth Cranham as a recently-demobbed RAF clerk?

EH What children's programme was the first to be screened on BBC2?

182

SD What was this group's biggest television related hit?

SS Which soap did *Softly Softly* actors Norman Bowler and Terrence Rigsby move on to?

FG Which cockney comedian discovered Sally Thomsett?

FF Which BBC newsreader interviews *HAL* the computer in *2001 A Space Odyssey*?

IP Which deputy's temporary New York City assignment is at Manhattan's 27th Precinct?

EH Which animated leading lady's vital statistics are 19-19-19?

183

SD What kind of music featured in the series *Honky Tonk Heroes*?

SS What did Fred Gee, Terry Bradshaw and Alf Roberts secretly keep in the cellar of the Rovers Return?

FG Which city was home to Ollie Beak, the puppet owl?

FF Which TV star called his autobiography *I Want To Tell You A Story*?

IP What was *Amos Burke: Secret Agent* the follow up to?

EH Which country was the setting for the climax of the TV film *Raid on Entebbe*?

184

SD Which singing-dancing former model now has the surname Lawson?

SS Which *Coronation Street* actor is an expert swordsman who arranges fights for films and TV?

FG Where did Doberman, Ritzig and Paparelli do their army service?

FF Which 1980 series based on a J. B. Priestley novel starred Judy Cornwell as a member of the Dinky Doos?

IP What colour hat did Hopalong Cassidy always wear?

EH Which writer of the successful play *The Ghost Train* played Private Godfrey in *Dad's Army*?

(185)

SD Who was the boss of Melody Ranch?

SS Which *Coronation Street* role has Eileen Derbyshire filled since the third episode?

FG Which town on the River Tum gives amusement to children?

FF Which famous comedy actor retired from showbusiness in January 1988?

IP Which continent was the setting for *Daktari*?

EH Which war was the subject of *The Quiet Man*?

(186)

SD Who was the first man to play the role of Dolly in *Hello Dolly*?

SS Which regular *Coronation Street* character originally moved into the Street pretending to be Mrs. Harry Bates?

FG What five words did Harry Corbett always close *The Sooty Show* with?

FF Which former member of *Ralph Reader's Gang Show* went on to host his own programmes including *Up the Elephant, Round the Castle*??

IP Which island was the setting for *Elephant Boy*?

EH Which member of the Redgrave family starred in *Maggie*?

(187)

SD Which *Opportunity Knocks* winner starred in *Gypsy* on Broadway?

SS Which *Angels* actress was married to Simon MacCorkingdale?

FG Which member of the Royal Family masterminded the *Grand Knockout Tournament*?

FF Which actress went from *Yes Honestly* to *Pig in the Middle*?

IP Which school did John Steed of *The Avengers* attend?

EH Which *Apollo 11* astronaut was the subject of the documentary *Return to Earth*?

(188)

SD Which of this singer's songs went to number one after appearing in a jeans commercial?

SS Which member of the *Educating Rita* film cast is probably best known for her *Telecom* commercials?

FG Who was the Frank in *Let's Be Frank*?

FF Which famous interviewer supervised, but didn't take part in *At Last the 1948 Show*?

IP Which 1971 Glenda Jackson series had episodes called *The Lion's Club* and *Sweet England's Pride*?

EH Which actress brought her imaginary friend Marlene from radio to televison?

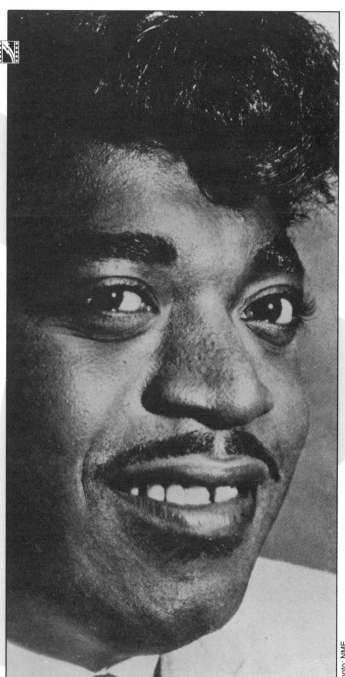

SD Which channel broadcast the heavy rock *Colour Me Pop* series in the '60s?

SS Which *Howard's Way* sexpot played a Dr. Who baddie in *The Mark of the Rani*?

FG Which is the only quiz on TV that pits one contestant against two?

FF Which actor left his junk behind to open a corner shop in *Grundy*?

IP What was the name of the Welsh pirate in the *Buccaneers* series?

EH Who has directed TV films including works on Elgar, Debussy, Bartok and Delius?

---

(190)

SD Which band borrowed their name from *The Flintstones* to have a hit with the Beatles song *Ob-La-Di-Ob-La-Da*?

SS Whose son did Kenneth Farringdon occasionally appear as on *Coronation Street*?

FG Who was the first host of *Ultra Quiz*?

FF What science does Heather Couper regularly discuss on TV?

IP Which city do Jonathan and Jennifer Hart live in?

EH Who sat next to Phones at the controls of *Stingray*?

---

(191)

SD Which TV series' theme was *Heaven and Hell-Third Movement* which was a hit for Vangelis?

SS Which early soap featured Dr. Ed Nelson?

FG What film is showing at the drive-in movie that *The Flintstones* are seen leaving at the end of each show?

FF Which game show host's father became rich by selling custard powder?

IP Who does Peter Ritter carry out investigations for?

EH Which city was the setting for the thrice repeated *Armchair Theatre* play *No Trams to Lime Street*?

---

(192)

SD Which TV pop show was co-presented by a green alien called Gilbert?

SS Who gave Mike Baldwin a thousand pounds towards her husband's gambling debts?

FG Which female duo received complaints after using 70 real babies in a sketch about multiple births?

FF Which film critic was Channel 4's anchorman for the 1988 Olympics?

IP Which crime-busters were under the control of a sergeant played by Ian Hogg?

EH Which family were featured in the most-watched documentary ever to appear on British television?

---

(193)

SD Which pop group appeared on the *Ed Sullivan Show* in 1964 when Mitzi Gaynor topped the bill?

SS What colour were Hilda Ogden's plaster ducks?

FG What breed of dog is this cowardly canine?

FF Which alternative comedian played Conny Kujau in *Selling Hitler*?

IP What was Regan's rank in the final episode of *The Sweeney*?

EH Which TV Western hero was created by legendary writer O.Henry?

---

(194)

SD Which soap star told newspapers in 1957 that she was taking lessons to become a pop singer?

SS What change of headgear did George Cole make when he played an Arthur Daley-style role for the *Leeds Permanent Building Society*?

FG Which programme might find Arthur Bostrom giving directions to the "Shit-eau"?

FF Which member of the cast also co-wrote *Black Adder*?

IP Whose real-life pregnancy was written into the plot of *Cagney and Lacey*?

EH Which children's series was written by Elizabeth Beresford?

©1985 Hanna

195

SD What type of holidays were promoted by White Plains singing *Step Into A Dream*?

SS Which soap starred Kylie Minogue as Char and Jane Hall as Regina?

FG What was the name of the Maplins Welsh yellowcoat?

FF Which star of *Red Dwarf* presented the game show, *Cyberzone*?

IP Which troop was stationed at Fort Courage?

EH Which area of which city was the setting for *Please Sir*?

196

SD Which TV comedian is actually quite a talented pianist and used to play with a jazz band?

SS Which product's commercials included the exchange: "Do you know the piano's on me foot dad?" ..."You 'um it son and I'll play it"?

FG Which was British televison's first quiz show?

FF Who does Janette Charles bear a striking resemblance to?

IP Name this character's motor-cycle riding sidekick?

EH What two people's pictures hung on Alf Garnett's living-room wall?

197

SD Which DJ was Britain's first American football presenter?

SS Which soap had just ended when the SAS raid on the Iranian Embassy began and became the world's longest news flash?

FG What do the knobs do at the end of Edith's mother's bed in *'Allo 'Allo*?

FF Which *Army Game* actor became Adrian Mole's grandfather?

IP What kind of business provided the main setting for the drama series *Thin Air*?

EH What role did Michael Keaton fill on film that Adam West rose to fame in on TV?

198

SD What was the title of Johnny Logan's second Eurovision winner?

SS Why was Krystle Carrington given her first name?

FG Which country did Shelley's daughter emigrate to?

FF Who once said that the person he'd most like to meet was "Des O'Connor's music teacher because he needs some encouragement"?

IP What punctuation mark decorated the costume of Batman's enemy, The Riddler?

EH Which superhero attends Shuster University?

199

SD Which *Man from UNCLE* actor had a hit with *Communication*?

SS Which Carrington died in the hotel fire?

FG Which series features Carstairs and Fairfax?

FF Who once said "I can train a dog in five minutes. It takes longer to train the owner"?

IP What was the name of Silver's girlfried in *The Adventures of Long John Silver*?

EH Which two characters spoke in a language known as 'Oddle Poddle'?

200

SD Which British cop theme was a hit for Ken Mackintosh?

SS Which Carrington lost a lover, Luke Fuller, in a massacre?

FG Why doesn't Richard O'Sullivan's *Me and My Girl* character have a wife?

FF Which two 'foods' forecast the weather?

IP What was the name of *A Perfect Spy*?

EH Who try to keep things clean when The Smoggies cause pollution?

201

SD Which '50s TV trio saw their *Mummy Kissing Santa Claus*?

SS What was the profession of Ken Barlow's younger brother?

FG What is the family relationshp between the two main characters who live together in *Don't Wait Up*?

FF Which romantically named actor played Raffles?

IP What job did Suzi Kettles' husband do in *Tutti Frutti*?

EH What is the name of the egg-shaped cuddly toy in *Playschool*?

202

SD How many weeks did Acker Bilk's *Stranger on the Shore* spend at number 1 in the BBC top ten?

SS Which TV soap celebrated its 2000th edition first — *Crossroads*, *Coronation Street* or *EastEnders*?

FG What two words complete the catchphrase "Smile please you're on............."?

FF What did Carol Hersee do to be seen on television for more hours than anyone else in Britain?

IP What was Master Po's disability in *Kung Fu*?

EH Who presented *The First Eden*?

203

SD Who appeared on *Top of the Pops* in fairy tale dress to promote *Prince Charming*?

SS Which *Dallas* character married the same man twice?

FG Which New Zealand-born comedienne married a funny man after starring in *Funny Man*?

FF What TV series was Ward Bond making when he died on location?

IP Which TV series telling of the Hapsburghs' story starred Curt Jurgens as Bismark?

EH Which sport is Bill McLaren best known for commentating on?

204

SD Which TV cartoon band became the only non-existent group to have a number 1 hit when they scored with *Sugar Sugar*?

SS Who's "tough and strong and can't go wrong"?

FG Which series had its main character living next door to Abner and Gladys Kravitz?

FF Who married Rula Lenska in 1987?

IP Which *Minder* character left the police to work for a private security firm?

EH Which sport is Clive Everton best known for reporting on?

205

SD Which American all-female band sang *Walk Like an Egyptian* on UK TV in 1986?

SS What is advertised on Chinese TV by someone ringing a doorbell and saying: "Ai fang lai la"?

FG What was Peter Vaughan's *Porridge* role?

FF What was Pete Duel of *Alias Smith and Jones* standing by when he shot himself in December 1971?

IP Which TV title character drinks in a bar called Danny's Place?

EH Where do Doozers do their building?

206

SD Who has held the *Top of the Pops* number one slot for longer than anyone else?

SS Which former Labour deputy leader appeared in Cross-Channel Ferry TV commercials?

FG Who played Adrian Mole's grandmother?

FF Who played Claire Bloom's husband in *Brideshead Revisited*?

IP Which TV title character has a girlfriend called Lee Potter?

EH What is Alice's job?

207

SD Which song saw Rolf Harris prancing around on three legs?

SS What was the name of Matt's first wife on *Emmerdale Farm*?

FG Which comedy series starred Milo O'Shea and Anna Manahan as his mother?

FF Who played *Gunsmoke*'s Matt Dillion on US radio but didn't get the TV part because of his size?

IP Which department of the US government employed Elliot Ness?

EH Which actor committed suicide five months after the death of his wife, Diana Dors?

208

SD Which programme saw the first meeting between 16-year-old Jane Asher and David Jacobs?

SS Which soap has an actor and a character called Burnside?

FG Which husband and wife team were voted 1978's Comedy Act of the Year?

FF Which *Star Trek* actor starred in *Airplane II — The Sequel*?

IP Which cake decorating ex-fiance of a Beatle shared a man with Felicity Kendal in *The Mistress*?

EH Who played Alf Garnett's wife?

209

SD What two words appeared inside brackets after Paul Shane's hit record title *Hi De Hi*?

SS Which *Emmerdale* character accidentally killed himself in 1989?

FG What kind of animal is Kissyfur?

FF What is the final name of Lenny Henry's character Algernon Winston Spencer Churchill Gladstone Disraeli Pitt the Younger?

IP What was the name of the Marchmain's family seat?

EH Which star wears a TV costume which includes $300,000 of gold chains which he claims to own himself?

210

SD Which London Palladium game sequence gave Sparks a top-10 hit title?

SS In which country did Alec Gilroy propose to Bet?

FG Who had an octopus called Aristotle?

FF Who was the Jewish daughter of a Hawaiian painter and decorator who tried to get Michael Parkinson to strip on TV?

IP Which *Star Trek* baddies had sonic disrupter pistols?

EH Which of the *Muppet Show* hecklers was bald?

211

SD Which '60s hit guitarist played the theme for *Have Gun Will Travel*?

SS Who makes J.R.'s favourite chilli?

FG Which comedy series had a sequel called *Whoops Baghdad*?

FF Who started a regular hunt for crooks after presenting *Out of Court*?

IP What language was ITV's 1962 production of *Electra* broadcast in?

EH What began on US TV in 1952 with Ralph Edwards and on UK TV in 1953 with Eamonn Andrews?

212

SD Who, according to her signature tune, "Makes them look like a bunch of fairies"?

SS In which city was Brian Tilsley stabbed to death?

FG Whose comedy show saw Susie Baker botching announcements between sketches?

FF Who was the *Grandstand, Football Focus* presenter prior to Sam Leitch?

IP What is Columbo's rank?

EH What was Bilko's *Formula 7* supposed to remove?

213

SD Which TV lane does ex-Bonzo Dog musician Neil Innes take young children down?

SS Who did Mike Baldwin try to bribe not to turn up when she won a night out with him in a raffle?

FG Which newspaper's readers are the regular butt of Jasper Carrott's jokes?

FF Which American joined the cast of *Colditz*?

IP Which county was the setting for *Rich Tea and Sympathy*?

EH Which TV series followed GP Barry Brewster about when he visited his patients?

214

SD Which member of Duran Duran began his entertainment career as the little boy in a *Pepsi* commercial?

SS Which *Coronation Street* character was offered fifteen thousand for a house she'd paid less than six hundred for?

FG Which game show puts people in *Contestants' Row* before they can take part in the actual games?

FF Who took on Reg Varney's role in the remake series of *The Rag Trade*?

IP What was the series if Ed Asner played a newspaper editor?

EH What is Malcolm's surname in *Watching*?

Photo: Hulton Deutsch

(215)

SD Which dance team replaced Pan's People on *Top of the Pops*?

SS Which *EastEnder* took to using a *Walkman* after winning it in a competition?

FG Which Henry Kelly daytime quiz is played between competitors from all over Europe?

FF What was the subject of this TV presenter's 1967 documentary for *Survival?*

IP What kind of *Practice* did Bob Buzzard appear in?

EH Who is He-Man's deadliest enemy?

(216)

SD Who came fourth in the Eurovision Song Contest with *Power To All Our Friends*?

SS Who owns *The Denver Mirror*?

FG Which role did Paul Shane build into his own in *Hi De Hi*?

FF Which poet presented *An Englishman's Home*?

IP What is Lovejoy's business?

EH Which city was the setting for *Family Affair*?

(217)

SD What seven words follow: "The Six-Five Special coming down the line"?

SS Which soap's very first lines were spoken by Jane Rossington?

FG What is the name of the premises below Melville's seafood restaurant?

FF Who went from being a TV producer to become the last leader of the Liberal Party?

IP What does Bruce Wayne call his underground laboratory?

EH Which anniversary did *Dr. Who* celebrate in 1981?

(218)

SD Which TV theme was a hit for both Duane Eddy and the Ray Anthony Orchestra?

SS Where would you be if Rolly bit Willie?

FG Which TV quiz gave its young contestants as many prizes as they could hold?

FF What was Anthony Hopkins' role in *The Bunker*?

IP Which series starred Ronnie Barker and Patricia Brake as husband and wife?

EH Which country's resistance movement was the subject of *Secret Army*?

219

SD What colour shoes did Sandie Shaw wear when she sang *Puppet on a String* in the Eurovision Song Contest?

SS Where did Angie Watts go to when Anita Dobson left *EastEnders*?

FG Who withdrew his book of collected speeches from Faber and Faber when they published a *Spitting Image* book picturing a naked Prince Andrew?

FF Which sports reporter was brought in as a main presenter of TVam because he was ordinary?

IP Which decade was the setting for *We'll Meet Again*?

EH Who presented a Sunday evening series which looked at *Castles Abroad*?

220

SD What kind of animal was a hit for the Goodies?

SS What was the name of *Crossroads* extended to towards the end of its life?

FG What was the series if Timothy West was Bradley Hardacré and Caroline Blakiston played his wife?

FF Which *Young Ones* actor had bright orange hair and studs on his face?

IP Which 1981 hit drama series was set in the Vatican of the fifteenth century?

EH Where did BBC cameraman Mick Burke die?

221

SD Which comedy series had *Liberty Bell* as its theme music?

SS Which cinema super-star became Jason Colby?

FG Who took over *Treasure Hunt* from Anneka Rice?

FF Which pseudo-science series was hosted by Miriam Stoppard and Rob Buckman?

IP Which state provided the setting for *Knots Landing*?

EH Whose funeral was televised as *The Valiant Man*?

222

SD Who was the first presenter of *The Old Grey Whistle Test*?

SS Which TV despatch rider was in commercials for alcohol-free lager whilst trying to overcome a drink problem?

FG Which quiz show was originally part of *Wednesday Night Out*?

FF Who starred opposite her real-life husband in *A Fine Romance*?

IP Which TV copper made his appearance in *The XYY Man* before getting his own series?

EH Which was the first regular half-hour news bulletin?

223

SD Which member of The Who starred in *How to be Cool*?

SS Which Government sell-off was advertised by telling you to tell Sid?

FG What did the *Auf Wiedersehen Pet* characters call Germans?

FF Which knock-about comedian starred in the drama *Going Gently*, in which he died of cancer?

IP Which cops and robbers series was set in Seven Dials?

EH Which series did Bernard Braden win the 1964 BAFTA award for?

224

SD Who sang *All Night Long* during the televised closing ceremony of the 1984 Olympics?

SS What was the name of Bet and Alec's first dog at the Rovers Return?

FG Who replaced Arnold in the *Happy Days* cafe?

FF Which former footballer sent Julian Clary twelve red roses after calling him a "poofter"?

IP Which Evelyn Waugh novel became a TV play with Donald Pleasance and Denholm Elliott working for the *Daily Beast*?

EH Which royal event held the record for the biggest TV audience until *Live Aid* came along?

225

SD Which Eurovision winner had a hit version of 10 CC's *I'm Not In Love*?

SS How was Monica Colby's baby written out of the series almost as soon as it was born?

FG What does Fred Flintstone wear around his neck?

FF Who lost his job in the Shadow Cabinet for taking a job on Sky Television?

IP What was the job of the people who starred in the documentary *The Duty Men*?

EH Which church is in the centre of the Thames Television logo?

226

SD Whose 1991 TV video saw her duetting with her long-dead father?

SS Who stole the clocking-in clock as a souvenir when the *Coronation Street* factory closed down?

FG Which long-haired rock star appeared on *That's My Dog* with a dog he'd never actually seen before?

FF Which traveller presented *Living with Waltzing Matilda*?

IP Who was Carol Royle living life without, in her series with Simon Cadell?

EH Why was the Queen's Silver Jubilee shown only on BBC television?

227

SD Which song flopped for TV presenter Jonathan King but was a smash for Laura Branigan?

SS Who cleaned for the Lowthers and the Baldwins?

FG Which TV quiz show's adult and junior versions were hosted by Jeremy Hawk?

FF Which Sidney Poitier cinema role was re-created for TV by Howard Rollins?

IP What was the title of the programme if Nigel Havers was playing the role of Gorse?

EH Which televised sport is Peter O'Sullivan most famously associated with?

228

SD Name this 1960s TV dance group, who had a hit with *Lover Please?*

SS Which soap's minor characters include factory workers Marg Butler and Josie Philips?

FG Which *Golden Shot* role has been filled by Derek Young, Alan Bailey and Johnny Baker?

FF Who played *Shoestring* and is married to the woman who borrows *Gold Blend* from her neighbour?

IP What was the follow-up series to *Rockliffe's Babies* called?

EH What does Ali Bongo often appear in TV credits as being the adviser in?

229

SD Which pop series did NBC launch on the same day as *Star Trek?*

SS Who is the best hotpot cook at the Rovers Return?

FG Whose real wife played Oscar's ex on *The Odd Couple?*

FF What name did Norma Sykes adopt when her 42-19-35 figure started to attract attention?

IP Which 1981 assassination attempt featured in the play *The Most Dangerous Man in the World?*

EH Which TV company's closing caption included boiled eggs?

230

SD Which TV band became the only act with Roman numerals in their name to have a UK number 1?

SS Which film star took the *Dynasty* role of Lady Ashley?

FG What was Warren Weber's *Happy Days* nickname?

FF Which member of the *Blue Peter* team once climbed up Nelson's Column?

IP Which series based on a Chris Mullin novel saw left-wing steel-worker Harry Perkins become prime minister?

EH What is St.Clare the patron saint of?

Photo: Hulton Deutsch

231

SD In which British holiday resort did Abba win the Eurovision Song Contest?

SS Which *EastEnder* character's assassin was hidden in the daffodils?

FG How many milk bottles are standing on the porch when Fred Flintstone puts the cat out?

FF Who was the subject of *This Year's Blonde*?

IP Which cop show's outdoor shots are filmed at Chicago's Maxwell Street precinct?

EH Whose *Glass Menagerie* was adapted for television in 1974?

232

SD Which *Six-Five Special* regular's proper name was Gordon Langhorn?

SS Which American soap was almost called *The Vintage Years*?

FG Which comedian tried his hand at acting in *Up the Elephant, Round the Castle*?

FF Which series married Julia McKenzie to Anton Rodgers?

IP Which famous detective was first played by Joan Hickson in 1984?

EH Which Bill Tidy cartoon strip had a title inspired by *The Forsyte Saga*?

233

SD Who made his US national TV debut on 28th January 1956 on The Dorsey Brothers Stage Show?

SS Which soap's characters have included Connie, Louella, Serena and Sly?

FG Who was the first compere of *Telly Addicts*?

FF Who played Tripper in *Tripper's Day*?

IP Which TV detective was played by Stacey Keach?

EH How many programmes in the *Talking Pictures* series were dedicated to silent movies?

234

SD Who received a standing ovation after making a speech during a televised rock concert from Wembley at Easter, 1990?

SS Who did Cliff Barnes marry in an attempt to control two-thirds of Ewing Oil?

FG How many dates do *Blind Date* contestants have to choose from?

FF Who went from Regan to being journalist Mitch?

IP Who was the television play *Amy* about?

EH Whose novel was *The Moneychangers* based on?

235

SD Which female pop singer turned down a multi-million dollar deal to appear in *Diet Pepsi* commercials in 1989?

SS Which of the Colbys was almost killed by paint fumes?

FG In which role did Peter Howitt become a heart-throb?

FF Who was television's *Freud* until he became an Agatha Christie sleuth?

IP Which TV sci-fi series had a one-letter title?

EH What topped the TV viewing charts for the week ending 16th June in 1971, 1981 and 1991?

236

SD Which instrument does Victoria Wood usually play on her shows?

SS Who got *Coronation Street's* Andrea Clayton pregnant?

FG Which alternative comedian became a *Black Adder* writer from the second series on?

FF Which Hollywood heart-throb played a spaceship captain in *The Martian Chronicles*?

IP Which TV adaptation of a Daphne du Maurier novel starred Joanna David as the second wife?

EH Which channel's early-morning programme displays its clock at the top of the screen?

237

SD Who was the first rap artist to have his own cartoon series?

SS Which *Falcon Crest* actress was formerly Mrs. Ronnie Reagan?

FG How many saddles were there on the Goodies' bicycle?

FF Which of the *Monty Python* team had an acting role in *G.B.H.*?

IP What was the name of Doug McClure's character in *The Virginian*?

EH What did Davy Crockett call *Old Betsy*?

238

SD What chat-show host and sports reporter had a hit with *Shifting Whispering Sands*?

SS Who was given the Dallas police Department number 6306 when suspected of murder?

FG Which puppet series featured the Soup Dragon?

FF Which role did young Martin Harvey fill in the 1991 TV adaptation of *Great Expectations*?

IP Which series starred Adam Faith as Gordon Shade?

EH What was the American series *Sugarfoot* called in the UK?

Photo: Hulton Deutsch

(239)

SD Which member of the *That's Life* team had a hit under the name Ivor Biggun?

SS What was Paul Collins of *Brookside* timed at taking more than 5 hours to do in 1987?

FG Why did Steve Nallon's TV career look to be in danger when John Major became prime minister?

FF Who took over from Jenny Seagrove as *A Woman of Substance*?

IP What school does this *Miss* teach at?

EH Which quiz show host headed a controversial 1990s working-party on the future of the Cairngorms?

(240)

SD Which TV hero's name was adopted by Stephen Duffy?

SS Who was Mike Baldwin living with when he began his affair with Jackie Ingram?

FG Which *Happy Days* dude was studying to become an eye doctor?

FF Who received a warm response for hosting *Global Village*?

IP What is Templeton Peck's *A-Team* nickname?

EH Which Hywel Bennett series had the same title as a drama about a poet?

(241)

SD Who left *Neighbours* "To concentrate on my singing career"?

SS Which *Emmerdale* role is filled by Stan Richards?

FG Which section of the brewery do Laverne and Shirley work in?

FF Whose regular lead into a commercial break is "We'll be back in a trice"?

IP Which show lost Henry Blake when his plane crashed in the Sea of Japan?

EH What was Galton and Simpson's next major comedy series after they parted with Hancock?

(242)

SD What name does August Darnel go by when he stands in front of his Coconuts on TV?

SS Which *EastEnder* took a bar job after working in a travel agency?

FG What programme had Jillian Comber handing out cabbages?

FF Which American cop series starred John Ritter, son of the cowboy Tex?

IP Which city was the setting for *Rockliffe's Babies*?

EH Whose only TV words were: "You killed the President, you rat"?

(243)

SD Which opera singer appeared on TV singing *Perhaps Love* with John Denver?

SS Which family lived in a caravan when they first arrived in Emmerdale?

FG Which member of the *Monty Python* team wrote a children's book called *The Saga of Eric the Viking*?

FF Which Man from UNCLE starred opposite Diana Rigg in *Mother Love*?

IP Which islands were the setting for *Tumbledown*?

EH Which dog's statue stands in the BBC's *Blue Peter* garden?

(244)

SD Which pop presenter and performer devised BBC's *No Limits*?

SS Why was this character once fined by the courts?

FG Who took over Sid's Cafe in *Last of the Summer Wine* when Sid died?

FF Which of the *Bread* boys is played by Nick Conway?

IP What was wrong with the girl in the drama-documentary *Dummy*?

EH Which member of the Redgrave family became a star in the American *House Calls* series?

Photo: Scope Features

(245)

SD Which mother of a *Blue Peter* presenter didn't have much success with her recording of *True Love*?

SS Who became Mayor of Weatherfield in 1973?

FG What was Ollie Beak's doggy friend called?

FF Who was the main female presenter when *Wish You Were Here* was first broadcast in 1973?

IP Which cop series followed the exploits of Baker and Poncharello?

EH Which British TV series was shown in America with the title *My Partner the Ghost*?

(246)

SD Who went on a *Summer Holiday* with Cliff Richard before settling down as *Worzel Gummidge's* girlfriend?

SS Which soap star has been married to Myron Frutterman, Ronald Reagan and Fred Karger (twice!)?

FG How did Rigsby always refer to his female tenant?

FF Who was the Scottish presenter of *Frocks on the Box*?

IP Which son rode Beauty in *Bonanza*?

EH What was *The Royalty* in the TV series of that title?

(247)

SD Which *Bread* brother was played by Jonathan Morris?

SS Which British soap received a new shopping mall in 1990 to celebrate its 1000th episode?

FG What did a Routh do in the UK that a Funt did in the USA?

FF Which British DJ presented *Foul Ups, Bleeps and Blunders* on American TV?

IP Why does Kojak suck lollies?

EH Which colourful Hollywood dancing queen starred in the 1959 BBC musical *Carissima*?

(248)

SD Which *Adrian Mole* actress was married to Maurice Gibb of the Bee Gees?

SS Which 1991 film starring Sally Field was a send-up of TV soaps?

FG What was the mechanical drawing device on Billy Bean's wonderful machine called?

FF What is the family relationship between Lord Grade and Michael Grade?

IP What can you board by using the shuttle *Galileo*?

EH Which French author's works were serialised in *Roads to Freedom*?

• G A M E 5 •

249

SD Which TV pop show was hosted by Stevi Merike, followed by David Jensen and then Mike Reid?

SS Which Clash hit reached number 1 in 1991 after being used in a *Levi's* commercial?

FG What three words appear at the end of a *Looney Tunes* cartoon?

FF Which Maplins entertainer became theatrical agent Harry James?

IP What did Simon Locke become when he moved to the big city?

EH What is Janet Waldo's contribution to the *Penelope Pitstop* cartoons?

250

SD Which children's TV pop show was hosted by Alistair Pirie?

SS Which 1970s Donna Summer hit was rehashed in 1991 by soap star Sophie Lawrence?

FG Which TV series won Marty Feldman a BAFTA award?

FF Which TV comedy duo were once billed as the Harper Brothers?

IP Who adopted the name of a car whilst hitch-hiking from Betelgeux to Orion?

EH Which movie superstar stood in for a sick Raymond Burr in Perry Mason's *The Case of the Constant Doyle*?

251

SD Which Radio One DJ was voted into the Gunk Tank during the 1989 *Comic Relief* show?

SS Which *Coronation Street* character often talked about her daughter, Joan?

FG Which famous *Carry On* comedian narrated *Will O' The Wisp*?

FF What is the name of the sheep who interviews guests on *Ghost Train*?

IP Which city's patients are treated at St Elsewhere?

EH How many great paintings were the subject of the biggest TV series ever devoted to art?

252

SD Which classic pop show was based on the earlier *Pop Inn*?

SS Who was known as 'Queen of the Soaps' and appeared in *Crossroads* on 3521 occasions?

FG What did The Fonz do for a living?

FF Who lists his favourite memory as: "Seeing car stickers 'J.R. for President' outnumbering those for Carter and Reagan"?

IP Which character was assisted in his various travels by Ace, Mel, Peri, Nyssa and K9?

EH Which US state did *Rumpole of the Bailey* retire to?

253

SD Which musical TV star called his autobiography *From Drags to Riches*?

SS Which *Coronation Street* character fell foul of his wife when he shaved off his moustache for a bet?

FG Who played the chauffeur in *Home James*?

FF Which impersonator hosted his own TV *Sketch Pad*?

IP What kind of surgery was the setting for *The Eleventh Hour*?

EH Which country was the setting for *The Regiment*?

254

SD Which all-singing-all-dancing-all-grinning female made her first appearance on *Opportunity Knocks* at the age of 6?

SS Which soap found *T.J.Hooker* girl, Heather Locklear, in the role of Sammy Jo?

FG Who built a machine out of sticks and stones and nuts and bolts and glue?

FF Which '60s TV detective was played by John Gregson?

IP What was the central piece of action in the TV film *Enola Gay*?

EH Which soap star had top billing in *The Return of the World's Greatest Detective*?

255

SD Which of Jean-Michel Jarre's works was his biggest hit and most regularly used composition for TV backing tracks?

SS What operation did Miss Ellie undergo?

FG Which quiz show involves a gigantic typewriter keyboard?

FF Which Western hero was the first guest on *Rowan and Martin's Laugh-In*?

IP Which Victor Hugo novel inspired *The Fugitive*?

EH Which cartoon series is set in the desert in America's Southwest?

256

SD Which vacational TV title gave *Human League* a hit in 1980?

SS Which TV oil company was first formed in 1930?

FG Which former DJ hosts *All Clued Up*?

FF Which flamboyant TV interviewer failed to win Hereford for the Liberals in 1959?

IP Which respected actress played Barbie Batchelor in *The Far Pavilions*?

EH Who did Barney find living on the dump?

(257)

SD Which *Equalizer* actor had a top-50 hit with *The Way You Look Tonight*?

SS Which soap was wound up after only a hundred episodes in 1986?

FG What nationality did Manuel become when *Fawlty Towers* was sold to Spanish television?

FF Which conjuror was a regular *What's My Line* panelist?

IP What is Thomas Magnum's middle name?

EH What was Laurence Olivier's first TV role?

(258)

SD Which top-ten folk singer presented the children's programme *Tickle on the Tum*?

SS Which *Coronation Street* character will be 60 on 8th May 2000?

FG How many illuminated lights win the star prize in *Every Second Counts*?

FF Which kid's TV presenter began his broadcasting career in New Zealand?

IP What is a star constellation visible from Australia and the name of Clayton Farlow's ranch?

EH Who sometimes called himself Don Pedro O'Sullivan when he took off his mask?

(259)

SD Which Glaswegian hippy appeared on six consecutive *Ready Steady Go's*?

SS What job has been done by Mr. Chumley, Mr. Sparrow and Mr. Willmott-Brown?

FG What was Paula Wilcox's character called in *The Lovers*?

FF Which specs-wearing lady hosted Channel 4's *Wine Programme*?

IP What is the name of the chauffeur in *Hart to Hart*?

EH Which cartoonist's work was the basis for *My World and Welcome To It*?

(260)

SD Which TV programme has the same name as a Rezillo's top-twenty hit?

SS Who was the only original *Coronation Street* character still in the show at the end of 1991?

FG Which *I Love Lucy* cast member's contract stipulated that she remain 20 pounds overweight?

FF Which film director is this actress married to?

IP Which John le Carré series starred Peter Egan as Magnus Pym?

EH Why has the road surface of the Mall been red since 1953?

Photo: Hulton Deutsch

Photo: Scope Features

261

SD What are the words to the first line of this creepy family's theme tune?

SS Where did the Rev. Donald Hinton take over from the Rev. Edward Ruskin?

FG What is the first thing that *What's My Line* contestants are always asked to do?

FF Which TV sports commentator was editor of the *Cheshire County Express* at the age of 23?

IP Which TV cop was known as T.S. to his friends?

EH What does *Thunderbird 1* launch from?

262

SD What drink was promoted by Bobby Goldsboro's *In The Summertime*?

SS Which soap is set in Erinsborough?

FG What score must be obtained or beaten to win a *Bullseye* star prize?

FF Who, in 1991, became the first psychic investigator to be given his own British TV series?

IP What did the Six Million Dollar Man do for a living before he had his accident?

EH Whose was the first and the last head to be seen in the opening credits of *A Prime Minister on Prime Ministers*?

263

SD Which '50s and '60s music game was presented by Marion Ryan and Jackie Ray?

SS What is Billi Corkhill's *Brookside* trade?

FG How many contestants are there at the beginning of a 3-2-1 programme?

FF Who was the most senior member of the Royal Family to head a team in the heavily criticised *It's A Knockout*?

IP Which country's fleet did 'The Heroes' attack?

EH Which was the first TV Western to be broadcast in colour?

264

SD Who was the "king of the wild frontier"?

SS What were advertised as being "mighty meaty matey"?

FG Which great comedy character had a girlfriend called Joan Hogan?

FF Which TV star made money as the owner of Motorvation, the company that transported guests to his show?

IP What four letters appear on T.J.Hooker's uniform?

EH Which series developed from a pilot film called *Regan*?

265

SD Who was the only regular female presenter of *The Old Grey Whistle Test*?

SS What is Alexis Colby's favourite food?

FG Who replaced David Vine as the *It's A Knockout* commentator?

FF Which member of the Royal Family asked Terry Wogan why he didn't think up his own questions?

IP Which gambling series saw the Dragon Club renamed Olivers?

EH Who played Sally Geeson's father in *Bless This House*?

266

SD Which TV presenter ended the documentary *Viva Elvis* by singing: "You ain't never caught a wabbit and you ain't no fwiend of mine"?

SS Which of the Carrington's shacked up with Ted Dinard in Greenwich Village?

FG What is the name of the German General in *'Allo 'Allo*?

FF In which show did Ed Asner get the title role after his success as Mary Tyler Moore's boss?

IP Which British TV series never set foot outside the UK but had a sheriff as one of its main characters?

EH What is the significance of the number at the end of the series title *Beverly Hills, 90210*?

(267)

SD Which Welsh cabaret artiste made a comeback after singing Prince's *Kiss* on a Jonathan Ross show?

SS Who completed the Rovers Return snug trio with Minnie Caldwell and Ena Sharples?

FG Which David Jason comedy series saw the bridegroom's dad bedding the bride's mum at the reception?

FF Which newsreader has a brother who plays Hercule Poirot?

IP What is the name of the company that *Boon* rides for?

EH Which TV cop series was a spin-off from the movie *Prescription Murder*?

(268)

SD Which oft-televised video begins: "Is this the real thing, or is this just fantasy"?

SS Which county did Hilda Ogden retire to?

FG Which household servant boasts the surname DuBois?

FF Who drew the outline of Alfred Hitchcock that appeared at the start of his shows?

IP Which crime-busting show once had former Presidential press secretary Pierre Salinger in the role of the villain Lucky Pierre?

EH What are you watching if Scully is in Scarborough scrutinizing scrap?

(269)

SD What was the Partridge family's dog called?

SS Which *Woolpack* regular was never given any lines?

FG Who hosted *Masterteam*?

FF Who created the *Peter Gunn* TV series and is married to the star of *Mary Poppins*?

IP What did the Lone Ranger make from his dead brother's waistcoat?

EH Which TV series was successfully sued by a circus performer called Paladin?

(270)

SD Why did Britain stand even less chance than usual of winning the Eurovision Song Contest in 1956 and 1958?

SS What car accessory did Charlie Cotton give to Frank and Pat Butcher as a wedding present?

FG Which member of a very famous puppet trio had a voice provided by Gladys Whitred?

FF Which *Black Adder* actor presents *Stay Tooned*?

IP Which Greenwich Village precinct was the setting for *Barney Miller*?

EH In which comedy series did this actor appear as an impresario?

271

SD What position was Great Britain lucky enough to achieve on the first occasion it entered the *Eurovision Song Contest*?

SS Who won the Queen Vic's first 'glamorous grandmother' competition?

FG What colour sweaters were worn by the *Sporting Triangles* teams?

FF Who went from being Harvey Moon to starring in *Chimera*?

IP What is Seymour's surname in *Last of the Summer Wine*?

EH Which glamorous TV sleuth series was based on the '30s film, *The Thin Man*?

272

SD Which piece of music became a major hit after Thames Television pulled it out of their library for a 1972 cop series set in Europe?

SS What was the name of the fictional quiz show that *EastEnder* Arthur Fowler appeared on?

FG What was Fliss and Chris's surname in *The Cuckoo Waltz*?

FF Which former member of Britain's Ryder Cup team went on to present *Pro Celebrity Golf* on television?

IP What seasonal plant gave its name to the computer in *Red Dwarf*?

EH Whose novel was the basis for *Anna Karenina*?

273

SD Which Sex Pistols video was banned by the BBC as an insult to royalty?

SS What was the name of Ali's Cafe changed to in *EastEnders*?

FG Which scriptwriting comedian chaired *Jokers Wild*?

FF Which member of *The A-Team* appeared in the film *Rocky*?

IP Which city's streets would you expect to find Karl Malden and Michael Douglas patrolling?

EH What traumatic experience was Jason Colby going through at the start of the series that Frankie Colby was going through at the end?

274

SD Which alternative fat guy made a record called *Didn't You Kill My Brother*?

SS What is Mrs.Pearce's first name in *Coronation Street*?

FG Which famous TV army camp was in the city of Roseville?

FF Which movie star played the role of Inspector Abberline in the 1988 TV production of *Jack the Ripper*?

IP What was Peter Barkworth's job in *Telford's Change*?

EH Which American highway did George Maharis and Martin Milner travel along in a TV series?

275

SD Who joined Bonnie Tyler to sing *A Rockin' Good Way* on TV in the 1980s?

SS How many times has *Coronation Street's* Alf Roberts been married?

FG In which sport did Lucy Ricardo become an unwilling participant during an *I Love Lucy* trip to Mexico?

FF Whose more serious roles have included Chrissie's wife in *The Boys from the Blackstuff*?

IP What make of car does Magnum drive?

EH What does it say on a *Jim'll Fix It* medal?

276

SD Which TV show had a hit with *Santa Claus Is On The Dole*?

SS Who was pregnant in the very first episode of *EastEnders*?

FG What word means 'Hello' on the planet Ork?

FF Who was the first British chat show host to admit that TV made him a millionaire?

IP What was Hudson's first name in *Upstairs Downstairs*?

EH Which Muriel Spark novel was adapted for TV with Geraldine McEwan in the title role?

277

SD Which member of the Maplins team had a freak number 2 hit with *Starting Together*?

SS Who upset patriotic Albert Tatlock by buying a German car?

FG Which TV comedy actor narrated *The Perishers*?

FF Who appeared on TV at Christmas 1958 and said of her family: "We have no plans for space travel — at the moment"?

IP Which Californian town was *Sunset Strip* set in?

EH Who went *Solo* after a spell of *The Good Life*?

278

SD Which TV scientist featured on Thomas Dolby's hit *She Blinded Me With Science*?

SS What did Elsie Tanner's husband Steve do for a living?

FG Which *Dad's Army* character had the nickname 'Napoleon'?

FF Who was *World of Sport's* main presenter for 16 years?

IP How did King and Castle earn their living?

EH What name was given to the children's version of *Krypton Factor*?

279

SD Which comedy show theme makes the observation: "Every inch of him is limp. He's a fourteen carat wimp"?

SS Who divorced Jill Harvey and married Frea Offermans?

FG What book does the celebrity guest always have on hand on *Countdown*?

FF What is the first name of Michael Parkinson's wife?

IP What was The Baron's name?

EH Which common christian name was selected as a surname by the leader of the aliens in *V*?

280

SD Which *TW3* singer appeared in the film *Alfie*?

SS Which watery soap setting was originally owned by Jack Rolfe?

FG Whose alter-egos include Gizzard Puke?

FF Who played film star Gene Bradley in *The Adventurer*?

IP What delicate material was the title of a Shirley Conran mini-series?

EH Which game show host lists his favourite memory as: "30 seconds of excruciating pain when I was attacked by a marauding ferret"?

281

SD Who joined Patrick MacNee on his *Kinky Boots* hit?

SS Which country had a king called Galan, according to *Dynasty*?

FG Which *Gilligan's Isle* castaway was also the voice of cartoon character Mr.Magoo?

FF Which female presenter of the '60s became Granada's Head of Children's Programmes in the '70s?

IP Who was the landlady of Jim Bergerac's local The Royal Barge?

EH Who played Luke in *Luke's Kingdom*?

282

SD Which TV theme was a hit for Yannis Markopoulos and his Greek orchestra?

SS Who raped Fallon of *The Colbys*?

FG What was Marigold's real name in *In Sickness and in Health*?

FF Who played the Mayor of Casterbridge in the TV series?

IP What does Mabel deliver in *Chico and the Man*?

EH What was *The Third Man's* name?

283

SD Which mini-series' love theme was a hit for Spanish guitarist Juan Martin?

SS What name appeared next to GAV on the windscreen of Gavin Taylor's car in *Brookside*?

FG What kind of coat did Del Boy's Uncle Albert wear?

FF Which troop did Forrest Tucker and Larry Storch belong to?

IP Which John Buchan character was played on TV by Robert Powell?

EH Who titled his autobiography *I'm Not Spock*?

284

SD What is the British title of the popular French Eurovision loser *L'Amour Est Bleu*?

SS Why didn't *Brookside's* Sheila Grant want her husband to have a vasectomy?

FG What is the name of Lenny Henry's crucial DJ character?

FF What did newsreader Brian Connell have that no previous newsreader has displayed on screen?

IP What kind of creature was Tattoo's friend Chester on *Fantasy Island*?

EH Which TV personality had Government Minister John Nott walk out on him part-way through a 1983 TV interview?

285

SD Who had the best start ever by any solo artist, when her first six singles all reached the top two?

SS Where did *EastEnders* Colin and Barry first meet?

FG How many TV editions of *The Army Game* were made in colour?

FF Who was chosen from 70 candidates to replace Angela Rippon at the BBC in 1981?

IP Who featured in the title of a book, the title of a film and then the title of a TV series starring Jeff Rawle?

EH What had *The Man from Atlantis* lost when he was first found washed up on a beach?

286

SD Which comedy theme was a hit for Michael Medwin, Bernard Breslaw, Alfie Bass and Leslie Fyson in 1958?

SS Who did Harry and Edna Cross buy their *Brookside* bungalow from?

FG What was the only word the *That's Life* talking dog was apparently able to say?

FF Who was the first British newsreader to lose an earring on television?

IP Which TV sleuth has a partner called Tinker?

EH Which author was the subject of the documentary *Mirror of Maigret*?

SD Which early pop show's original theme was *Love and Fury* by the Tornadoes?

SS Which *Emmerdale* character gave birth to a baby on Christmas Eve 1982?

FG What did Roger de Courcey call the racehorse purchased with the earnings made from his Nooky Bear act?

FF Who was the human star of *Cuddles and Co*?

IP Which of John and Sue Peters' friends has the ability to swap heads?

EH What kind of building stood at Petticoat Junction?

SD Which Welshman was the first person to clock up 50 *Top of the Pops* appearances?

SS What relationship did Joan Legget claim to Charlie Cotton

FG What childish decision did Bernie Winters ask Su Pollard, Matthew Kelly and Beryl Reid to make?

FF Who ended up on a 'Desert Island' after presenting *Nationwide*?

IP What four words were printed on Paladin's business card?

EH Which 49-part series began with *The Galaxy Being* and ended with *The Probe*?

SD Which theme from a film did the BBC borrow for the 1984 Olympics?

SS What colour coat is the woman wearing when the dog runs past her at the start of *Coronation Street*?

FG Which TV comedy features Simon and Samantha Harrap?

FF Which series stars Tony Britton as Toby Latimer?

IP What kind of foreign toy was seen to come apart at the beginning of *Tinker, Tailor Soldier Spy*?

EH Who had a career as a TV sleuth after being Donald Sinden's housekeeper in *Our Man At St. Mark's*?

SD Who made her first stage appearance at a Beatles concert when the Fab Four couldn't appear?

SS What was Gelda of *Crossroads* doing when she was raped?

FG Where were the scrap dealers hoping to get a huge haul of junk from in *Salvage*?

FF Which comedian and game show host had a double-act with his former wife, Penny Calvert?

IP Which series sees Irwin Bernstein prosecuting on behalf of the District Attorney?

EH Which city was *The Onedin Line* based in?

Photo: Scope Features

SD Who were the first female vocal duo to perform their number one hit on British TV when they scored in 1977 with *Yes Sir I Can Boogie*?

SS Which character taught this motel worker to read?

FG What was Sam's mother called in *Bewitched*?

FF Who played Timothy Dalton's sister in *Sins*?

IP How did Ken Masters win ten thousand pounds in *Howard's Way*?

EH Which DJ thought it was a little gay prank to bend Wogan's microphone on *Blankety Blank*?

SD What year was it when TV newsreaders told us that it was twenty years ago today since *Sgt.Pepper* was released?

SS Which TV sports personality signed a £220,000 contract with Courage Brewery in 1982?

FG What was the name of Sam's husband in *Bewitched*?

FF Who was the first British TV star to have a programme named after him even when he didn't appear on it?

IP Which university was the setting for *The Glittering Prize*?

EH Which fictional town was the setting for *Crown Court*?

Photo: Syndication International Ltd

(293)

SD How old, according to the theme song, was Davy Crockett when he killed his first bear?

SS Which *Coronation Street* character had an affair with his future wife's stepmother?

FG Which comedy series moved to Camp Fremont from Fort Baxter?

FF Which chat show host did Sir Robin Day describe as "Even more boring than I am"?

IP What is the surname of the family in *Butterflies*?

EH Who was the first of his relatives to have contact with *The Fugitive*?

(294)

SD Who was asked to sing *The Twist* on American TV when the original twister, Hank Ballard, didn't turn up?

SS Which *Dallas* character has had a fling with Eddie Cronin, Ray Krebbs, Mickey Trotter and Roger the photographer?

FG Which radio presenter hosted *The Newly Wed Game*?

FF Who received a credit as a consultant for *Bob Says Opportunity Knocks* but apparently wasn't consulted at all?

IP Which Jeffrey Archer novel became a series in which an MP ignored a blackmail attempt by a prostitute?

EH Which of these Angels married the Bionic Man?

(295)

SD Which long-running rock show did the BBC announce the end of in 1987?

SS Who proposed to Deirdre Barlow in 1983?

FG Which cartoon series sometimes sees a TV host called Ed Sullystone?

FF Which actor was *The Fall Guy*?

IP What kind of machine can be heard under the opening credits of *The Rockford Files*?

EH What was Klinger's rank at the end of the War?

(296)

SD What was the name of Simon Dee's early evening chat show?

SS What 'Prolonged Active Life'?

FG Which 'camp' actor had the catchphrase "I'm free"?

FF Which two Lewis Carroll characters were played by John Gielgud and Malcolm Muggeridge in TV's *Alice in Wonderland*?

IP What headdress was seen at the opening of each episode of *An Age of Kings*?

EH Where were TV cameras allowed for the Coronation of Elizabeth II that they hadn't been allowed for that of her father?

297

SD Which 54-year-old organist was known as 'The Bishop' and had an affair with 22-year-old actress Anita Kay?

SS Which soap saw window cleaner Walter Potts change his name to Brett Falcon in an attempt to become a pop star?

FG Which was Alfie Bass and Bill Fraser's follow-up to *The Army Game*?

FF Which comedy series saw Robertson Hare as the archdeacon and Derek Nimmo as the curate?

IP Which author was the subject of the TV drama *Alice*?

EH Which commentator said "Goodnight" at the end of the thirteen and a half hour Coronation broadcast in 1953?

298

SD Which great elderly British comedy actress was a keen member of the Elvis Presley Fan Club?

SS Which soap had the working title *Midland Road*?

FG Which quiz show was hosted by Robert Robinson and featured parents with their children?

FF Who played Crane and then rose to new heights advertising houses from a helicopter?

IP Who was Britain's equivalent of America's Archie Bunker?

EH Which 1950s children's puppet series caused controversy due to the language of the two main characters?

299

SD Which pop series took its name from the myth that a song would be a hit if the theatre doorman could whistle it?

SS Which *Crossroads* character was imprisoned for dangerous driving?

FG Which cartoon spy had a partner called Squiddly Diddly?

FF What was Andy Pandy's girlfriend called?

IP Which country provided the setting for *Animal Doctor*?

EH Which 1950s children's BBC TV series became a major video hit in 1988?

300

SD Which precocious brat from Utah appeared on *Top of the Pops* singing *Long Haired Lover from Liverpool* in 1972?

SS Which British soap saw Jane Rossington pregnant for eleven months?

FG Which panel game has been chaired by David Jacobs, Penelope Keith and Angela Rippon?

FF Who became the star of *The Antiques Roadshow* after a long stint on *Going For A Song*?

IP What was the British inspiration for the American shop-based comedy *Beane's of Boston*?

EH What event dominated every British newspaper on the day in 1963 that *Dr.Who* was first broadcast?

301

SD What words did Elvis sing to the tune of the *Just One Cornetto* commercial?

SS Which soap's characters tune in to the 3PA radio station?

FG Who is assisted by his wife, Debbie McGee?

FF Whose odd accent went through keyholes and presented *Masterchef*?

IP Which *Avengers* character stirred coffee counterclockwise?

EH What kind of wood gave its name to the first British TV programme for and by people of West Indian origin?

302

SD Which '60s teen idol flopped when his TV role in *Budgie* became a West End musical?

SS What was Lofty's surname?

FG Which comedy enjoyed a guest appearance by Robin Williams when Richie dreamed that Mork was about to take him into space?

FF Which real-life author played Allen Mallory on *Columbo*?

IP Which cop show often intoned: "In a moment, the results of that trial"?

EH What news bulletin did Granada Television broadcast at 7.40pm on November 22nd, 1963, 20 minutes ahead of the rest of the network?

303

SD What did the New York Dolls drummer Billy Murcia do that got mentioned on the TV news on the band's first visit to London?

SS What day sees the showing of the *Brookside* omnibus edition?

FG Who is Carla's ex-husband on *Cheers*?

FF What is the first name of Magnus Magnusson's broadcasting daughter?

IP Who often uses the alias Sonny Burnett?

EH What colour is Noddy's hat?

304

SD Which TV comedian first tasted chart success with *Gather In The Mushrooms*?

SS Who lived at Inglebrook before moving to the Woolpack?

FG Who was in charge of the chalet maids at Maplins Holiday Camp?

FF Which former swimmer played Jungle Jim in the TV series?

IP What was Commander Henry's three-letter nickname in *The Winds of War*?

EH What vehicles are used for the final *Fun House* race before actually entering *The Fun House*?

305

SD What TV dancer announced his retirement in 1989 at the age of 41?

SS What did Albert Tatlock always order if someone bought him a drink in The Rovers Return?

FG Which hall did the ghosts played by Arthur English and Sheila Steafal live in?

FF Which comedy actor was the unusual choice for TV's Dick Turpin in the 1980s?

IP Which cop show's better moments are the appearances by officers Bonnie Clark and Kathy Linahan?

EH Which of Dr.Who's enemies threatened to "Exterminate-exterminate-exterminate"?

306

SD Which *EastEnders* star did Mike Sarne ask to 'Come Outside'?

SS Which soap is set close to a town called Braddock?

FG Which cartoon character takes his legal problems to Perry Masonry?

FF Whose catchphrase is "And it's over to you, David"?

IP Which outdoor survivor's friends included Nakuma and Mad Jack?

EH Which series of television plays began on BBC in 1956 and ended on Thames in 1974?

307

SD Which 1975 Dickens drama was planned as a musical but screened without any songs?

SS Whose *Coronation Street* husband Ernest was shot by raiders in 1978?

FG What did both John Stonehouse M.P. and Reginald Perrin do in an attempt to escape from the lives they were living?

FF Which famous farce actor is the brother of *Emmerdale's* Annie Sugden?

IP Which TV series was based on a book by American surgeon, Dr.Richard Hornberger?

EH Which British naval vessel was the subject of *Sailor*?

308

SD Which soap star had a hit with *Every Day I Love You More*?

SS Which soap star made a name for himself as an astronaut in *I Dream of Jeannie*?

FG What was the better-known name for *Today is Saturday Wear A Smile*?

FF Which comedian wrote scripts under the name Gerald Wiley?

IP Who was on the British throne when *The Adventures of Black Beauty* was being filmed for TV?

EH What day is it if *The Antiques Roadshow* is being screened?

309

SD Which TV dance team was founded by Arlene Phillips

SS Which *Dallas* character died but was then resurrected in a shower when the actor playing him got a pay rise?

FG Which *Celebrity Squares* host answered questions himself for charity as part of the programme?

FF Who did Bruce Forsyth meet at a Miss Longest Legs contest, made her his hostess, then made her his wife?

IP What kind of business did *The Brothers* operate?

EH Which Peter Barkworth drama series did Mary Whitehouse admit to liking even though she found it sexy?

310

SD Who was the lead female dancer in *The Hot Shoe Show*?

SS Which piano-playing comedian plugged *Heineken's* part-refreshing virtues?

FG Whose boss was known as C.J.?

FF Who played television's *Hamlet* in 1971 but was better known as a soap doctor?

IP Which TV series lasted for eight years longer than the war it was about?

EH What job did unlikely TV star Fred Dibnah do?

311

SD Which song always closed *The Andy Williams Show*?

SS Which former Commissioner of the Metropolitan Police became even better known for his tyre commercials?

FG Who was Jim Henson's co-creator of *The Muppets*?

FF Who, collectively, were Robert Vaughan, Tony Anholt and Nyree Dawn Porter?

IP Which Michael Crawford character was created by cinema cleaner Raymond Allen?

EH What was the subject of the BBC programme *Coming Out*?

312

SD Which comedy show's theme ends: "You're gonna make it after all"?

SS Which mountain range was pictured on Hilda Ogden's 'murial'?

FG What kind of creature is George on *Rainbow*?

FF Who was Stan Butler if Doris Hare was his mum and Anna Karen was his sister Olive?

IP Which British drama series was the basis for the American programme called *Beacon Hill* about a rich Boston family?

EH Which 1977 drama series was plugged on Michael Parkinson's chat show by author Alex Haley?

(313)

SD Which cop show's theme clicked with the lyric: "You meet the highbrows and the hipsters, the soda jerkers and twisters"?

SS Which fictional hospital was the setting for *Angels*?

FG What was *Mastermind* Fred Housego's job?

FF Which of *The Goodies* is a doctor?

IP Who got the *Upstairs Downstairs* role of Sarah only because the show's co-deviser, Eileen Atkins, wasn't available?

EH Which British TV production did the Pope give a plug for in his 1977 St.Peter's Square blessing?

(314)

SD Which band's *Drive* became a hit after gaining massive TV exposure as the *Live Aid* anthem?

SS Which character made a surprise re-appearance in *Crossroads* after sailing off on the *QE2*?

FG Which quiz show presenter's real surname is Sigursteinnson?

FF What is this chat host's first name?

IP What male name is written on the Batpole?

EH What did Michael Angelow do to get himself on TV during a 1975 cricket match from Lords?

(315)

SD Which long-running Noel Edmonds Saturday morning variety show for kids first took to the air in 1976?

SS Which 'smart Alec' pulled his last pint at the *Rovers Return* in 1992?

FG Which game show was inspired by the legend of William Tell?

FF Who completed the early '50s announcing trio with Mary Malcolm and McDonald Hobley?

IP Which oil company featured in *The Troubleshooters*?

EH Which rocket ship was controlled by Captain Troy Tempest?

(316)

SD What did ageing rocker Frank Zappa sell in an episode of *Miami Vice*?

SS What was said to make the going easy?

FG What did Hughie Green move to after *Double Your Money*?

FF Which eccentric scientist interviewed fellow-eccentrics in his own programme *One Pair of Eyes*?

IP Who played opposite Irene Handl in *For the Love of Ada*?

EH How many episodes of *Fawlty Towers* were made?

317

SD Which former member of the Eagles played a drug-running pilot in *Miami Vice*?

SS What was lipsmackinthirstquenchinacetastin' motivavatin'good-buzzincooltalkin'highwalkin' fastlivin'evergivin'coolfizzin"?

FG Who starred in BB2's *The World of Beachcomber*?

FF Who became Bergerac after gaining fame as Nerys Hughes' boyfriend in *The Liver Birds*?

IP How many parts was the TV series *The Six Wives of Henry VIII* divided into?

EH What were advertisers talking about in 1975 when they told you to *Save It*?

318

SD Whose last chat show interview was given to Tom Snyder?

SS What were you using if you let your fingers do the walking?

FG Who camped his way through *Shut That Door*?

FF Which female author and university lecturer co-presented *Nice Time* with Jonathan Routh and Kenny Everett?

IP Who was Chief Navigator of the *Starship Enterprise*?

EH Which science show was presented by Derek Griffiths, then by Adrienne Posta and then by Miriam Stoppard?

319

SD Which instrument does Hawaiian Eye cabbie Kazuo Kim play?

SS Who made the chocolate bar advertised with the jingle: "Nuts — Whole Hazelnuts"?

FG Which comedy series had John Alderton living next door to Hannah Gordon?

FF Which television roving reporter was reported dead during the Korean War but lived on to use his credit card?

IP Which county was the setting for *Hadleigh*?

EH Which year first saw video cassette recorders available for home use in Britain?

320

SD Which instrumental did Tony Holland waggle his muscles to?

SS Which soap were you in if you were under Dr.Bywaters?

FG What, collectively, were Garden, Oddie and Brooke-Taylor?

FF Which popular comedy actor starred in the series *Mr 'Aitch*?

IP What was the *Iron Horse* in the Western series of that name?

EH Who became the first male newsreader to have his name above the title and not wear a tie when he read a children's bulletin in 1972?

321

SD Which show's theme song began by asking: "Who can turn the world on with her smile"?

SS Which soap role was played from a wheelchair by cancer victim Roger Tonge?

FG Which comedy series found Paula Wilcox defending her virginity against attacks from Richard Beckinsale?

FF Which dizzy blonde from *Laugh-In* became a major movie star?

IP Which TV drama series starred Anthony Quayle as Adam Strange?

EH Which great chat show host died of hepatitis in 1988?

322

SD Who sings the *Love Boat* theme?

SS Which *Coronation Street* character was said to be having an affair with "her at number 19 Inkerman Street"?

FG Who was Cliff Morgan's opposing captain on the first edition of *A Question of Sport*?

FF Which actor was the youngest member of *Dad's Army*?

IP Who were Captain Scarlet's main enemies?

EH Which programme scooped the world with news of Margaret Thatcher's elevation to the leadership of the Tories?

323

SD Who sang: "We're the young generation and we've got something to say"?

SS Which *Coronation Street* character became the father of twins in 1965?

FG Which programme heard Bruce Forsyth introducing: "The eight who are going to generate"?

FF Who played the womanising widower in *Father, Dear Father*?

IP Which 220-part series starred Jack Lord as Steve McGarrett?

EH Which comedy series was once referred to as *Are You Being Stereotyped* by gay-libbers?

324

SD Which cop show once featured hit-maker Leonard Cohen as an international drug dealer?

SS What did Christian Toma and Jennifer Clulow advertise together for the first time at Christmas, 1973?

FG Who upset chat show host Michael Parkinson by dragging him to the floor and messing his hair?

FF Who played Bernard Hedges in *Please Sir*?

IP What was the 1982 follow-up to 1969's *Take Three Girls*?

EH Which *Magic Roundabout* character, when told that he didn't skip like a rabbit, said: "We're re-thinking the image"?

Photo: NME

 325

 SD What was Illya Kuryakin's favourite kind of music?

SS Which *Coronation Street* character's long-lost son visited the Rovers in 1974 and left without introducing himself to his mother?

FG Which children's TV quiz about the cinema was hosted by Chris Kelly?

FF Who was the typical teenager on the first edition of *Juke Box Jury* who went on to present *Magpie*?

IP Who lived at Melford Park

EH Whose was the first major royal wedding in colour?

326

SD Which show's theme song pined "All the things I'm missin', good vittles, love and kissin', are waiting at the end of my ride"?

SS Which soap set in the Blue Ridge Mountains of Virginia was narrated by Earl Hammer Jr.?

FG Which comedy series followed up the activities of the *Please Sir* pupils after they left school?

FF Which actor once said: "I'd be pleased if a big crane fell on Hedges' car and splattered him into the (play)ground"?

IP What, in 1969, became the first British series to be axed part-way through due to its excessive violence?

EH What did *Magic Roundabout* rabbit Dylan always carry?

327

SD What are the first two words of the *Welcome Back Kotter* theme song?

SS Which of this man's hits went back to number 2 in the charts after appearing in a *Levi's* commercial?

FG What item is always included on *The Generation Game's* conveyor belt?

FF Who was Nellie Pledge if Jimmy Jewel was Eli?

IP Which 1969 series took Liza Goddard, Angela Down and Susan Jameson as its three main characters?

EH Which British TV channel was the first to broadcast in colour?

328

SD Which Irish song did the cast sing as the lights were turned out at the end of the final *Mary Tyler Moore Show*?

SS Which tyre company advertised itself with the help of the Groundhog?

FG What was the name of the *Magic Roundabout* rabbit?

FF Which consumer programme first thrust Esther Rantzen upon us?

IP Which 1937 Francis Durbridge character came to TV in the form of Francis Matthews in 1969?

EH Who narrated *The World At War*?

(329)

SD Which cop show had Kiss rock star Gene Simmons in the role of Newton Blade?

SS Which soap was launched in New York in 1972 with a special programme to explain such terms as "ecky thump" and "barm-cake"?

FG Who was the first member of the Royal Family to take part in a TV panel game?

FF Who was *The Laugh-In* sock-it-to-me-girl?

IP What, collectively were, Stuart Damon, William Gaunt and Alexandra Bastedo?

EH Which series saw Geoffrey Hayes take over as host from David Cook?

(330)

SD Which TV star wrote the book that taught Eric Clapton and John Lennon how to play the guitar?

SS Who was Emily's bridesmaid when she married Ernest Bishop?

FG Whose *On the Buses* catchphrase was: "I hate you Butler"?

FF Which radio DJ was given his own Saturday chat show in 1967?

IP Which Western series starred Lief Erickson as Big John Cannon?

EH Which lunchtime chat programme did the BBC start to broadcast from its Birmingham studios in 1972?

(331)

SD Which children's show saw Pip Hinton singing with Peter Glaze?

SS Which British soap did Les Dawson describe as *Dallas* with dung?

FG Whch TV series starred Spike Milligan as a Pakistani?

FF Who was *The Forsyte Saga's* Irene?

IP Which city was the setting for the short-lived *Market in Honey Lane*?

EH Which German camp became the venue for tourist trips after it featured in a 1972 TV series?

(332)

SD Who composed the *Neighbours* theme tune?

SS Who was held hostage by Steve Tanner's killer, US Army Sergeant Joe Donnelli?

FG Which member of the original team was missing from the 1974 series of *Monty Python*?

FF Which popular 1960s puppet series was written and narrated by Emma Thompson's father Eric?

IP Which night of the week was it if the pubs were empty because everyone was watching *The Forsyte Saga*?

EH Which children's hero did Australian thugs try to kill in 1970?

(333)

SD Which former Page Three Girl joined Mick Fleetwood in an attempt to co-host the 1989 Brit pop awards?

SS What killed Ken Barlow's wife Valerie?

FG Which Goon starred in *Q5*?

FF Which programme first brought together the Monty Python team of Cleese, Chapman, Idle, Jones and Palin?

IP What was *The Prisoner's* number?

EH Which former prime minister stopped an interview when David Dimbleby asked him about the money he'd made from his memoirs?

(334)

SD Which Scottish folk duo sang regular news-inspired ditties on *Tonight*?

SS Which is the closest village to *Emmerdale Farm*?

FG Who was the voice of *The Wombles*?

FF Which *Batman* villain was played by Frank Gorshin?

IP Which 1960s secret agent made a 1981 return to television in *Wet Job*?

EH What was the sign above the door of the Commerical Inn at Esholt near Bradford changed to when it appeared in *Emmerdale Farm*?

(335)

SD Which Scottish club did Robin Hall and Jimmie Macgregor host for five years?

SS Which *Emmerdale* sheep farmer lost his wife, Peggy, because she wanted out of the series and then lost his twin daughters?

FG Which comedian said of the 1960s: "It was the permissive society but someone forgot to tell ITV, missis"?

FF Which actress played Fleur in *The Forsyte Saga*?

IP Which popular British actor had his ear bitten by a rat whilst filming *The White Rabbit* for television?

EH Which TV series was based on the books of Major Pat Reid who was the escape officer at a World War II German prison camp?

(336)

SD Who rode *Sidesaddle* into the charts after being a TV favourite with Billy Cotton?

SS Who received complaints in 1971 when they exchanged their chimps for a human vicar?

FG What was Dick Dastardly's dog called?

FF Which *It's A Knockout* presenter was found not-guilty of shoplifting in 1991?

IP Who was Callan's sidekick, said to stink like a skunk when he was nervous?

EH Who presented *Film 89, Film 90, Film 91, Film 92* etc.?

337

SD Which song was Madonna paid three million pounds to sing in a *Pepsi* commercial that was then dropped for being blasphemous?

SS Which *Coronation Street* duo bought a colour TV in 1971 and had it repossessed by the finance company?

FG Which actor sent letters in *Dear Mother...Love Albert?*

FF Which folk singer entertained each week on *The Frost Report?*

IP Who did Number 6 have to outwit in *The Prisoner* if he was to discover the identity of Number 1?

EH How many contestants took part in each edition of *The Generation Game?*

338

SD What was Kylie Minogue's role on *Neighbours?*

SS What was the surname of Elsie Tanner's second husband?

FG What was the title of *Monty Python's Flying Circus* changed to in 1974?

FF Which former Radio Luxemburg disc jockey called his TV son-in-law "Shirley Temple"?

IP Which 1967 drama series by Patrick McGoohan cost seventy-five thousand pounds per episode, almost double the usual cost?

EH Why did Gordon Jackson do everything left-handed in the first episode of *Upstairs Downstairs?*

339

SD Which member of this group was previously in Co Co and subsequently became a TV presenter?

SS What was the name of Minnie Caldwell's cat?

FG Which puppet character did Ivan Owen base on Terry Thomas?

FF Who was David McCallum if Robert Vaughan was Napoleon Solo?

IP Which 1966 TV play was named the best drama of 1985 by TV critics?

EH What tragic TV first did Gareth Jones achieve during a 1958 live transmission of a play?

340

SD Which was the first show presented by Cilla Black in which she didn't sing?

SS What brand of mints were "A minty bit stronger"?

FG Which magician's TV show led to stardom for Basil Brush?

FF Which duo were the stars of *Not Only ... But Also?*

IP Which show were you in if you came face to face with Clarence the Cross-eyed Lion?

EH What number completed the title of Cliff Michelmore's first *Holiday* series visiting countries with foreign tongues?

341

SD Which comedian sang the *Supergran* signature tune?

SS Which brand of peanuts tasted "Jungle fresh"?

FG Which puppet's human partners have included Rodney Bewes, Derek Fowlds and Howard Williams?

FF Who was the first presenter of ITV's *World of Sport*?

IP Which series was set in Dr.Marsh's Wameru Study Centre in Africa?

EH Which series introduced snooker to the world of colour television?

342

SD Which drama series followed the fortunes of the Majestics pop group?

SS What was the name of Betty Turpin's husband?

FG Which future comedy show saw three of its team making an early stab at television on the children's programme *Do Not Adjust Your Set*?

FF Which 1965 18-part series starred Douglas Wilmer and Nigel Stock?

IP Which drama series starred Steve Forrest as John Mannering, an undercover agent in the guise of an antiques dealer?

EH Who do *Star Trek* fans call themselves?

343

SD What was the surname of Kate in *Kate and Ted*?

SS Which character died suddenly when *Coronation Street* was about to celebrate its 1000th episode?

FG Which TV series' working titles included *Vaseline Review* and *Owl Stretching Time*?

FF Who said "Yus, m'lday" to Lady Penelope?

IP Which was the last major British TV series to be made in black and white?

EH Which actor once said of Henry VIII: "He is the reverse of myself — but I admire his excesses"?

344

SD What was the name of the duo who played the music on *French and Saunders*?

SS What was advertised as "The bright one-the right one"?

FG Which cast member from *The Darling Buds of May* was a regular on the kid's show *Do Not Adjust Your Set*?

FF Which literary duo were played by Ian Carmichael and Dennis Price in a 1985 TV series?

IP Which '60s series featured a charlady who inherited ten million pounds?

EH What did Stephanie Rahn do in the *Sun* in 1970 to find herself mentioned on television?

345

SD Which DJ hosted *First AIDS* the first British TV show to pass condoms around the audience?

SS What was the BBC's first twice-weekly series to be made in colour?

FG What is Basil Brush's two-word catchphrase?

FF Which panel game host once lost two false front teeth when trying to pronounce the unusual word "Kerseymere"?

IP What was the name of *Softly, Softly* extended to?

EH Which famous *Star Trek* props were made by make-up expert Fred Phillips?

346

SD Which pop singer became Adrian Mole's mum?

SS Which prime minister's wife complained when the London region dropped *Crossroads* in 1968?

FG What job was filled by veteran Desert Rat Norman Potter at Fenn Street School in *Please Sir*?

FF What was the last major state occasion to be reported on by Richard Dimbleby?

IP Which Stefanie Powers series was a follow-up to *The Man from Uncle*?

EH Which TV series saw Lord Kenneth Clark travel 80,000 miles to 117 different locations?

347

SD Which '60s pop star played a hairdresser in *Albion Market*?

SS Which product was advertised with commercials showing Martians laughing at humans for using real potatoes?

FG What product did the Pledges produce in *Nearest and Dearest*?

FF Who was ITN's first female newscaster?

IP Which 1966 television play was banned until 1985?

EH Who presented thirteen weeks of *Civilisation*?

348

SD Which newsreader sang *Hello Young Lovers* on the *Russell Harty Show*?

SS Who went on to become Ethel in *EastEnders* after being the originator of the silly old moo role in *Till Death Us Do Part*?

FG Who was the first host of the British version of *The Golden Shot*?

FF Who turned down the role of Simon Templar in *The Saint* because he didn't like the way he had affairs with different girls each week?

IP Which ocean is the headquarters of International Rescue?

EH Which Welsh village was the setting for *The Prisoner*?

349

SD Who moved in with Bob Geldof after presenting *The Tube*?

SS What kind of soap were you recommended to use if you had "B.O."?

FG Who made a career out of adding up the scores incorrectly on *The Golden Shot*?

FF Who provided the animals' voices in *Animal Magic*?

IP Who were International Rescue leader Jeff Tracy's sons, Scott, Virgil, Alan, Gordon and John named after?

EH What, in 1967, became the first news programme to enter the top ten ratings?

350

SD What did the initials of the late night variety show *OTT* stand for?

SS Who became famous as the "Sch — you — know — who" man?

FG Who was the only black compere of *The Golden Shot*?

FF Who was operating a cement mixer on a building site when he was given the role of Dr Who in 1974?

IP What was the registration number of Lady Penelope's pink Rolls-Royce?

EH Who co-presented the first *News At Ten* with Andrew Gardner?

351

SD Which '80s series with a name drawn from the '50s was presented by David Soul and Sally James?

SS Which *Coronation Street* character was fined for shoplifting in 1966?

FG Which comedy series starred John Bluthal and Joe Lynch as Cohen and Kelly the tailoring partnership?

FF Who commanded *Fireball XL5*?

IP What was Alf Garnett's job

EH Which newsreader claimed to wear his ill-fitting toupee "for medical reasons"?

352

SD Which beer gave rise to Chas and Dave's hit record *Rabbit*?

SS What was the name of the cat who ate *Kattomeat* with his paw?

FG What was the name of the bank manager who led *Dad's Army*?

FF Which famous scientist once dressed up in a spaceman's suit for a comedy spot on *Late Night Line-Up*?

IP Which TV character was a keen supporter of "Yer Mary Whitehouse" even though she wrote and complained about him?

EH What succeeded *Monitor* as the BBC's main arts programme?

353

SD Which 1985 musical performance was watched by 1.5 billion people?

SS What had you won if you were awarded a *CDM*?

FG Who accepted an invitation to say "Sock it to me" on *Laugh-In* when presidential candidate Hubert Humphrey turned it down?

FF Which top anchorman died in the same year as Winston Churchill?

IP Whose book *Cleaning Up TV* was seen burning in Alf Garnett's fireplace after she had complained about the programme?

EH What was ITV's flighty answer to *Blue Peter*?

354

SD After which singer was the pet alligator in *Miami Vice* named?

SS Who was buried alive under the wreckage when a train crashed off the *Coronation Street* viaduct in 1967?

FG Who gave us the phrase "What do you think of it so far?.....Rubbish"?

FF Who went from *Compact* to *United* to *Crossroads*?

IP What title was used when *Till Death Us Do Part* was resurrected in the 1980s?

EH What were 6 million Britons watching on TV at 3.56 a.m. on 21st July 1969?

355

SD Which Scottish singer appeared in four episodes of *Miami Vice* in which she married Crockett?

SS Which TV soap saw its central building destroyed by an old bomb in a 1967 episode?

FG Which actress once listed the highlight of her career as appearing with Morecambe and Wise?

FF Which programme has been presented by Howard Stableford, James Burke and Anna Ford?

IP Which 1966 award-winning play featured a homeless London family and starred Carol White?

EH Which 1969 royal occasion was the BBC's biggest outside broadcast since the Coronation?

356

SD Which British pop duo turned down roles as waiters in *Miami Vice*?

SS Who went to number 1 in the charts after Twiggy rang Paul McCartney to say she'd seen her on a TV talent show?

FG Who left a suicide note in Australia which read: "Thing seem to go wrong too many times"?

FF Who left *Tomorrow's World* because she didn't want to be a public figure only to become ITN's most famous face?

IP Which 1966 play led to the formation of the charity *Shelter* for the homeless?

EH Which year saw colour come to BB1 and ITV?

357

SD Which TV series once included Phil Collins in its cast as a conman?

SS Whose van killed *Coronation Street* resident Harry Hewitt?

FG Which comedian persuaded major actors to take part in "A play wot I wrote"?

FF Which *Tomorrow's World* presenter was described by the editor as "The last of the dinosaurs"?

IP Which Tory prime minister did Alf Garnett describe as "That grammar school twit"?

EH Which channel did the majority of British viewers watch the first moon landing on?

358

SD Which 1985 TV show raised fifty million pounds for famine relief?

SS Which commercial role was played by John Hewer and gained a *Times* obituary when dropped in 1971 even though he came back in 1974?

FG Which all-American hero wore a pink dress on *Laugh-In*?

FF Which singer claimed that he had cut off Mia Farrow's hair making her suddenly almost bald part-way through *Peyton Place*?

IP Which British programme had a German equivalent featuring the Tetzlaff family in which the wife was called a "silly goose"?

EH What was the name of the programme featuring a puppet dog which took over from *Magic Roundabout* for a spell?

359

SD Which pop singer received a lorra complaints about the dubious taste of broadcasting from the Zeebrugge ferry victims' hospital?

SS What three words complete the song: "A million housewives every day Pick up a tin of beans and say"?

FG Which two comedians were in charge of *Laugh-In*?

FF Who played Amos Burke in *Burke's Law*?

IP Who did Alf Garnett once suggest might have been on the pill, resulting in a BBC apology to Mary Whitehouse?

EH Which TV comedy series was inspired by the film *To Sir With Love*?

360

SD Which TV quiz show inexplicably ends with the studio audience trying to do the Hand Jive to the signature tune?

SS Who thought he'd come up on the pools in 1966 only to find that his wife hadn't filled in the coupon properly?

FG Which popular comedy series was set in Walmington-on-Sea?

FF Who did Frank Muir christen "the thinking man's crumpet"?

IP Who had nothing better to do than to count the fact that Alf Garnett once used the word "Bloody" 78 times in 30 minutes?

EH Which newsreader was often accused of being drunk when actually he was taking drugs to control his epilepsy?

361

SD Which stack-heeled Scottish pop singer was given his own chat show in 1982?

SS Who lugged teachests full of chocolate around as *Big Fry* before almost becoming a star in James Bond?

FG Which miniscule comedian starred in *No, That's Me Over Here*?

FF Who threatened to sue the BBC shortly before his death in 1991?

IP Which comedy series was developed from a *Comedy Playhouse* production about a London family called the Ramseys?

EH Which newsreader was the son of the England cricketer who invented the googly?

362

SD Which member of the Squeeze pop group presented *The Tube*?

SS What shape was happiness according to 1960 commercials?

FG Who took over from Jackie Rae as host of *The Golden Shot*?

FF Which actor played Simon Templar in *The Return of The Saint*?

IP Which puppet was the inventor of the Thunderbird vehicles?

EH What is still heard at the start of *News At Ten* that was only included because an engineer forgot to fade it at the start of the first edition?

363

SD Who shot back up the charts after singing the signature tune for the documentary series *Sailor*?

SS Which was the first American soap to find a place on British TV?

FG What colour stripes did Andy Pandy dress in?

FF Which member of the *What's My Line* panel even managed to have an argument with the puppet Archie Andrews?

IP Which TV villains were illuminated by indicator lights from old Morris Minors?

EH What was unique about *News Review* when it was first introduced in 1964?

364

SD Which top-ten group includes Andy Mackay who wrote the songs for *Rock Follies*?

SS Which fictional soccer club starred in *United*?

FG Which 1953 children's comedy series was broadcast live at 5.25 and then repeated (live again) at 7.25 for adults?

FF What kind of creature was Rag, of *Rag, Tag and Bobtail* fame?

IP Which popular TV series about an aircraft factory starred Patrick Wymark as John Wilder?

EH Which long-running programme was replaced by *24 Hours*?

Photo: Hulton Deutsch

SD Which *Starsky and Hutch* actor had several hit records?

SS Which '60s soap cast Haverhill in Suffolk as Angleton new town?

FG Which duo said: "Hello Aunty Jean" to Jean Morton?

FF What title came up on the screen when *Watch With Mother* was dropped?

IP Which TV series starred Leslie Phillips and later Donald Sinden as vicars?

EH What night of the week saw the first series of *Man from UNCLE* become compulsive viewing?

SD What was the name of the *Muppet Show* band?

SS Which actress lived next door to the Coopers in *The Newcomers* before moving to Albert Square?

FG Which comedian died in 1991 after giving the Beatles one of their early national TV plugs in a show he presented with his brother, Mike?

FF Which announcer once introduced: "The Chancellor of the Exchequer, Sir Stifford Craps"?

IP What did Rodney Bewes claim to have drunk nine pints of when he was supposed to be seen drinking beer on *The Likely Lads*?

EH What did ITV launch in 1965 as a rival to *Grandstand*?

SD On what American singer's show was this young pup a regular feature?

SS Which comedian said: "Roses grow on you"?

FG What was succeeded by *Not So Much a Programme, More A Way of Life*?

FF Which children's role was 11 stone 12 pound Gerald Campion typecast in?

IP Which British TV private eye was jailed after being framed for possession of stolen jewellery?

EH Which newly-elected prime minister gave an exclusive interview to ITN after a 1966 fall-out with the BBC?

SD Whose *Big Night Out* variety show flopped despite the revival of the fabulous radio *Glums*?

SS What was mummy using if her child asked: "Mummy, why are your hands so soft?"?

FG Which family moved into Beverly Hills after striking oil?

FF Which *Police 5* presenter is known in the underworld as *Whispering Grass*?

IP Who was Napoleon Solo's boss in *The Man from UNCLE*?

EH Which northern newsreader rose to fame due to his fits of laughter on *It's A Knockout*?

369

SD Which *It Ain't Half Hot Mum* duo topped the charts with *Whispering Grass*?

SS What kind of commercials did ITV ban in 1965?

FG Which member of this family originally made his living by putting fillings into *Bread*?

FF What kind of creature was Tag of *Rag, Tag and Bobtail* fame?

IP Who was on the British throne when Sgt. Cork was solving crimes?

EH Who was the first British politician to have his State Funeral televised?

370

SD What was the name of the girlie group in *Rock Follies*?

SS Which '60s British soap centred around the activities of a Midlands soccer club?

FG Which '50s puppet series ran to only 25 episodes but was still being repeated in 1970?

FF How many weeks did Annette Mills live for after Muffin the Mule's last TV programme?

IP Which TV series followed the search for a mysterious one-armed man?

EH Which acclaimed 1965 play by Nell Dunn was set in the Clapham area of London?

371

SD Which single letter was used as a name by Rula Lenska's character in *Rock Follies*?

SS Which American soap came into being only because US TV producers thought the yanks wouldn't understand *Coronation Street*?

FG What always ended with the song "Time to go home, time to go home, la la la la la la la la la"?

FF Which TV reporter was accused of blasphemy after he was heard to say "Jesus wept" during a broadcast?

IP What is the name of Dr.Who's time machine?

EH Which Tony Hart programme was the children's equivalent of *News Review* for the deaf?

372

SD Which Scottish folk singer co-hosted *The Generation Game* with Larry Grayson?

SS Which Goon provided the voice of Albert, one of the *Kennomeat* dogs?

FG Which popular puppet series was created by Serge Danot?

FF Why did Harry H. Corbett add the H in the middle of his name?

IP Which organisation was the main enemy of *The Man from UNCLE*?

EH Which annual sporting event did the BBC officially launch their colour television with?

373

SD Which game show host's *Travelling Music Show* flopped on Broadway?

SS Which company advised you to "Put a tiger in your tank"?

FG Who said *Meet the Wife* if the wife was Thora Hird?

FF Which 5-million pound epic starred Anthony Andrews and Jeremy Irons in opposite roles from those in which they were originally cast?

IP What did UNCLE stand for in *The Man from UNCLE*?

EH What was the French version of *It's A Knockout* called?

374

SD Which children's TV show cast recorded the anti-drug song *Just Say No*?

SS What do graded grains make?

FG Which of Dick Emery's characters said: "Ooh, you are awful — but I like you"?

FF How old was Gerald Campion when he first played Billy Bunter — 9, 19 or 29?

IP Which cop series featured down-and-out private eye Frank Marker?

EH Which puppets had their *You Too Can Be Prime Minister* programme temporarily banned before the 1966 elections?

375

SD Which pop band did Bill Grundy encourage to use four-letter words on his programme?

SS Who left *Coronation Street* because she was fed up with her character doing little more than ordering gin and tonics in the Rovers?

FG What was the name of the puppet series based on *The Goon Show*?

FF Which extremely popular early announcer was the grand-daughter of Lily Langtry?

IP Which county was TV detective *Cluff* from?

EH Which long-running children's story series was first shown in 1965?

376

SD What was the name of the dog who played piano on *The Muppet Show*?

SS Which soap followed the fortunes of the Cooper family who had just moved to East Anglia?

FG What was the name of Wilbur Post's talking horse?

FF What day of the week was it if *The Woodentops* were the main attraction on *Watch with Mother*?

IP Which comedy series featured characters called Terry Collier and Bob Ferris?

EH Who died before he could see Napoleon Solo, his last creation, on television?

377

SD Which musical programme became the first religious show to enter the top twenty?

SS What "cuts cleaning time in half" according to 1960s commercials?

FG Which TV comedy was the film *I Only Arsked* based on?

FF Who died after 37 episodes of *Alias Smith And Jones* to be replaced by Roger Davis?

IP Which TV series, based on *Butch Cassidy and the Sundance Kid*, starred Pete Duel and Ben Murphy?

EH Which politician was the main objector against TV cameras being allowed inside Westminster Abbey for the Coronation?

378

SD Which song found Middle of the Road's lead singer strutting her hot pants on *Top of the Pops* in 1971?

SS Which soap character was married three times — once bigamously — suffered two miscarriages and had a child by her stepbrother?

FG Which long-legged blonde appeared with Marty Feldman on *At Last the 1948 Show*?

FF Which puppet was accompanied by Maria Bird whenever he came out to play?

IP What was the title of *And Mother Makes Three* changed to when the cast got bigger?

EH What is the main link between Bill and Ben, Captain Pugwash, the Daleks and actor Peter Hawkins?

379

SD Which TV series gave Mike Batt four top ten hits?

SS What ended in 1988 after a twenty four year run?

FG Which chat show host refereed *Child's Play*?

FF Which Irish comedian had a TV dramatic acting role in *One Fine Day*?

IP Which TV drama based on books by James Herriot led to a stage play called *It Shouldn't Happen to a Vet*?

EH Which BBC news magazine programme began its long run in 1953?

380

SD What was a folk song and then soft drink TV commercial and then a hit for the New Seekers?

SS Who was the only *Crossroads* character to survive from the first episode to the last?

FG Who was supposed to chair alternate weeks of *What's My Line* with Gilbert Harding prior to being given the job every week?

FF Who played the king in the TV *King and I* follow-up *Anna and the King*?

IP What did the initials F.A. stand for in the programme title *Another Sunday and Sweet F.A.*?

EH Which TV star belonged to Shepherd's Bush brothers Arthur and Chris Arnold?

381

SD Who won the 1974 Eurovision Song Contest?

SS Who admitted that her face erupted when she first used *Camay* soap?

FG Which member of the *What's My Line* panel committed suicide after being accused of shoplifting merchandise to the value of 87p?

FF Who was the mother of actress Lucie Arnaz?

IP What night of the week was it if viewers were settling down to watch *Armchair Theatre*?

EH Which British TV programme's tribute to John F. Kennedy did Jacquie Kennedy ask for a recording of?

382

SD Why did Grace Jones bash Russell Harty with her handbag?

SS Which product was originally promoted by Dash and later by Digby with the help of three stunt doubles trained by Barbara Woodhouse?

FG Who had his hand up the original Sooty?

FF Which titled actress played Queen Mary in *Edward and Mrs. Simpson*?

IP What word beginning with 'CR' did Billy Bunter use 13 times in a single programme to bring accusations of bad language from an Enfield vicar?

EH Which comedy show was delayed until after the polls closed in the 1964 election, a move credited with winning the event for Labour?

383

SD Which BBC television signature tune became a hit after it was banned as being too morbid by BBC Radio?

SS Who jilted Leonard Swindley at the altar in *Coronation Street*?

FG What is the name of the Yorkshire snake on *Sooty*?

FF Which horse got its own TV series after co-starring with Gene Autry?

IP Which TV series had a follow-up called *Another Bouquet*?

EH Which channel was *Match of the Day* originally broadcast on?

384

SD Who wore tartan on *Top of the Pops* in 1974?

SS Which *Coronation Street* character died of a heart-attack in the Rovers Return snug?

FG Which TV puppet was born on the same day as *Watch With Mother*?

FF Which long-running four-legged puppet first went on air with his lady presenter in 1946?

IP Which village was the setting for *Dr.Finlay's Casebook*?

EH Who once advised young viewers to wash their cats' eyes with boracic acid when she should have said boracic powder?

385

SD Which *Whistle Test* presenter had the nickname Whispering?

SS Which cockney film star first saw his future wife on a TV coffee commercial?

FG What was the name of the caretaker at Fenn Street School?

FF Which former M.P. took over from former M.P. Brian Walden as presenter of *Weekend World*?

IP How did 'The Perfect Spy' die?

EH Who hosted *The Pyramid Game*?

386

SD Which series spawned the hit *Suicide is Painless*?

SS What product was promoted by a dog belonging to Cynthia Harrison who committed suicide a year after her dog died?

FG What is Sooty's magic spell?

FF Who took time off from wandering around jungles to become Head of BBC2 in 1965?

IP Whose main enemy was Mr.Quelch?

EH Which TV channel was blacked out by a power cut on its opening night?

387

SD Which Ken Russell work for television was about "The biggest dancer in the world"?

SS Which *Brookside* regular restored furniture in the garage?

FG Which TV series was inspired by *American Graffiti*?

FF Who did Harry Carpenter replace on *Sportsnight*?

IP What was the original British title of the series shown in America as *The Royal Victorians* or *Edward the King*?

EH What three-word snatch from a song did Granada borrow as the title of their film of the Beatles in New York?

388

SD Which weekly TV show established Cliff Richard?

SS Which heavily advertised product was named after its inventors Forrest Mars and Bruce Murrie?

FG Which TV series had an assistant headmaster called Oliver Pettigrew?

FF Who found fame in *Rainbow* after appearing in *Z Cars* as Detective Constable Scatliff?

IP Which series saw Miriam Karlin blowing a whistle and demanding: "Everybody out"?

EH What, in 1956, did Parliament decide must be broadcast simultaneously on both TV channels?

389

SD Which TV title completes the children's joke song that begins: "Dinner, dinner, dinner, dinner, dinner, dinner, dinner, dinner"?

SS Who was Deirdre Barlow's first husband?

FG Which 1960s comedy starred Larry Hagman as the master of a beautiful genie?

FF Which children's programme saw Huw Wheldon in charge of a weekly talent contest?

IP Which hero's life story was told in a TV play by Terrence Rattigan at the suggestion of Prince Philip?

EH Which drama series starred Barry Ingham as a British arms salesman?

 390

SD Which blonde bombshell sang the *Adam Adamant* theme song?

SS Which soap started topping the ratings again when Sunday repeats began in 1989?

FG Which politician became the only live person to appear on *Spitting Image*?

FF Which politician appeared on TV to condemn peace campaigners after the showing of *The Day After* nuclear attack film?

IP Which political party's rise was the subject of *Fame Is The Spur*?

EH Which city's immigrant population was the subject of *Shalom Salaam*?

391

SD Which member of the Scaffold was a *TISWAS* regular?

SS Which *Neighbours* star had a serious role as a sailor in *The Heroes*?

FG Which newsreader had an exploding nose on *Spitting Image*?

FF Who claimed that he took drugs partly to overcome the strain of getting up in the middle of the night to work on breakfast television?

IP Which '80s wartime series starred Susannah York and was named after a Vera Lynn hit?

EH Which TV channel's opening announcement was made by Denis Tuohy?

 392

SD Which film company made *Musical Mystery Tour* especially for television?

SS Which Colorado city is the setting for the Carrington home in *Dynasty*?

FG What was the show business version of *A Question of Sport*?

FF Who went from *Only Fools and Horses* to *The Two of Us*?

IP Which series saw Francesca Annis playing Fleet Street's first female editor?

EH Which decade saw the first episode of *Bonanza*?

393

SD Which Western theme asks: "Who is the tall dark stranger there?"?

SS Who first made love in this landlady's bar?

FG What was *Mastermind* winner Christopher Hughes's job?

FF Which actor was a policeman in *Family at War* before moving to *Coronation Street's* corner shop?

IP What was Lady Marjorie leaving for on her final *Upstairs Downstairs* appearance?

EH Whose idea was it to make the TV film *Jesus of Nazareth*?

394

SD Which show's theme song has the rather dubious lyrical ending: "We'll have a gay old time"?

SS Which type of chocolate bars did actor Martin Fisk advertise in the role of a truck driver?

FG Who was *Man About the House* if Paula Wilcox and Sally Thomsett were the girls?

FF Who shaved her forehead to play Elizabeth I in 1971?

IP Who played Diana Coupland's husband in *Bless This House*?

EH Which TV shows were broadcast live from Bolton Hospital in Lancashire?

395

SD Which 1990s pop star's father was a co-presenter of the 1950s show *Oh Boy*?

SS Which British programme did a Saskatchewan TV station buy 500 hours of in May 1971?

FG Which of the Fenn Street teachers was played by Joan Sanderson?

FF Which TV chef once stunned viewers with the fact that "a squid has ten testicles"?

IP Which TV detective was always yelling for Crocker?

EH Which TV series was a spin-off from the film *Wagonmaster*?

396

SD Which dancer starred in the series *Going My Way*

SS Which hairspray was that girl wearing if you couldn't tell if she was wearing any?

FG Which actress threatened to "Thkweam and thkweam and thkweam" in the TV adaptation of *Just William*?

FF Which was the only major *M*A*S*H* role to be played by the same actor in both the film and the TV series?

IP Which British detective series featured a man overcoming a drink problem?

EH What kind of creature was Nipper who pulled the TV cable underground from Buckingham Palace for the coverage of Prince Charles's wedding?

397

SD Who was the lead male dancer in *The Hot Shoe Show*?

SS Who flew from Luton Airport to drink *Campari*?

FG Which pudding company did Reginald Perrin work for?

FF Who was known as a comedy actress until she won awards as Edna the Inebriate Woman?

IP Which series, although set in Korea, was aimed at Vietnam?

EH Which David Attenborough series shot 1.25 million feet of film in 30 different countries?

398

SD Which *Neighbours* characters' wedding spawned a video and a hit single?

SS How many mistresses did J.R.Ewing have in the first six episodes of *Dallas*?

FG What was it if it was presented by Sally James, Chris Tarrant and Lenny Henry?

FF Which *Sale of the Century* host was voted 'switch-off of the week' in a newspaper poll?

IP Which series was Liza Goddard filming when she said: "I was wee'd on by a wombat and got lice from an emu or a koala bear"?

EH Which TV show once saw Arthur Negus drop and smash a viewer's clock?

399

SD Who wrote the theme tune for this pink cartoon character's TV series?

SS Which family had a feud with Digger Barnes?

FG What was Mrs.Fawlty's first name?

FF Which pop singer played the chirpy role of *Budgie*?

IP What was the children's series if William Lucas was the father and Judi Bowker was his stable-loving daughter?

EH Which author wrote to *The Guardian* when *Tinker Tailor Soldier Spy* ended to say that there hadn't been a mole in the first place?

400

SD What is the title of the hit record that was spawned by the *EastEnders* theme tune?

SS Which soap, launched in 1978, was written by, directed by and starred black people?

FG Which vast comedian hosted *The Wheeltappers and Shunters Social Club*?

FF Who retired from TV in 1988 to run an antiques shop?

IP Which Dutch detective created by Nicholas Freeling became a big hit in the '70s?

EH Whose novel was the basis for *Tinker Tailor Soldier Spy*?

Photo: Hulton Deutsch

(401)

SD Which of the Monkees wore that awful woolly hat?

SS Has Bet Lynch ever had an affair with Len Fairclough?

FG Which quiz show once refused to allow someone to answer questions on 'Routes to anywhere in mainland Britain from Letchworth'?

FF Who moved from the stage version of *A Funny thing Happened on the Way to the Forum* to TV's *Up Pompeii*?

IP Which children's series saw actor Geoffrey Bayldon transported from the eleventh century to present-day England?

EH What sport does this P.I. enjoy with his father?

(402)

SD Who promoted *Persil Automatic* with their song *Wouldn't It Be Nice*?

SS What unhappy event took place when Bobby Ewing and April were away on their honeymoon?

FG Which camp comic invited the men in his audience to: "Come on — chase me"?

FF Which actress is married to cartoonist Gerald Scarfe but is still better known for her relationship with Paul McCartney?

IP Which Superintendent found 'No Hiding Place' after starring in *Murder Bag*?

EH Who died soon after presenting the political *Pursuit of Power* series?

(403)

SD Who had a hit in 1959 with *Ragtime Cowboy Joe* and hit British TV in the early '90s as a kid's cartoon series?

SS What is normally found in the privacy of the bathroom but was clearly seen in model Meg Smith's hand during Britain's first TV commercial?

FG Which comedian's nickname is Lal?

FF Which *Z Cars* actor won an Oscar for a film about men in long shorts?

IP Which TV gambler called his mother "Sexpot"?

EH Which puppet's catchphrase is: "I wish I could fly, but I can't"?

(404)

SD Which Tony Christie hit re-surfaced as a jingle for sherry?

SS What did Mary Holland change her name to after becoming strongly associated with a TV commercial?

FG Which comedy series was based around the activities of the Luxton and District Transport Department?

FF Which newsreader was rumoured to be more than just good friends with Captain Mark Phillips?

IP Which city was *The Champions* based in?

EH How many different people's keyholes does each edition of *Through the Keyhole* peep through?

405

SD Which Eric Clapton composition became a jingle for *Vauxhall* car commercials?

SS Which is Britain's longest running series of TV commercials?

FG What was the name of Kenny Everett's space hero?

FF Which newsreader made headlines by throwing a glass of wine at a Tory MP in 1983?

IP Which famous American replaced Ernest Hemingway as the university's Vice Chancellor in *A Very Peculiar Practice*?

EH Which TV series sees its cops shopping at *Waverley's* supermarket?

406

SD What four words did Bill Haley sing on TV in 1956 that are still a popular catch-phrase in the '90s?

SS Whose son did Bobby Ewing tell Pam that their adopted child might be?

FG Which comedian introduced a West Indian called Chalky into his TV act?

FF Which series married Richard Briers to Penelope Wilton?

IP Which TV story of everyday coppers was almost called *Woodentop*?

EH What was Commander Shore's daughter called in *Stingray*?

407

SD What song did Elvis Presley sing to an animal when he appeared on American TV on 1st July 1956?

SS Which Ewing did Valene marry in *Knots Landing*?

FG Who was the first host of *Busman's Holiday*?

FF Which actor in a TV cop show spent time in Reading Jail on drugs charges?

IP Which legendary role did Michael Praed fill in a children's series?

EH What word completes the title of the Channel 4 movie: *P'tang Yang.................*?

408

SD Which bespectacled pop star did *Are You Being Served?* actor Mike Berry sing a hit tribute to?

SS What, according to the commercial, did "Ize drink when ize dry"?

FG What is Gerald and Tom's favourite sport in *You Must be the Husband*?

FF Who showed Princess Anne his Cocky when she visited the BBC TV studios in 1958?

IP Which of Ben Cartwright's sons was adopted?

EH What army rank did Foggy claim in *Last of the Summer Wine*?

409

SD Which TV cop theme gave Maggie Bell her only solo hit?

SS Who was the voice of Buzby?

FG Who starred in *Take a Letter Mr.Jones* when he was free?

FF Which TV presenter has a daughter named Fifi Trixibelle?

IP What non-medical instrument stood between Hawkeye and B.J.'s beds in *M*A*S*H*?

EH What is the relationship between Penny and Vince in the TV sit com?

410

SD Which brand of whisky was a hit title for TV theme writer John Barry?

SS How many nights a week was *Crossroads* aired when it first started?

FG Who played Miss Jones in *Miss Jones and Son*?

FF Which former review artiste was a founder of *TVam*?

IP What was the relationship between the Bionic Man and the Bionic Woman?

EH Which city was Logan on the run from?

411

SD Who sang the TV theme for the 1990 World Cup and attracted 100,000 to a free concert in Hyde Park?

SS What were "soft, strong and popped up too"?

FG Who married Joe Gerard?

FF Which cop series was narrated by newspaper columnist Walter Winchell?

IP Which country was the setting for *The Harp in the South*?

EH Which TV series was based on the book *Cyborg*?

412

SD What is Zoot's instrument in the *Muppet Show* band?

SS Whose TV commercial offered "Bright New Powder"?

FG What is Frasier Crane's job in *Cheers*?

FF Who played Maplins' Gladys Pugh?

IP Which series saw Simon MacCorkindale able to turn into the animal of his choice?

EH Which county was *The Likely Lads* set in?

413

SD What musical instrument can Warren Mitchell play to orchestral standard?

SS What was the name of Clement Freud's dog in the dog food commercials?

FG What does Yogi Bear's little pal Boo Boo wear around his neck?

FF Which great British actor made his TV debut in Ibsen's *John Gabriel Borkman*?

IP Which cop series was alternatively known as *Badge 714*?

EH What is the name of the beetle in the title of Andrea Arnold's environmental show for children?

414

SD Which country singer gave Joe Brown a pair of cowboy boots after they'd recorded on *Oh Boy* together in the early '60s?

SS Who was badly beaten up during the burglary that saw the death of Doctor Lowther?

FG Which Munster weighs 387 pounds?

FF Which *Partridge Family* regular resurfaced in *L.A.Law*?

IP What is Anton Rodgers supposed job in *May to December*?

EH What event, televised in May and June 1987, proved so unpopular that video tape rentals soared by 25%?

415

SD Which town are *The Flying Doctors* based in?

SS What did Minnie Caldwell always call her lodger Jed Stone?

FG Which club was run by Timmy, Tommy and Michaela?

FF Which of *Dr.Who's* young companions ended up supping pints in the Woolpack?

IP Which private eye has problems with a couple of Dobermans called Zeus and Apollo?

EH What kind of programmes compete for the Prix Jeunesse?

416

SD Which 1962 hit for Bryan Hyland was a chart topper 27 years later for *Neighbour* Jason Donovan?

SS What was Val Barlow just about to do when she died?

FG Who presents the old film clips in *Looks Familiar*?

FF Which TV presenter and former Liberal candidate married Moira Shearer?

IP Which *Upstairs Downstairs* character shot himself?

EH What were you travelling on if Nurse Chapel patched up your wounds?

417

SD Which British pop programme gave its name to the US band who had a 1988 hit with *Waiting For A Star to Fall*?

SS Who rose to fame in the soap role of Rodney Harrington?

FG Which Stalag were *Hogan's Heroes* held in?

FF Which son of a famous father patrolled *The Streets of San Francisco* with Karl Malden?

IP Whose lady friends have included Sergeant Whitfield and Sergeant Belding?

EH Who was the subject of the mini-series *King*?

418

SD Who joined George Michael on his 1991 Xmas hit video?

SS Which product's commercial claimed "A little dab'll do ya"?

FG Who wrote and starred in *Absolutely Fabulous* without her usual partner?

FF Which of his chat show guests called Michael Parkinson "A stupid white man"?

IP Which well-known writer was played by Peter Egan in *Lillie*?

EH Which *Upstairs Downstairs* actor died in 1990?

419

SD Who composed the *Coronation Street* theme?

SS Which member of *Dad's Army* was the voice of the *Homepride* chief flour grader?

FG Who partnered Les Dennis in a Vera and Mavis send-up?

FF Which future MP starred in the 1964 *Protectors* series?

IP Which king's mistress was the subject of *Lillie*?

EH Which newspaper does Lou Grant work for?

420

SD Which *EastEnders* actor once worked as a coalman?

SS Whose carpet commercials promised "This is luxury you can afford" before they went out of business?

FG What have Victor and Margaret Meldrew got according to the title of the series that features them?

FF Which two Olympic gold medallists had their own 1986 Christmas TV special?

IP Which septet had a computer called Orac?

EH Which TV cop hung out in Mother's nightclub?

421

SD Which chat show band is led by Steve Nieve?

SS Which DJ's distinctive voice advertised *Brentford Nylon* products?

FG Which of the services did Clive Dempster serve in before taking over Maplins Holiday Camp?

FF Which member of his family did John Mortimer take a television *Voyage Around* in 1969?

IP Which charlady played by Kathleen Harrison inherited the business?

EH Which classic comedy duo's TV voices were provided by John McGeorge and Larry Harmon?

422

SD Which comedy series featured a heavy metal band called Bad News?

SS Who thought he would be remembered not for *Hamlet* "but as that man who did the *Polaroid* commercials"?

FG Which comedy series starring Freddie Frinton and Thora Hird was a spin-off from the Comedy Playhouse production *The Bed*?

FF Which actress dictated letters to John Inman in *Take A Letter, Mr.Jones*?

IP Which TV private eye had occasional run-ins with Inspector Claude Eustace Teale?

EH Who had 'A Bit of a Do' in the role of Ted Simcock?

423

SD Which TV presenter comedian and multi-instrumentalist had a hit with *Little White Berry*?

SS What was the brush and tube of *Gibbs S.R.* stuck into on Britain's first TV commercial?

FG Who was "The oddest thing you ever did see"?

FF Who played the central role of Coral Browne in *An Englishman Abroad*?

IP What was Poldark's first name?

EH Which actor told TV's *Classic Ghost Stories*?

424

SD Which female singer's appearance in the Nelson Mandela Birthday Concert made her an international star?

SS What was the name of Blake's major corporation on *Dynasty*?

FG What was John's job in *Dear John*?

FF Which violent TV series auditioned Princess Caroline of Monaco and turned her down because she couldn't act?

IP Who, or what, was the subject of *Oscar*?

EH Which part of an animal's anatomy did Barbara Woodhouse claim to be able to blow up to gain control over it?

425

SD Which British band had the video of their hit *Wild Wild West* banned by UK TV when the disc was at No. 1 in the States in 1988?

SS Which *Dallas* character won custody of John Ross after Dusty had admitted to the court that he was impotent?

FG Which comedian hosts *Catchphrase*?

FF Which Middle-Eastern actor received (and then lost) thousands of letters when he appealed for a wife on the *Wogan* show?

IP Which TV series starred David Warner as a journalist known as The Poet Laureate of Sport?

EH Which Saturday morning show featured a friendly dinosaur called Posh Paws?

426

SD Which *Top of the Pops* presenter once sported tartan hair?

SS Who incurred Lucy Ewing's wrath by unplugging Mickey Trotter's life-support system?

FG Who played the pop singer opposite Liza Goddard's music teacher in *Roll Over Beethoven*?

FF Who played Megan 'The District Nurse'?

IP Which 1984 drama series brought complaints from Enoch Powell, Salman Rushdie and (perhaps not unexpectedly) Mary Whitehouse?

EH Which programme included the *Rough Guide* travel series?

427

SD Who starred as Gurney Slade after charting with *Why?*?

SS Which *Dynasty* damsel's lovers have included Nick the doctor, Peter the playboy, Mike the chauffeur and Jeff the junior executive?

FG What was the name of Rik Mayall's character in *The New Statesman*?

FF Which famous actress played Emma Hart during the latter part of her life in *A Woman of Substance*?

IP Which Jackie Collins novel was serialised on TV with 15 minutes missing from the final episode that no-one apparently missed?

EH What was the follow-up to *The Planets* called?

428

SD Which radio DJ presented *The Bottom Line*?

SS Which *Dynasty* character huffed: "Nobody takes me to the cleaners and to bed in the same night"?

FG What are the first names of French and Saunders?

FF Which *Dr.Who* actor was one of the She-Devil's victims?

IP What was the subject of *The Winning Streak*?

EH What do *Cadbury's* "take and cover in chocolate"?

429

SD Which Eurovision Song Contest winners were at number one in the UK charts on the day that John Lennon died?

SS Which actor announced in 1986: "It's really nice to be thought of as *the* Texan"?

FG What did Skullion try to dispose of by filling them with gas and floating them up the chimney in *Porterhouse Blue*?

FF Who chatted to the royals in *The Prince and Princess of Wales, in Private, in Public*?

IP What kind of headgear did Supergran wear?

EH What is Bob the ventriloquist's dummy called in *Soap*?

430

SD Which acclaimed TV show ended its run on Christmas Eve in 1965?

SS Who was arrested for the attempted murder of both J.R. and Bobby Ewing?

FG Which university refused to allow a *Porterhouse Blue* scene involving condoms to be filmed within its hallowed halls?

FF Who made news by telling Alastair Burnet that he talked to his plants?

IP Whose worst enemy was Scunner Campbell?

EH Which of *The Sullivans* married Kitty?

431

SD Which elderly TV singing trio produced daughters who perform as the Little Foxes?

SS How old was Alexis when she became Blake Carrington's child bride?

FG Who made quite an impression starring in *Now Something Else*?

FF What was the name of the 'half man-half make-up' character in the series *Beauty and the Beast*?

IP Which of these characters' real name is Hiram Hackenbecker?

EH Who was almost in tears when accepting the 1990 BBC Sports Personality of the Year award?

432

SD Which Eurovision winner was written by Anderson and Ulvaeus?

SS Who fielded a football team against Maurice Jones Builders when dithering Derek Wilton refereed the match?

FG Who took time off from minding to star opposite Jan Francis in *Stay Lucky*?

FF Who played the only male in Alan Bennett's *Talking Heads* series of monologues?

IP Which city was the setting for *Tutti Frutti*?

EH Which anniversary of J.F.Kennedy's death was commemorated by the drama series *Kennedy*?

(433)

SD Who had a hit with the theme from *Miami Vice*

SS Where was Meg supposedly heading for as she sailed away from *Crossroads* on the QE2?

FG What was hosted by Ted Rogers and became ITV's longest-running quiz in 1988?

FF What series did John Noakes 'go with' after leaving *Blue Peter*?

IP Which superb TV series was based on Mr. and Mrs Sinclair, Torquay Hotel proprietors?

EH Where were you supposed to get the special glasses to view the 1982 3-D version of *The Real World* science programme?

(434)

SD Who hosted *My Music*?

SS Which *Coronation Street* character wanted a cat destroyed because it knocked a cup of coffee over his jacket?

FG Who replaced Chris Langham when he left *Not the Nine O'Clock News*?

FF Which role required actress Annette Crosbie to age from a young girl to a dying old woman in *Edward the Seventh*?

IP Which Biblical TV series was held up when the film unit was caught in the Yom Kippur War?

EH Which bride was seen to wink at someone as she walked down the aisle after her 1986 televised wedding?

(435)

SD Which *Song by Song* singer has a role in *Fresh Fields*?

SS Which soap featured a family headed by Tom Bell?

FG Which game show awarded a cheque book cover and pen to its losers?

FF Which drama series saw Susan Hampshire as Lady Glencora, a role turned down by Hayley Mills and Pauline Collins?

IP Which novel by Andrew Newman introduced incest to television drama?

EH Which TV series did Edwina Currie think was left-wing propaganda?

(436)

SD Which role did Harry Secombe play in a musical adaptation of a Dickens novel?

SS Which Australian comedian sold *Foster's* lager?

FG Which game show has been hosted by the Michaels, Aspel and Parkinson?

FF What is this woman's catchphrase?

IP What was the inappropriate name of the little dog in *The Duchess of Duke Street*?

EH Which documentary series had *The Living Planet* as a sequel?

Photo: Hulton Deutsch

Photo: Syndication International Ltd

(437)

SD Who starred in the 1952 *Pet's Parlour* series?

SS Who was the first British athlete allowed to use his own name on a TV commercial?

FG Which member of the Royal Family was given Beryl Reid's voice on *Spitting Image*?

FF Who starred with his own wife in *Father Brown*?

IP What was the name of Angie Dickinson's spicy character in *Police Woman*?

EH What had happened the day before the action in the controversial documentary called *The Day After*?

(438)

SD What colour hair was Cher sporting when she appeared on a 1991 Wogan show?

SS Where do the Collins, Cross and Grant families live?

FG Which series saw Fletcher come out of prison after serving his *Porridge*?

FF Which member of the *Rising Damp* cast was an insurance inspector until he was thirty?

IP What was the name of Starsky and Hutch's hip informer?

EH What colour was the first *TVam; Good Morning Britain* sofa?

(439)

SD On whose TV show did this starlet make her US TV debut?

SS Which soap set consisting of real houses was bought with the aid of a Department of Trade loan?

FG Who made a successful game show comeback with new hair after flopping with his *Big Night Out*?

FF Who went on to become a major film star after playing Dobbs in *Thick As Thieves*?

IP Who was *The Naked Civil Servant* based on?

EH What colour was the sofa for the first BBC *Breakfast Time*?

(440)

SD Which *Blue Peter* presenter didn't make much chart progress with her single *Solomon Centipede*?

SS Which soap was set on a North Sea ferry?

FG What did *3-2-1* losers win?

FF Which director and which shareholder of Harlech Television appeared together in the company's *Divorce His, Divorce Hers*?

IP Where did Major Gowan live?

EH Which former ITN reporter wrote *Harry's Game*?

(441)

SD Which TV comedy duo reached the charts with *At the Palace*?

SS What is Brookside — an avenue, a crescent or a close?

FG Which game show's clues were once attempted by *Mastermind* champion Christopher Hughes who won a booby prize?

FF Who played Caine in *Kung Fu*?

IP Why was *The Sweeney* so called?

EH Who co-presented the first BBC *Breakfast Time* with Selina Scott?

(442)

SD Which *Billy Cotton Band Show* regular had a hit with *Dreamboat*?

SS Who played Blake Carrington in *Dynasty*?

FG What constituency does this B'stard represent at Westminster?

FF Who was a crook in *Thick As Thieves* and Regan in *The Sweeney*?

IP What was Quentin Crisp's job in the civil service to gain him the title *The Naked Civil Servant*?

EH Who was BBC *Breakfast Time's* first astrologer?

Photo: Scope Features

(443)

SD What is the better-known name of singer and chat show guest Cherilyn Sarkisian?

SS How many people died in the *Brookside* siege

FG Which spoof-soap featured the Campbells and the Tates?

FF What was Frances De La Tour's superb *Rising Damp* role?

IP Which 'Streets' starred Karl Malden

EH Which TV channel launched the *Daily* breakfast programme in 1989?

(444)

SD Who conducts Max Bygraves' band and has appeared as Manuel with his Music of the Mountains?

SS Who was paid thirty thousand pounds for *Horlicks* commercials and told he couldn't have the money until he retired from athletics?

FG Who was the best-known captain of the men's team if Una Stubbs was the best-known women's captain?

FF Which series launched Miriam Stoppard and Magnus Pike?

IP Which drama series followed the fortunes of the maid, Rosa Lewis, who went on to run the Cavendish Hotel?

EH Who was seen on TV in his pyjamas because the television lights were needed to help with his rescue from the Grand Hotel?

(445)

SD Who were the *Black and White Minstrel Show* chorus?

SS What was the end product of the company featured in *King's Royal*?

FG Which game show did Les Dawson take over from Terry Wogan?

FF Which hard-times series saw James Bolam as Ford Seaton and Susan Jameson as his lady Jessie?

IP Which TV adaptation of a Robert Graves black comedy saw a snake slither across mosaic paving at the start of each episode?

EH Who beat Steve Davis in the 1985 snooker match that kept 18 million viewers glued to their sets until well after midnight?

(446)

SD Who hosted *Face the Music*?

SS What is the end product of the Californians who appear in *Falcon Crest*?

FG How many personalities were there on a *Blankety Blank* panel?

FF Which prime minister was played by Sir John Gielgud in *Edward the Seventh*?

IP Which series found Prue in bed with dad with a follow-up in which Prue's mum hit the sack with Prue's husband after Prue had died?

EH Which female reporter won an award after Norman Tebbit had said that her Libyan reports were biased?

SD Who sang about "Mud, mud, glorious mud" and appeared on *My Music*?

SS What event in 1983 prompted John Betjeman to write "Ken's a nice man; he deserves better"?

FG Which two members of the *Not The Nine O'Clock News* team shared the same surname initial?

FF Who was John Cleese's former wife and co-writer of *Fawlty Towers*?

IP Which novels by Arnold Bennett became, in 1976, ITV's longest-ever drama with a total running time of 26 hours?

EH Whose resignation from the Marines was a major topic of news and TV discussion in 1987?

448

SD Which two brothers can be blamed for the *South Bank Show* theme?

SS Which Italian company put an end to a classic series of commercials because they didn't like to see their drink being spilled?

FG How many patients were there in the ward that featured in *Only When I Laugh*?

FF Which star received one of his big breaks as Carter in *The Sweeney*?

IP What was the name of the nurse that Arkwright lusted for in *Open All Hours*?

EH Which member of the Royal Family talked about carriage driving on the *Wogan* programme?

449

SD What was the title of the *Van der Valk* theme which reached number one in the charts?

SS Which soap gave a part to Down's Syndrome victim Nina Weill?

FG Which comedy series was about a female undertaker?

FF Who won a well-deserved BAFTA Award as *The Naked Civil Servant*?

IP Who had to be hauled up on a cross five times in 1977 before the director had the shot he wanted for his production of *Jesus of Nazareth*?

EH Which member of the Royal Family talked about her Nazi father on *TVam*?

450

SD Which TV cast's first British hit was called *Hi'Fidelity*?

SS Which *Dynasty* character died after marrying Alexis from an oxygen tent?

FG Which decade was the setting for *In Loving Memory*?

FF Who played Caligula in television's *I, Claudius*?

IP Which major drama series starred John Amos as Kunte Kinte?

EH Who wrote *Talking Heads*?

451

SD Which Scandinavian duo had a hit with *Sucu Sucu*, the theme from *Top Secret*?

SS Which TV series had a rule that every scene should include at least one police character?

FG Which comedy series starred Dinsdale Landen caught between wife, Joanna Van Gyseghem, and mistress, Liza Goddard?

FF Who filled the role of shopkeeper Arkwright in *Open All Hours*?

IP Who was Bodie and Doyle's boss in *The Professionals*?

EH Which regularly featured sport did ITV decide to drop from the screens in 1988?

452

SD Which member of The Who played McHeath in a TV adaptation of *The Beggar's Opera*?

SS Which country did Elsie Tanner move to when she left *Coronation Street*?

FG Which TV comedy series was partly based on *The Crossman Diaries*?

FF Which great actor presented a series of other people's best plays in 1976?

IP Which TV play was based on the life of football pools winner Viv Nicholson?

EH Who sent a letter of apology to Ronald Reagan after US servicemen were depicted taking drugs in *Airbase*?

453

SD Which film did the Beatles make for television?

SS What did Joanne not want to say goodbye to when David went into business alone?

FG Which British MP took part in a specially written *Yes, Minister* sketch at a 1984 awards ceremony?

FF Which 1977 biblical work starred Laurence Olivier, Ralph Richardson and Peter Ustinov amongst others?

IP Which 1977 drama series saw Jack Hedley and Betty Arvaniti messing about on boats in Greece?

EH Which TV channel had problems when they charged to see the Tyson/Bruno fight and then found they couldn't broadcast it in some areas?

454

SD Which former pop singer presented *Enterainment USA*?

SS What couldn't Ian Botham eat three of?

FG What did the American game, *Card Sharks*, become when it reached Britain?

FF Which American president was the subject of a series of David Frost interviews in 1977?

IP Which Dickens work was adapted for television starring Timothy West, Edward Fox and Patrick Allen?

EH Which TV company launched the *Squarial*?

455

SD Who was the first person to win two Eurovision Song Contests?

SS What breakfast cereal did Henry and George Cooper eat?

FG What did the American show, *Family Feud*, become when it reached Britain?

FF Who went from *Bonanza* to become a slave-owner in *Roots*?

IP Which character became a partner in a restaurant after leaving *Man About The House*?

EH Which TV channel was launched in a blaze of glory with such superstars as Keith Chegwin and Austin Mitchell?

456

SD Which quartet won an Emmy for their programme *Head*?

SS Which *Dallas* role did Donna Reed suddenly step into in 1984?

FG What was the name of the MP who became PM in later series of *Yes, Minister*?

FF Who played the Virgin Mary in *Jesus of Nazareth* when she was nine years younger than the actor playing Jesus?

IP Which TV series had characters called Siegfried and Tristram?

EH Which football stadium's overcrowding brought scenes of horror to a 1989 Saturday afternoon's TV programmes?

457

SD Who had a hit with *Rat Rapping*?

SS Which *Coronation Street* duo both failed to turn up for their wedding to each other?

FG Which quiz show host presented a television history of *The Viking*?

FF Which *New Avengers* role was filled by coffee bean shaker Gareth Hunt?

IP Which all-action series ended with the two heroes crashing a rubber dinghy into the boat they were chasing?

EH What sport did Channel 4 begin to screen weekly in the year that ITV dropped wrestling?

458

SD What was the Muppets' first chart hit?

SS Which series of hour-long police stories became a twice-weekly soap?

FG What was the supposed relationship between Thora Hird and Christopher Beeny in *In Loving Memory*?

FF Which biblical character was played by Burt Lancaster in a major 1970s TV drama?

IP Which 1970s H.E.Bates adaptation saw Mel Martin reject advances from Christopher Blake, Jeremy Irons and Peter Davison?

EH Which 1988 drama did Defence Secretary George Younger ask for changes to be made in?

459

SD Whose theme did Paul Henry record with the Mayson Glen Orchestra?

SS What was Cecil Colby of *Dynasty* doing when he had his 1983 heart attack?

FG Which county was the setting for *In Loving Memory*?

FF Which comedy duo once played themselves in *The Sweeney*?

IP Which two Sundays in 1977 saw the television screening of *Jesus of Nazareth*?

EH What did Adam West insure for $1 million against damage, when he opened a Birmingham record store in 1988?

460

SD Which pop show was introduced by Peter Cook as the manager of the hall?

SS Which car rental company features the Two Ronnies in their commercials?

FG Which children's comedy starred Irene Handl and was produced by Mickey Dolenz of the Monkees?

FF Who was killed off as Dennis Waterman's wife in *The Sweeney* and resurrected in *Juliet Bravo*?

IP Which 1970s drama series about Cambridge University saw Sarah Porter win absolutely nothing after revealing her breasts for almost ten minutes?

EH Which member of the Royal Family starred in the horse racing documentary *Royal Champion*?

461

SD Which city is the setting for *Fame*?

SS Which family's parents are played by Lynda Bellingham and Michael Redfern?

FG Which member of the *Not The Nine O'Clock News* team went out with Fergie on her hen party?

FF Who played the part of Mrs. Basil Fawlty

IP What was Arkwright's nephew called in *Open All Hours*?

EH Which member of the Royal Family wrote and presented *The Duke's Award*?

462

SD Which TV series saw Leslie Crowther transforming labourers into singing superstars?

SS Which soap was praised by Edwina Currie when it sent women rushing for breast X-rays after a character's cancer scare?

FG What were the lowest odds on the *Winner Takes All* board?

FF Which presenter became a star when *Aquarius* was replaced by *The South Bank Show*?

IP Which TV character could change his character by swapping heads?

EH Which of the *Odd Couple* remarried at the end of the series?

Photo: Syndication International Ltd

463

SD Which pop record title included a TV weatherman's name?

SS Who was the father of Michelle's baby on *EastEnders*?

FG What was the title of *Variety Madhouse* changed to?

FF Which 1978 series, set in Edinburgh, won plaudits for Geraldine McEwan?

IP Which Western series was set in a Wyoming trading post?

EH Which very famous TV star was made from a green coat that belonged to Jim Henson's mother?

464

SD Which hitmaker moved to the States and had a straight acting role in *McKenzie*?

SS What is the programme if the main characters are the Beales, Fowlers and Watts?

FG Whose many superb comedy roles included *Potter*?

FF What is the name of the Australian who filled Horace Rumpole's wig?

IP Which detective wasn't much liked by CID officer Choc Minty?

EH Which TV cowboy's height varied from 6 feet 5 to 6 feet 8 if contemporary news reports were correct?

465

SD With what pop group did this comedy duo perform a hit version of *Help*?

SS Which soap includes characters with names taken from East End tomb stones?

FG What was the head of the household's job in *Keep It In The Family*?

FF Who was *Dallas's* Pam Ewing?

IP Which 1978 drama series is said to have been hated by the Queen Mother because scenes depicted George VI?

EH Which city is 6,133 miles away accordng to the singpost in *M*A*S*H*?

466

SD What instrument did Johnny Staccato play when he wasn't out sleuthing?

SS Which fictional London borough is the *EastEnders* Albert Square situated in?

FG Which quiz game allowed contestants to go "higher" or "lower"?

FF Which TV series was being filmed when Christopher Timothy had a romantic involvement with his leading lady, Carol Drinkwater?

IP Whose TV wife was played by Peggy Bates and then by Marion Mathie?

EH How many teeth did Mr.Ed have left on the last occasion he had his oats?

467

SD What is the title of the *Minder* theme?

SS Which brand of tea did Cilla Black dress up as a waitress to promote?

FG Who took over *Family Fortunes* from Bob Monkhouse?

FF Which *Dynasty* actor was the voice of Charlie on *Charlie's Angels*?

IP Which famous ITV barrister was first seen in a BBC *Play For Today*?

EH Which book did Patricia Driscoll read to children on Monday afternoons?

468

SD Which radio DJ introduced *The Roxy*?

SS Who liked his electric razor so much that he bought the company?

FG How many members are there in each *Family Fortunes* team?

FF For which actor did *The Professionals* production team delay filming, so that he could finish work on *Upstairs Downstairs*?

IP What was the title of the 1978 John Mortimer series about the life of the Bard?

EH What subject's history was traced in the documentary *In the Club*?

469

SD Who conducted the Eric Morecambe assassination of Grieg's Piano Concerto?

SS What must snooker referee Len Ganley have been drinking if he could crush a snooker ball in his white-gloved hand?

FG Which game show presents its questions on a computer called Mr.Babbage?

FF Which US president received $600,000 and 10% of the profits for being interviewed by David Frost?

IP Which school's pupils have included Gripper Stebson and Tucker Jenkins?

EH Which 1989 documentary series saw an armed robber being shot dead by police?

470

SD Which children's song has been a hit for Danny Kaye and *EastEnder* Mike Reid?

SS Which electricity company sponsored weather forecasts?

FG Who once gave a contestant one of his 12 inch LPs when she won a cassette recorder on his quiz show?

FF Which star refused to permit repeats of *The Professionals* because he thought they were losing him film parts?

IP Who was married to "She who must be obeyed"?

EH Which year first saw *Prime Minister's Question Time* on TV?

471

SD Which pop star's version of the *Crossroads* theme was used on the rare occasions that something dramatic happened?

SS What was advertised as 'new' in 1985 but then went back to its old style when consumers didn't like the new flavour?

FG Who took over *Family Fortunes* from Max Bygraves?

FF What role was filmed by John Alderton and Simon Ward that was played on TV by Christopher Timothy?

IP Who worked alongside Phillida Trant, as played by Patricia Hodge?

EH Who had been shot when 4 out of 5 American TV viewers tuned in to find out who'd done it?

472

SD Which song was the subject of an entire edition of the arts programme *Arena*?

SS Which TV star had to be shot with a tranquiliser dart when he went missing whilst filming a loo paper commercial?

FG Which comedy series featured the Tooting Popular Front?

FF Who refused to take part in a stage version of *Last of the Summer Wine* because he couldn't get on with Bill Owen?

IP What's the programme if "You can have a fishy in a little dishy"?

EH What is this dog's job when he isn't trying to be a super-sleuth?

Photo: Scope Features

473

SD Which French singer was played on TV by Jane Lapotaire?

SS What kind of animal said "My name is Bond — Brooke Bond"?

FG What deformity was suffered by the dishwasher in *Robin's Nest*?

FF Who won Emmy awards for *M*A*S*H* as a director, a writer and an actor?

IP Which TV detective has one glass eye?

EH Which outside broadcast had by far the biggest audience of any programme in 1981?

474

SD Which Welsh pop singer had a role in the TV movie *Pleasure Cove*?

SS Which former model advertised *Honda*?

FG What was George and Mildred's surname?

FF Which chat show host did Alan Bennett describe as being "untouched by expertise"?

IP Which TV drama series was set in Stone Park Women's Prison?

EH Which Mediterranean island was used as the set for Mars in *The Martian Chronicles*?

475

SD Which radio DJ introduced *The Golden Oldie Picture Show*?

SS What is "happiness"?

FG Which series starred Diane Keen and Trevor Roper as Fliss and Chris with Lewis Collins as lodger Gavin?

FF What colour are Zippy's eyes?

IP Which fictional store was the setting for *Are You Being Served?* ?

EH What did Barbara Woodhouse use when training dogs that the RSPCA said was cruel?

476

SD Which city was *Top of the Pops* originally broadcast from?

SS Which *Crossroads* character was declared innocent after being charged with Lynda Welch's murder?

FG Which comedy series starred Arthur Mullard and Queenie Watts?

FF Which heart-throb played *Arthur of the Britons*?

IP What is the name of the *Last of the Summer Wine* cafe?

EH Which company won their franchise from Westward Television in 1980?

477

SD Which *Neighbours* star had a hit with a re-issue of a Little Eva song?

SS Which tyres did Sir Robert Mark recommend?

FG Who starred as Selwyn Froggitt?

FF Which current affairs interview show has been hosted by Peter Jay, Brian Walden and Matthew Parris?

IP Which *Avenger* popped up in *The Upper Hand*?

EH Who gave us the one-word catchphrase "Sit!"?

478

SD Which chat show's resident band is Steve Nieve and the Playboys?

SS Which cigarette brand sponsored the superb Dennis Taylor v Steve Davis 1985 World Championship competition?

FG Who became known as the "rat who joined a sinking ship" after he was brought in to help save *TVam*?

FF Who devised *Nanny* under a male pseydonym and then played the starring role?

IP Which TV drama led to the loss of two hundred million pounds in exports and the cancellation of a royal visit by King Khaled?

EH What was the subject of the 1980 series *Diamonds In The Sky*?

479

SD Which TV comedian appeared in the very first *NME* top twenty with the song *Cowpuncher's Cantata*?

SS Who was Pete Beale's first wife on *EastEnders*?

FG Which former DJ asked *Whatever Next*?

FF Which very large funny man played the leader of the Majestics in *Tutti Frutti*?

IP Which political party won the election at the end of *First Among Equals*?

EH Which country was the subject of Keith Floyd's second series?

480

SD What six-letter word means "bribery to play a record on radio or TV"?

SS Which *Dallas* character did Luther Frick force at gunpoint to strut her stuff in her Miss Texas swimsuit?

FG Which newspaper cartoon character was played on TV by James Bolam?

FF Which actor complained about having to drink real ale in his role as Inspector Morse because he prefers vodka?

IP What was postponed in the title of John Mortimer's drama about Simeon Silcox?

EH Which series saw Harry Dodson restore a 100-year-old garden?

481

SD Which final number 1 of the 1970s had an animated video and expressed the sentiment: "We don't need no education"?

SS What did *Dynasty's* Alexis disguise herself as in an attempt to smuggle King Galen out of Moldavia?

FG Who went from *Rising Damp* to *A Kind of Living*?

FF Who became Brond after being Barlow?

IP What was there an epidemic of in *A Very Peculiar Practice*?

EH What did an Old English Sheepdog do in a *That's Life* April Fool gag?

482

SD Which superb guitarist had the plugs pulled on him for not playing what he'd been told to play on a *Lulu Show*?

SS Who is Amy Barton's *Coronation Street* son-in-law?

FG Which Page Three Girl appeared on *That's My Dog* with someone else's dog?

FF Who went from radio to TV to present *The People Show*?

IP Which '60s children's series became a hit in the '80s when it was put out on *TVam* to fill in gaps during a strike?

EH What did *The Magic Roundabout* stand in?

483

SD Which was the first song to reach number 1 whilst banned by the BBC?

SS Who took his wife to Italy on the *Orient Express* because he thought she was dying?

FG Which animated character will only allow rock music to be played on his hi-fi?

FF Which actor was the subject of *In From The Cold* in which Elizabeth Taylor refused to appear?

IP Which country was the setting for *Fields of Fire*?

EH Which TV commentator once observed: "It's not easy to get a snooker when there's only one ball on the table"?

484

SD Which Don MacLean track had frequent TV airings during Van Gogh's 1991 anniversary year?

SS What were the Henry and Amos in *Emmerdale Farm* that didn't run the Woolpack?

FG Which *Beverly Hillbillies* character went back home to find a mate for Ellie May?

FF Which Tory co-presented a Sky chat show with Labour's Austin Mitchell?

IP Which part did Ian Richardson fill if Anthony Hopkins was Guy Burgess?

EH Which object took almost seven televised hours to rise dripping from the Solent in October 1982?

485

SD Who had a hit with *Magic Moments* after giving the song plugs on his weekly TV show?

SS Which actress shot herself in the foot when she was supposed to shoot in the air to make Linda Evans fall off a horse?

FG What was the name of the robot who appeared in *3-2-1*?

FF Which famous director of Harlech Television died in 1984?

IP Which TV series stemmed from an occasion when the *Monty Python* team spent some time filming in Torquay?

EH Which Rantzen-produced series saw Chris Searle and Paul Heiney making fools of themselves doing other people's jobs?

486

SD Which TV comedian had a hit with *The Ballad of Spotty Muldoon*?

SS How many years old was *Crossroads* when it died?

FG Who had his own name in the title of his show but played a character called Rob Petrie?

FF Which *TVam* presenter was the 1986 television Personality of the Year?

IP Which Italian-sounding lawyer was played by Barry Norman?

EH Which journalist and polo fan was a regular panellist on *What's My Line*?

487

SD Which TV talent show winners had their first hit with *Hey Rock and Roll* and their last with *Who Put The Bomp*?

SS What did Nick Cotton break in the first episode of *EastEnders*?

FG What job do 'Roy's Raiders' do?

FF Which comedian was known as 'The Lad Himself'?

IP What housed a crew of 430 on its eight decks?

EH Which *Laugh-In* star said: "I never resented the dumb, fluffy blond image until I was confronted with it when I wasn't in a playful mood"?

488

SD What position did Sandie Shaw's Eurovision winning *Puppet On A String* reach in the UK charts?

SS Which *EastEnder* said formal goodbyes to her family and then died?

FG What is the surname of Barry, the baddie on *Ghost Train*?

FF Which duo held the British record for the biggest TV audience for a comedy programme in 1980?

IP What was the subject of the drama series *Intimate Contact*?

EH Whose pink-covered autobiography is called *My Gorgeous Life*?

Photo: Hulton Deutsch

489

SD What did this celebrated singer like to have taped down when he was in front of the camera?

SS Who left Deirdre alone in *Coronation Street* and headed for Holland?

FG Who begins her show with the words: "I was born in the Bronx, New York, in December of 1941"?

FF Which of the Goodies was the patriotic coward?

IP What was special about *Wonder Woman's* lasso?

EH Which TV interviewer became known as St. Mugg?

490

SD Which presenter of TV religious programmes had his biggest solo hit with *This Is My Song*?

SS In which village did Joe Sugden marry Kate Hughes?

FG Which kid's programme was subtitled *The Fairly Pointless Show*?

FF What was William Conrad's follow-up fat detective role after *Cannon*?

IP What was the first British cop series to be filmed in the streets of London?

EH Which puppet superstar warned her admirers: "Never be seen wearing yellow lipstick"?

491

SD Which member of *The Young Ones* cast had a hit with *Ullo John Got A New Motor?* ?

SS Which *Emmerdale* character is sometimes called Jenny and sometimes called Amos?

FG Who did Spike Milligan describe as "One of the greatest clowns the world has ever known"?

FF Which dancer occasionally appeared in *To Catch A Thief* as the greatest thief of all time?

IP What did the initials of the computer SID stand for in *UFO*?

EH Who won the 1978 Best Actor award for his role in *Porterhouse Blue*?

492

SD Who frequently used the word 'Wow!' when being interviewed on TV and went on to have a hit with that title?

SS Which high-pitched-voice *Coronation Street* character wears an earring and caused a fuss by shaving off his moustache?

FG Who lives in Moosylvania?

FF Which cook took over Clive James's weekend TV slot?

IP What was Charlene's job in *Neighbours*?

EH What colour are the stripes on Big Ears' trousers?

493

SD Which Irish band provided the music for *Harry's Game* and *Robin of Sherwood*?

SS Whose husbands included Sean and Blake who were shot, Cecil who had a heart attack and Dex who fell off a balcony?

FG Which *Taxi* character's surname is Nardo?

FF Which famous actor starred as Uncle Silas in *Dark Angel*?

IP Whose crimes did a 1988 TV series claim had been carried out by Queen Victoria's surgeon Sir William Withey Gull?

EH What is Benjamin Franklin said to have invented that Val Doonican made regular use of on TV?

494

SD What was Karen's instrument on Carpenters' TV broadcasts?

SS Which family went to Southend to look for Mark on the last day of 1985?

FG What included *The Showcase Showdown*?

FF Who played Danny Kane, co-owner of *The Paradise Club*?

IP Which tennis term gave Len Deighton the title for a spy series?

EH What was the first TV communications satellite called?

495

SD On which Cliff Richard song did The Young Ones join in, for charity?

SS Who went to work in Spain after borrowing money for the fare from Alec Gilroy?

FG Which series sees Anton Rodgers in love with a gym mistress who is half his age?

FF Which record-breaker was played by Anthony Hopkins in *Across the Lake*?

IP Which English town's tourist trade was boosted when it became the setting for *Inspector Morse*?

EH Who was the first British politician to have his funeral televised live?

496

SD Which family had a hit with *I Think I Love You*?

SS Which *Dynasty* character managed a football team?

FG Which golfing comedian starred in *The 19th Hole*?

FF Which megastar came from Moonee Ponds?

IP What was this actress later to find under her settee in *Talking Heads*?

EH Which famous author was one of the originators of *The Man from UNCLE*?

(497)

SD How many times did the Clash feature in the *Top of the Pops* 'top ten' between 1970 and 1990?

SS What chilly product was the first to be advertised in colour on British TV?

FG What was the name of the chef at this hotel?

FF Which fictional character's TV pals were played by Archie Duncan and Alexander Gauge?

IP Which TV series with 'Swift' connections starred Andrew Burt in a huge role and Jonathan Cecil in a tiny one?

EH Which TV superhero is a vegetarian because he was brought back to life by ketchup instead of blood?

(498)

SD Who is the boxing son of Ireland's 1967 Eurovision singer?

SS What was punk Mary's surname on *EastEnders*?

FG Who commanded Fort Baxter in *The Phil Silvers Show*?

FF Which former holder of the Britain's Best Bottom title played Gemma in *Solo*?

IP What sort of car does Bergerac's former father-in-law, Charlie Hungerford, drive?

EH Which cartoon mouse claims to be 2000 years old?

(499)

SD Which city's music was featured in *I Feel Fine*?

SS How did Angie Watts try to commit suicide?

FG Which fictional TV station did Eric Idle create?

FF Who filled the TV role of the P.D.James character, Adam Dalgleish?

IP Who cooked for the Bellamy family?

EH What is Cliff's job in *Cheers*?

(500)

SD Which channel broadcasts *The Tube*?

SS Who paid Alf Roberts twenty pounds a week to live in the flat over the shop in 1989?

FG Which colour hexagons have to be joined across the *Blockbusters* board?

FF Which film actress played TV's Eva Peron?

IP What did Mrs.Bridges of *Upstairs Downstairs* steal to end up in the dock?

EH Which two Beatles took part in the 1965 *The Music of Lennon and McCartney* TV spectacular?

Photo: Hulton Deutsch

SD What was the family relationship between the Eurovision songsters The Allisons?

SS Who bought Stan Ogden's window cleaning round?

FG Which *Opportunity Knocks* winner was known as Mr. Parrot Face?

FF Who went from live creatures to dead ones in *Lost Worlds, Vanished Lives*?

IP Which city was the setting for *Family Pride*?

EH Which TV comedy theme was a hit for Gary Portnoy?

SD Who wrote the *Dr. Who* and *Steptoe and Son* theme music?

SS Why was Frank Butcher's mother, Mo, sacked as Brown Owl of the Albert Square Brownies?

FG Which house had a cat called "Zaza" and a frog called "Kiki"?

FF Which all-purpose sports commentator turns up at the Horse of the Year Show when he isn't on the piste?

IP Who were led by Dr. Tiger Ninestein?

EH Which series of American murders were fictionalized in *Helter Skelter*?

503

SD For which regular programme did *Top of the Pops* musical director, Johnny Pearson, write the theme tune *Arabesque* ?

SS Which *EastEnder* has worked at the Queen Vic, the launderette and for Dr. Legg?

FG Which *Robin's Nest* actress was once married to Tony Blackburn?

FF Which *Blue Peter* Peter was in *Space 1999* and *Fallen Hero*?

IP What was the name of the girl who joined *The A-Team* in their first series?

EH What was the name of Edward Woodward's character in *The Equalizer*?

504

SD Which top ten hit was sung by Jerry Nelson but always featured a green puppet on camera when performed on TV?

SS Which *Neighbour* was known as Superbrain?

FG What was Jim Hacker's first ministerial post in *Yes Minister*?

FF Who won a 1978 BAFTA award for the most important contribution to factual televison, even though they probably couldn't understand him?

IP Which state was *Cades Country* set in?

EH What was the job of the 'Man of the World'?

505

SD Which comedy duo had a top-50 hit with *Fan'dabi'dozi*?

SS What is the name of Richard Channing's *Falcon Crest* newspaper?

FG Who is Morticia Addams's husband?

FF Which racing commentator is known as "Lord"?

IP Who played the American Jew, Natalie Jatrow in *The Winds of War*?

EH Which Australian sent TV postcards from Chicago and Rio?

506

SD Which TV series gave Lynne Hamilton a hit with *On The Inside*?

SS What building did B.B. Blake re-design?

FG What make of car did Joey Boswell drive?

FF Which support actor in *The Prisoner* went onto individual fame as a TV legal eagle?

IP What was tough-guy B.A. Baracus extremely frightened of?

EH Who wakes up the Gods with the *Horn Resounding*?

507

SD What theme gave Jan Hammer his second hit after the *Miami Vice Theme*?

SS What is the name of Ernie Shuttleworth's pub near to *Emmerdale Farm*?

FG What is Joey Boswell's traditional one-word salutation?

FF Which US TV series starred Grey Morris and Peter Graves throughout its seven-year run?

IP Which MP shares his office with Fletcher Dervish?

EH What is Mrs. Boswell's alternative name for "That Tart" in *Bread*?

508

SD Which 1986 event gave Heads a hit with the BBC theme *Aztec Lightning*?

SS Which member of the Sugden family returned to *Emmerdale* from Italy?

FG Which comedian was 'Diced' in the title of a series?

FF Who won the TV equivalent of an Oscar for his nine minute small-screen debut in *Roots, the Next Generation*?

IP What was Jennifer Hart's job when she wasn't out amateur sleuthing?

EH Which former *TVam* anchorman and sports commentator presents *Hitman*?

509

SD How much money did the cast of *Grange Hill* receive for their *Just Say No* hit record?

SS What did *Crossroads's* Salvation Army member Jane Smith's mother do for a living?

FG Which comedy series starred Richard Briers as a vicar called Philip?

FF Who gained fame talking about stolen goods but also presented a series on how to play bridge?

IP What was the name of Roger Moore's *Persuaders* character?

EH What kind of crawly creature is Nero in *Dangermouse*?

510

SD Which American country and western radio show moved to TV in 1955?

SS Which *Dallas* character spent a wild weekend in Waco with Luther Frick's wife, Wanda?

FG Which '80s comedy series, based on a best-selling book, made a star of schoolboy Gian Sammarco?

FF Which *Bill* character's large boots are filled by Christopher Ellison?

IP What was the nationality of *The District Nurse*?

EH Which drama series starring Ben Cross was based on a novel by M. M. Kayes?

511

SD What was the name of this rodent's record label?

SS Which cars were "Tested by dummies — driven by the intelligent"?

FG Which famous funny man died during his act on *Live from Her Majesty's*?

FF Which *Cagney and Lacey* actress admitted that she'd had an alcohol problem the same as her character?

IP Which decade was *Hi De Hi* set in?

EH Which Sheffield theatre is the World Professional Snooker Championship broadcast from?

512

SD Which TV comedian did Whitne Houston want dropping from th Nelson Mandela Wembley bill because she'd never heard of him

SS What is the surname of the Kylie who appeared in *Neighbours* if w aren't talking about Kylie Minogue?

FG Which radio DJ co-presented *That's Showbusiness* with Gloria Hunniford?

FF Who became chairman of the England selectors after being a cricket commentator?

IP How many joggers run past Mar in the opening sequence of *The Mary Tyler Moore Show*?

EH In which holiday resort did John Logie Baird finally win his battle to transmit a TV picture?

513

SD Which *Juke Box Jury* chairman's style was described by Bill Cotton as "like a veritable Rock of Gibraltar"?

SS Which *Coronation Street* actress died on Boxing Day 1983?

FG Where did Jumblie sleep?

FF Who lists his most cherished possession as: "Slack Alice's secret recipe for elderberry wine"?

IP What was the name of Matt Dillon's deputy?

EH What kind of creatures are Ruff 'n' Reddy?

514

SD Which male DJ recorded *It Takes Two, Baby* with Liz Kershaw?

SS What kind of flowers does *Knots Landing* TV announcer Ben Gibson grow as a hobby?

FG Which comedy series features Malcolm who met Jackie in a singles bar?

FF Which TV chat show host comes from Barnsley?

IP Which country was Hitler heading into at the start of *The Winds of War*?

EH What are Bonnie and Willow?

515

SD Which TV actor copped out from his usual image to have a number one hit with *If*?

SS Which village is patrolled by Sergeant McArthur?

FG Which TV quiz show was based on BBC producer Bill Wright's wartime grillings by the Gestapo?

FF Which cricketer was the 1981 BBC Sports Personality?

IP Which war did Jim Rockford serve in?

EH Who didn't use his licence to kill in the title role of *Sherlock Holmes in New York*?

516

SD Which TV theme by Ken Barrie is one of radio's most requested children's songs of all time?

SS Who wrote-off the Rover that was Annie Walker's pride and joy?

FG Which superhero does Eric turn into after a mouthful of fruit?

FF Which *New Faces* winner became a member of The Copy Cats?

IP Which series penned by Ted Willis featured fictional French murder trials?

EH Which family pop group's members were appointed goodwill ambassadors by the US Music Committee in a '70s cartoon series?

517

SD Which Scottish TV discovery had her first hit with *Modern Girl*?

SS Whose *Coronation Street* wife died in a 1980 car crash?

FG What do Oliver and Simon sell in *Never the Twain*?

FF Which 'where there's muck there's money' series married Timothy West to Caroline Blakiston?

IP Which city is the setting for *Taggart*?

EH Which quiz show asks you to link the letter and connect the clue?

518

SD Which regular on America's *Porter Wagoner Country Show* became famous for her big hits after first charting with *Jolene*?

SS What did *Coronation Street's* Myra Dickinson's surname become when she married?

FG Who had been left without George in *Life Without George*?

FF Which *Blue Peter* star was described as "nervous, bad-tempered, toothless and shortsighted"?

IP Whose boss was Captain Frank McNeil?

EH Which British sports programme was shown live in many European countries on Saturday afternoons, but not until the evening in Britain?

519

SD Which 1970 Free hit made a 1990 chart come-back via a chewing gum commercial?

SS What opened on TV eighteen months after it was supposed to have first opened its doors to paying customers?

FG What was the top number on the bingo cards in *Bob's Full House*?

FF Which son-in-law of James Callaghan became a TV presenter?

IP How many different mothers were involved in producing Ben Cartwright's three sons?

EH Who made his final ITN appearance in August 1991 at the age of 63?

520

SD Which pop group included Bruce Forsyth's daughter Julie?

SS What product was promoted on television by the dog, Jenards Likely Lad of Lardama?

FG Which *Crackerjack* host's catchphrase was "Crush a grape"?

FF Who always reads out the Miss World results "in reverse order"?

IP What was the title of the series that starred Jemma Jones as Louisa Trotter?

EH Which regular member of the *Dad's Army* cast comes next alphabetically after John Laurie?

521

SD Which DJ obtained the nickname Medallion Man?

SS Which chocolate biscuit had a commercial in which a Mexican sang *I can't stand it*?

FG Who did Ian Botham replace on *A Question of Sport*?

FF Which former MP for Birmingham, Ladywood, presented *Weekend World*?

IP Who survived to be assisted by Georgina Jones?

EH Which TV panel game has been described as "Charades by any other name"?

522

SD Which famous Lancastrian was the first person to sing on a synchronised TVam and radio programme?

SS Who shot Kate Hughes' dog?

FG Which *Carry On* actor was in both *The Army Game* and *Secret Army*?

FF Which German-born TVam personality was mostly famous for his odd taste in sweaters and went on to become a Tory candidate?

IP What was Grizzly Adams's first name?

EH Which country was the setting for *The Flame Trees of Thika*?

523

SD Which country singer provides the *Dukes of Hazzard* theme song?

SS Which company did Maurice Westrop bring to Beckindale?

FG How many contestants take part in each edition of *Mastermind*?

FF Which former *Avengers* girl played Doris Asterman in *Voice of the Heart*?

IP What was Granny Trellis's favourite game in *Rich Tea and Sympathy*?

EH Which ITN defence and diplomatic correspondent has a name that sounds like that of a political novelist?

524

SD Which pop singer played Leather Tuscadero in *Happy Days*?

SS Which soap starred Howard Duff as Titus Semple?

FG Which army series did Clive Dunn serve in before taking up arms with *Dad's Army*?

FF Which star of *Moonlighting* was voted CBS Model of the Year in 1968?

IP Which US state was patrolled by the *Highway Patrol*?

EH What is the Telly of Telly Savalas a shortened version of?

525

SD Which day in 1967 saw the first showing of the Beatles' *Magical Mystery Tour* on television?

SS What regal title did Dirty Den always use when addressing Sharon?

FG What was the name of Harry Enfield's Greek kebab store owner?

FF Whose chat show really was *The Last Resort*?

IP What disease did Dennis Potter and his creation *The Singing Detective* both suffer from?

EH Which children's series once included a sci-fi cartoon called *Bleep and Booster*?

526

SD What are the first eight words of the *Laverne and Shirley* theme?

SS Which of the *Carry On* team told us to buy *Bloo Loo*?

FG What Saturday evening talent show saw Tony Hatch and Mickey Most become even more unpopular by criticising the acts?

FF Who was Henry VIII in the '70s and made a come-back as Captain Beaky?

IP Which 1970s TV drama series starred the beautiful *Charlotte Rhodes*?

EH Who looked at his predecessors in *A Prime Minister on Prime Ministers'*?

527

SD Which BBC DJ moved to Independent Radio and then popped up on Sky's *Lifestyle Coffee Break*?

SS Who is said to make "exceedingly good cakes"?

FG Which comedy series is claimed to be based on a previously undiscovered diary by Prince Edmund, Duke of Edinburgh?

FF Which 70-year-old woman was receiving 300 fan letters a day in the early 1980s?

IP Who is the Mayor of Hazzard County?

EH Which programme called itself *The Window on the World*?

528

SD Which *Happy Days* actor co-hosted the 1976 tribute to Richard Rogers with Gene Kelly?

SS Which soap was ordered by the IBA to drop one of its four weekly episodes in 1979?

FG Which entertainment supremo was the *Muppet's* Dr.Bunsen Honeydew said to be modelled on?

FF Which Dorothy L.Sayers role was filled by Ian Carmichael?

IP Which series has turned the Yorkshire town of Holmfirth into a place of pilgrimage?

EH Which northern prison was the setting for an eight-part BBC documentary in 1980?

529

SD Which *Top of the Pops* presenter was nicknamed Fluff?

SS Which very famous role did nine-year-old Terry Brooks don specs and a stetson for?

FG Which comedy series went on and on and on, but was supposed to take place during a fortnight's Spanish holiday?

FF Which actor spent two days in bed to safeguard against catching a cold after filming *King Lear* under a rain machine in 1983?

IP Which TV spy with an Irish name was played by New Zealander Sam Neill?

EH What were the names of BBC2's kangaroo mascots?

530

SD Which pop singer was Wogan about to welcome to his first TV show when he tripped up?

SS What did J.R. describe as "Just another Ewing possession, like an oil lease in the Midlands — easily disposable"?

FG Which series first saw Griff Rhys Jones and Mel Smith involved in one of their famous head-to-head talks?

FF Who became a 'Hooker' after captaining the *Starship Enterprise*?

IP Which country was the setting for *Saigon - The Year of the Cat*?

EH What two colours is Rupert the Bear's scarf?

531

SD Which former DJ presented *The Multi-Coloured Swap Shop*?

SS What is the name of *Coronation Street's* closest large supermarket?

FG Which member of the original *What's My Line* panel returned with the show in 1984?

FF Which historic duo was played by Martin Sheen and Blair Brown in a 1983 TV drama?

IP Which TV series saw Peter Bowles playing a country magistrate?

EH How many parts of the *Tripods* trilogy were screened?

532

SD What is the name of the *Mission: Impossible* theme music?

SS How many words per minute could Krystle type when she became Blake Carrington's secretary?

FG Which spoof-soap featured in *Victoria Wood - as Seen on TV*?

FF Which of the *Rock Follies* cast played a rock singer in *No Excuses*?

IP Which sport featured in the play *Singles*?

EH Which children's Saturday morning show came from a grounded spacecraft called the *Millenium Dustbin*?

533

SD Who danced to *Let's Face the Music and Dance* on the *Morecambe and Wise Show*?

SS Which two foreign languages can Fallon Carrington respond to her lovers in?

FG Which comedy series teamed French and Saunders with Ruby Wax, Tracey Ullman and Joan Greenwood?

FF Which actor appeared on *Aspel and Co* holding a jug of orange juice and accused Aspel's other guests of being drunk?

IP Which drama series saw riots at an Indian station that were actually filmed in Buckinghamshire?

EH What new name was given to the *Day to Day* programme?

534

SD Which pop star was ditched by Dame Edna for being boring?

SS What colour flower did the *Santa Barbara* Carnation Killer leave behind?

FG Which funny female performer and writer won the 1985 BAFTA Award Comedy award?

FF Which drama series won Tim Piggot-Smith the BAFTA Best Actor award for his portrayal of a policeman called Merrick?

IP Which 1984 Granada series took four months to film in India?

EH What was the title of *The Big Match* changed to?

535

SD Which Welsh cabaret singer had a role in the TV movie *Pleasure Cove*?

SS Which building was being handed over to a new owner in the very first scene of *Coronation Street*?

FG What should the reply be if Timmy Mallet and Michaela Strachan ask: "What are we"?

FF Which tragic funnyman was the subject of the play *The Comic*?

IP How did Superintendent Lockhart like to take his tobacco?

EH Which county was the setting for *Sam*?

536

SD Which American singer had an acting role in *Condominium*?

SS Which regular *Coronation Street* role did Peter Dudley fill after being Alec Smith, Duggie Bowker and a jeweller?

FG Which TV comedian supported an election campaign by suggesting that Margaret Thatcher should bomb the Russians?

FF Which cop actor is married to Sheila Hancock?

IP Which police chief's headquarters were in the Iolani Palace in Honolulu?

EH What did Isla St. Clair do before she became a TV presenter?

Photo: Scope Features

(537)

SD Which TV pop programme stopped miming in 1965?

SS Which *Crossroads* star was used as a model by John Logie Baird?

FG Which piece of film studio equipment gave its name to a Chris Kelly quiz show?

FF What is Hale, of Hale and Pace's, first name?

IP Which '50s children's series featured a large animal called Bimbo?

EH Who returned from retirement in a 1981 TV special to win a case in front of Mr.Justice Bullingham?

(538)

SD Who made their first television appearance on Granada's local *People and Places* programme on 17th October 1962?

SS Which soap star's daughters are Sacha, Tara and Katyana?

FG Which duo's animated offerings include *Huckleberry Hound* and *Pixie and Dixie*?

FF Which northerner presented the outside broadcast sections of *The Multi-Coloured Swap Shop*?

IP How many Robinson children were *Lost In Space*?

EH What links the members of a team in *Busman's Holiday*?

(539)

SD Who, in 1980, became the first British conductor to have his life dramatised on television?

SS Where did this couple go for their honeymoon?

FG What is the first name of the Boswell's father?

FF Who played Dick's wife in *The Dick Van Dyke Show*?

IP What facial alteration took place in Perry Mason between the end of black and white production and the start of colour?

EH What colour is the head of Timmy Mallett's mallet?

(540)

SD What words did Elvis sing to the tune of the *Just One Cornetto* commercial?

SS Which soap is set in the town of Harmon Springs?

FG What is the name of the TV set in *Will O' the Wisp*?

FF Which actress played Telford's wife in *Telford's Change*?

IP What was Banacek's percentage?

EH What was the radio equivalent of TV's *Horne A' Plenty*?

541

SD Which night of the Proms was first broadcast in 1953?

SS Who shot J.R. (the second time)?

FG What are the red circles that appear on the *Strike it Lucky* losing screens called?

FF Which political reporter played his own great-great-grandfather in *Black Adder the Third*?

IP What is the series if Sarah works for Julian at Bygone Books?

EH Which long-running radio series was brought to television with the title *Home Town*?

542

SD What was the imaginative name that the BBC gave to their first Television Orchestra?

SS Who secretly sent his son to Ballard Intermediate School to avoid him being kidnapped?

FG What is the name of the doctor played by Richard Wilson in *Only When I Laugh*?

FF Who was blessed with the *Z Cars* role of Fatty?

IP What was the programme if the twins in the family were called Buffy and Jody?

EH What make of car was involved in the accident in the series *Hit and Run*?

543

SD Which drinking song became a hit after being sung in the 1948 TV production of *No, No, Nanette*?

SS What was the former use of the *EastEnders* pizza parlour?

FG Which town's fire brigade always ends its show by playing on the bandstand?

FF Which chat show host's final series took in a *Grand Tour*?

IP What was the name of the Admiral in *Voyage to the Bottom of the Sea*?

EH Which of Lucille Ball's TV series had Lucy as a widow?

544

SD Who was pictured in the background with his back to the camera on Abba's *Waterloo* record sleeve?

SS Who always refers to the *EastEnders* launderette as *The Bridge Street Washeteria*?

FG Which Goodie played Derek in *Me and My Girl*?

FF Who was the first *Nationwide* anchorman?

IP Which city is the setting for *The Justice Game*?

EH Where did Maxwell Smart carry his secret telephone in *Get Smart*?

545

SD Which Doors hit was used in a 1985 commercial for *Pirelli* tyres?

SS Which *Neighbour* was offered a job as a model in America?

FG Which show hosted by Tim Brooke-Taylor gave Harry Enfield his first TV appearance?

FF Which comedy actor is the voice of *Count Duckula*?

IP Which professor was assisted by Judith Carroon?

EH Who wrote *Beethoven's Tenth*?

546

SD Which pop singer became famous on TV due to his eye patch and died in a 1966 car crash?

SS Which organisation did *Coronation Street's* Lucille Hewitt do voluntary work with?

FG Which *Laugh-In* catchphrase was always spoken in a heavy German accent?

FF Which former *Game For A Laugh* star travels on *The Animals Roadshow*?

IP Which European island did Sophia of *The Golden Girls* originate from?

EH Which member of the *TISWAS* team hosts *Everybody's Equal*?

547

SD Who played lead guitar on the theme for *Peter Gunn*?

SS What was the name of the son whom Pam and Bobby Ewing adopted?

FG Which comedy series was introduced by Gary Owens?

FF Which Goon presented *Golden Silents*?

IP Which sci-fi series saw Interceptors launched against visitors from outer-space?

EH Which sci-fi TV character was originally going to be called Captain Robert April?

548

SD Whose baby did Mia Farrow announce she was expecting in October 1969?

SS Which number in Brookside Close is a bungalow?

FG Which of the *Three of a Kind* played Old Scrunge?

FF Which actor devised *Lytton's Diary*?

IP Whose life was totally changed when he was bitten by a radioactive insect?

EH Which TV personality is the agony aunt for the *Sunday Mirror*?

549

SD Which father of a future TV executive charted twice with the theme from *Friends and Neighbours*?

SS Who was driving the car in which Bobby Ewing was supposedly killed?

FG Which early question and answer show was chaired by Michael Flanders?

FF Which *Dad's Army* star was married to Hattie Jacques?

IP Which series saw Robert Colbert and Jane Darren locked in a machine?

EH Which *Last of the Summer Wine* actor played his own father in *First of the Summer Wine*?

550

SD Which TV star became a record breaker by playing *Whistle While You Work* on 40 different instruments in 4 minutes?

SS Which film star played Sammy Jo's *Dynasty* dad?

FG Which duo's final applause was often stolen from them at the end of their show by Janet Webb?

FF Who was the Shirley in *Shirley's World*?

IP Which series featured fast breeding Tribbles?

EH Which actor directed the movie *Star Trek V*?

551

SD Which of Batman's adversaries was played by singer Eartha Kitt?

SS Who was Jamie's mum in *Neighbours*?

FG What name is given to the group of prizes that can be won at the end of *The Price is Right*?

FF Which of Shirley Temple's vintage co-stars reached an even wider audience in *The Beverly Hillbillies*?

IP What were *The Survivors* trying to survive?

EH Who acted with his own son, Jeremy, in *Never the Twain*?

552

SD What is the Eurovision link between Lulu, Salome, Lennie Kuhr and Frida Baccara?

SS Which of *The Likely Lads'* actresses became Elsie in *Sharon and Elsie*?

FG What is Alfie Atkins's invisible friend called?

FF Who played Father Ralph de Bricassar in *The Thorn Birds*?

IP What is Spiderman's daytime job?

EH Which member of the Pertwee family played Air Raid warden Hodges in *Dad's Army*?

553

SD Which *Tonight* reporter went on to write a musical with Andrew Lloyd Webber?

SS Which soap featured an aircraft designer who went into boats?

FG What kind of creature is Hong Kong Phooey?

FF Which enthusiastic northerner went *Up A Gum Tree*?

IP What was the *Tomorrow People*'s computer called?

EH Which chat show host wrote the book *Cricket Mad*?

554

SD Which TV cop-series theme was dragged into the charts on 5 separate occasions by the Ted Heath Orchestra?

SS Which *CATS Eyes* actress sulked her way through *Renault* commercials?

FG Which superstar is managed by Darcy McFarcy?

FF Who went hitchhiking around the galaxy and is married to a former *Dr. Who*?

IP What is Peter Parker's other identity?

EH Which sports commentator is married to former Olympic long jump champion Jean Desforges?

555

SD Which comedian won a *Golden Rose* at Montreux for conducting and playing all the parts in the *1812 Overture*?

SS What was the relationship between Miss Ellie and Garrison

FG Who did B.J.Hunnicut replace in *M*A*S*H*?

FF Who was replaced by Kenneth Robinson on *Points of View*?

IP What was the name of *The Love Boat*?

EH Which member of the *That Was The Week That Was* team wrote a book called *French Letters*?

556

SD Who was *Ready Steady Go's* 'Queen of Bluebeat'?

SS Which soap has featured Glyn Owen and Kate O'Mara who both also appeared in *The Brothers*?

FG Whose brother is a game show producer and researched for game shows himself before becoming a chat show host?

FF Who fills the role of Hooperman?

IP How did Alec meet Zoe in *May to December*?

EH Which *Fawlty Towers* actress is married to actor Timothy West?

557

SD What four words followed "Double Your Money" in the last line of the show's theme song?

SS Which 'Allo 'Allo star had a role in Compact?

FG What is the name of the block of flats in which Del and Rodney Trotter live?

FF What was Tom O'Connor's day job before he became a full-time entertainer?

IP Which train provided the setting for a Minder Christmas special?

EH Which member of the Not the Nine O'Clock News team had a role in Superman III?

558

SD What did the England World Cup team sing on Top of the Pops in April 1970?

SS Who was the Lassiters' housekeeper?

FG Who hosted Scribble and died in 1991?

FF Which actor narrated Hollywood?

IP Which sci-fi series featured a space craft called the Heart of Gold?

EH Which deep-voiced actor was always portrayed begging for a knighthood on Spitting Image?

559

SD Which 1960s TV personality was known as "Mr. Guitar"?

SS Which soap featured racetrack owner Richard Channing?

FG What colour was Goldie Hawn's hair when she appeared on Laugh-In?

FF Which former footballer previewed forthcoming TV shows for TVam?

IP What kind of headgear did Skullion usually wear when he went out cycling?

EH Which comedian scripted, directed and acted in The Plank?

560

SD Which programme won the NME Best TV Show award each year from 1972 to 1977?

SS Which eastern university did Kelvin leave EastEnders for?

FG What was Radar O'Reilly's first name on M*A*S*H?

FF Which was Edward Woodward's first series as a secret agent?

IP What is this Vulcan's blood group?

EH Which actor wrote the book My Russia and presented a TV series on the same subject?

(561)

SD Which early *Top of the Pops* presenter didn't have much success with his own recordings of *So Much Love* and *It's Only You*?

SS Which were the "too good to hurry mints"?

FG Who took over from Una Stubbs as captain of the ladies on *Give Us A Clue*?

FF Which star of the early series *Buccaneers*, sailed to sea in *Jaws*?

IP Which city had Hazell solving its crimes?

EH Who was the very famous comedy actor father of the girl who played Jenny Piccolo in *Happy Days*?

(562)

SD Which Paul McCartney hit was performed on TV by a group of singing frogs?

SS What was the name of the whisky drinker who moved in to number 5, Coronation Street in 1976?

FG Which show's cast had to make the clothes, planned for a three week holiday, last for three seasons?

FF Which northern actor played C.S.Lewis in *Shadowlands*?

IP How many law books appear in the closing credits of *Perry Mason*?

EH How many helicopters landed during the opening credits of *M*A*S*H*?

(563)

SD Which fifties TV star had her first hit with *Bell Bottom Blues* and last with *Cowboy Jimmy Joe*?

SS Which soap was devised by *Grange Hill* creator Phil Redmond?

FG What is the basic colour of Elmo's Wine Bar?

FF What was stuttering Baron Glenavy's stage name?

IP Which mystery series features the characters Inspector Burden and Inspector Wexford?

EH Which film had TV cartoon spin-offs called *Droids* and *Ewoks*?

(564)

SD Which very famous big band had a hit with the BBC World Cup Grandstand Theme in 1982?

SS What job had Nicola Freeman done in a night club before moving to *Crossroads*?

FG Who starred in *Cool It*?

FF Who was warned of an encounter with J. F. Kennedy: "Don't build him up by appearing with him on television"?

IP What answer was always given when *The Prisoner* asked: "Where am I?"?

EH Which musical quartet won the 1966 Best Comedy Emmy?

(565)

SD What product did *Shades*, a hit for the United Kingdom Orchestra, sell on TV?

SS What does *Neighbours'* Clive Gibson play with when he wants to relax?

FG What newspaper do *The Flintstones* take?

FF Which newsreader once said that the happiest thing he'd ever announced was Stalin's death?

IP What century do the Star Trekkers do their trekking through?

EH What job did Bilko have in *The New Phil Silvers Show*?

(566)

SD Who was interviewed on the thousandth edition of *Wogan*?

SS Who was the father of the child that *Coronation Street's* Maggie Dunlop gave birth to in 1982?

FG Whose show was Yogi Bear a part of before getting his own series?

FF Which super-hero's tights were filled by the legs of Nicholas Hammond?

IP What is the nickname of Kizzy's son on *Roots*?

EH What was a boy called David the first child to appeal for, on television, when he appeared on 8th February 1982?

(567)

SD Who were the resident band on *The Last Resort*?

SS What have both Mike Baldwin and Jack Duckworth been charged with?

FG Whose sidekick is Benny the Ball?

FF Which large actor played the title role in *John Silver's Return to Treasure Island*?

IP Which show saw Calderon finally wasted after he had killed Lieutenant Lou Rodriguez?

EH Whose was the first televised Royal funeral?

(568)

SD Whose vocal version of *The Howard's Way* theme was used for one series?

SS Which club was Alec Gilroy running when he first got to know Bet Lynch?

FG Who was the first person to host *Crackerjack*?

FF Which *Saturday Superstore* regular went on to become the 'Son of God'?

IP Which US state did the *Rawhide* cattle drive first start rolling, rolling, rolling in?

EH What date in 1981 first saw the Queen's Christmas message with subtitles for the deaf?

569

SD Which medical series had *Sleepy Shores* as its theme music?

SS Who wasn't expected to attend Mike Baldwin's wedding to Susan, but did?

FG Who is the voice of Emu?

FF Who played the role of Piggy Malone?

IP Which of Dempsey and Makepeace isn't American?

EH Which famous building's interior was first seen on television on 21st February 1969?

570

SD Which TV show's theme song is *There's A New Girl In Town*?

SS Which soap newspaper did the Clarion Group buy a majority shareholding in?

FG What name was given to the masked character who threw custard pies around in *TISWAS*?

FF Which duo are *The Management*?

IP Which show's fantastic adventures were filmed in a Los Angeles public park called "The Arboretum"?

EH What was the address of the first British house to have a TV set installed as part of the lounge furniture?

571

SD What colour was Madonna's hair when she appeared on the 1000th *Wogan* show?

SS What operation did Alison of *Crossroads* have at Benny's expense?

FG What is the name of the Hazzard County sherriff?

FF Who is Frank Muir's most regular writing partner?

IP Who was aided in his flight from the law by his sister Donna?

EH What did Margaret Thatcher say was her favourite TV programme?

572

SD Which pop singing actor wrote the theme music for *Roy's Raiders*?

SS What was Jill thinking of calling her small West Country hotel as she spoke the final words in *Crossroads*?

FG Who was the butt of Basil Brush's "Boom-Booms" before he became a *Likely Lad*?

FF What was this man's chat show called?

IP Which mini-series featured arch-rivals Ishido and Toranaga?

EH Which BBC programme gave live 'uncoverage' to Erica Roe's famous streak at Twickenham?

Photo: Hulton Deutsch

573

SD What was Morecambe and Wise's theme song?

SS Why did *EastEnder* Pete Beale lose his driving licence?

FG Which classic comedy duo lived in Oil Drum Lane?

FF Which wartime commentator was known as "The Voice of America"?

IP What was the name of the hotel in *Hotel*?

EH Which TV detectives were served their drinks by Huggy Bear?

574

SD Whose weekly show always included the song: " Letters, we get letters, we get stacks and stacks of letters "?

SS Which *EastEnder* had the middle name Ada?

FG Which host spins the *Wheel of Fortune*?

FF What was Bert Ford's job?

IP What nationality was Victoria who swept up at *The High Chapparal*?

EH After which city was Alexis Carrington's dog named?

575

SD Which non-European country won the Eurovision Song Contest with *Hallelujah*?

SS Which legendary sailor shares his name with the *Brookside* window cleaner?

FG Who were the two stars of *Dear Ladies*?

FF Who played the Sultan in the series *Harem*?

IP Which cop series starred Alfred Burke as Marker?

EH Which feminine cop series saw Danny die in a fire in its final episode?

576

SD Which TV dance team lost their hearts to a starship trouper?

SS What is the nearest city to *Falcon Crest*?

FG Which Radio One DJ gave schoolchildren the opportunity to *Beat the Teacher*?

FF Which *Dad's Army* actor played Ron in the TV version of *The Glums*?

IP Which Welsh drama starred Sian Phillips and Stanley Baker?

EH What colour hair grows on Edd the Duck's head?

577

SD What did Damon Grant send to his *Brookside* cookery teacher to warrant a threatened suspension one February?

SS Which soap's first death came when Gavin Taylor suffered a brain haemorrhage?

FG Which army featured in *Hallelujah*?

FF Which role was played by Ian Richardson in *Mountbatten, The Last Viceroy*?

IP What were George Dixon's final words?

EH What was the name of the featured family in *Father Knows Best*?

578

SD Which aerobatic pilot appeared on *Top of the Pops* singing *Cars*?

SS What was the name of Jason Colby's father?

FG Where does Polly Sherman work?

FF Which member of the Starship Enterprise acting crew played an undercover agent in *Cash and Cable*?

IP Which jail did Callan meet Lonely in?

EH Which three-sided area of the world was the setting for *Fantastic Journey*?

579

SD Which character found the Firm saying "He's Alright" in their 1982 hit single?

SS Which *Coronation Street* character had an affair with her husband's Australian cousin?

FG Which comedy series was set in an agency called "Maggie's Models"?

FF What had Brian Blessed apparently lost between leaving *Z Cars* and starting *Return to Treasure Island*?

IP Which drama series featured a female warden nicknamed 'The Freak'?

EH Which sci-fi series' characters were treated by Dr. Helen Russell?

580

SD Which large-scale game-show gave Peter Gabriel a hit single title?

SS What was the closest rival to Fairlawns Hotel?

FG Which quiz show heard Les Dawson asking for the legend to be revealed?

FF Which TV series featured Herbert Lom as a psychiatrist?

IP Which TV ranch was set in the middle of the Comstock Lode silver mining area?

EH What is Kate's surname in *Kate and Allie*?

SD Who had a 1984 hit with the *Fraggle Rock Theme*

SS Who broke up the fight between Alf Roberts and Malcolm Reid when Alf thought Malcolm was having an affair with Audrey?

FG Which game show were you watching if the names were in the frames and the scores were on the doors?

FF Which TV presenter wrote *Jacobs Ladder*?

IP What four bits did Steve Austin have replaced when he became bionic?

EH Which of his regular stooges was in the next bed to Hancock in *The Blood Donor* sketch?

SD Which Berlin hit was used to help sell cars on TV?

SS Who left *Coronation Street* with Linda Jackson?

FG How many people were involved in the survey that provided each *Family Fortunes* question?

FF Which radio presenter saw David Frost performing in a club and gave him his break on *TW3*?

IP What was the limit to *The Champions'* amazing powers?

EH Which famous footballing surname is Rodney Trotter's middle name in *Only Fools and Horses*?

SD Which 1987 hit for the Firm had a chorus which included: "Klingons on the starboard bow, starboard bow, starboard bow"?

SS Who ran away from *Coronation Street* to stay with Susan Barlow when her parents wouldn't let her have a pet dog?

FG What was Hugh Laurie's role in *Les Girls*?

FF Who was the black member of *Three of a Kind*?

IP Which Western's characters were regularly whacked over the head by bottle-wielding Kitty Russell in the Longbranch Saloon?

EH Which of Del Boy's *Only Fools and Horses* friends is named after a cowboy's horse?

SD What was the Flying Lizards' follow-up hit to *Money*?

SS Who kidnapped Nicky Tilsley?

FG Which TV lawyer does Anton Rodgers have ambitions to emulate in *From May to December*

FF Which television lady married Desmond Wilcox?

IP What did Robert Culp and Bill Cosby pretend to be as a cover for their real activities in *I Spy*?

EH What is the family relationship between Don Henderson and Leslie Grantham in *The Paradise Club*?

SD Which TV cartoon was featured in Michael Jackson's *Black and White* video?

SS Why did Jack Sugden return to Emmerdale Farm?

FG Who had his mail delivered by Pop it in Pete?

FF Who was discovered by Armchair Theatre in 1959 and went on to become *Superman's* mum?

IP What was Gerald Lloyd Kookson III's nickname?

EH What is the name of the dog who makes a better job of presenting Children's ITV than his human assistants?

SD Whose song was a hit for Jon Pertwee?

SS Who does the R stand for in J.R. Ewing?

FG Which game show hears Tony Green shouting the scores?

FF Who quit a role in *The Rockford Files* because the stunts and fights had damaged his knees?

IP What did Joe Beck do before he became a policeman with a female boss?

EH Which George Webley actor died in 1988 when he fell off a horse whilst filming in Spain?

SD What type of music was featured in the 1980s series *And the Band Played On*?

SS Which soap's characters get their Chinese take-aways from the Green Lantern?

FG Who was always trying to borrow food in *Sykes*?

FF Who filled the role of Pappy Beau Maverick?

IP What year was the setting for *Rocket Robin Hood*?

EH Which film company had its own hour-long House of Horror series?

SD Which musical TV programme began in September 1950 and is still running?

SS Which soap's residents read the *Liverpool Echo*?

FG What breed of dog was the *Beverly Hillbillies'* pet Duke?

FF Which New Zealand-born actress had a starring role in *The Forsyte Saga*?

IP Which series had a spin-off called *Tucker's Luck*?

EH Which of the services was the setting for *Get Some In*?

Photo: Hulton Deutsch

589

SD Who sang *Laughter In The Rain* on an *Earth Born* Shampoo commercial?

SS Who was forced to marry hillbilly Cally Harper when her brothers discovered he'd had an affair with her?

FG Which series linked Nerys Hughes with Polly James?

FF Which *Lou Grant* actor won the Anne Frank Human Rights Award in 1986?

IP What was Kim's job on *Hawaiian Eye*?

EH What everyday object was referred to as a 'predictor' when *Quatermass* was made in 1953?

590

SD Who sang *Memories Are Made of This* on *Kodak* commercials?

SS What did J.R. claim that Afton Cooper was in order to have her leave town?

FG Whose brain went missing on *Spitting Image*?

FF Who ended up on a 'Desert Island' after presenting *Nationwide*?

IP What was B.J.'s surname in *B.J. and the Bear*?

EH Which TV series had Lorna Patterson in a 'Goldie Hawn film role'?

591

SD Which classy band sang *You Make Me Feel Brand New* on a Candide perfume commercial?

SS Where did this couple spend their first honeymoon?

FG Which puppet hosted *The Joke Machine*?

FF Which quiz host wrote and presented *The Archaeology of the Bible Lands*?

IP Who is the Hazzard County girl if the boys are Bo and Luke?

EH What particular branch of Scotland Yard was the subject of *The Pursuers*?

592

SD Which of Dexy's Midnight Runner's hits had the catalogue number *BRUSH I*?

SS What was the name of the sporting club, named after a local landmark, that early *Coronation Street* members attended?

FG Which of the Likely Lads had a sister called Sheila?

FF Who was the first British TV interviewer to have two sons doing the same job?

IP What is Hooperman's first name?

EH Which fictional village would you visit to meet Alf Thompson and Granny Dryden?

SD Which *EastEnders* actress was backed by the Simon May Orchestra on her biggest hit?

SS What nickname did Terry Wogan give to Lucy Ewing?

FG What was Timothy's job in *Sorry*?

FF What two letters and two numbers identify the most famous cop role played by Brian Reece?

IP Which drama series followed John Blackthorne's adventures as a prisoner of the Japanese?

EH Which husband and wife duo starred in *Forever Green*?

SD Which phrase from *The Secret Diary of Adrian Mole* was a hit for Ian Dury?

SS What were the people who shot Ernie Bishop trying to steal from the *Coronation Street* warehouse?

FG How many actors were included in each group of six people in *Sweethearts*?

FF Which actress did Noel Coward refer to as "The three worst actresses in the English speaking world"?

IP Which British series featured John Drake and was called *Secret Agent* when shown in the States?

EH What was *War and Rememberance* the sequel to?

SD Which Electric Light Orchestra hit title was also a TV comedy series featuring Nigel Planer?

SS Who lost his wife in the 1975 *Coronation Street* fire and then married Eunice Nuttall in the hope that this would help him get a pub?

FG Which ventriloquist hosted *Three Little Words*?

FF Which female presenter co-conducted Andrew and Fergie's pre-wedding interview?

IP What is the name of Taggart's daughter?

EH Who was the oldest Womble?

SD Which Paul McCartney composition did this young performer sing as the theme for her 1968 series?

SS Who raised eyebrows by camping out with Victor Pendlebury?

FG Which Tom O'Connor quiz show is based on crossword puzzles?

FF Which talent scout hosted the *Junior Discovery Show*?

IP Which *Kojak* character grew plants on his desk?

EH Which TV sisters were played by Mildred Natwick and Helen Hayes?

Photo: Hulton Deutsch

597

SD What was the name of the rapper who joined Fab on their *Thunderbirds* hit?

SS Which *Coronation Street* characters' grandchildren included Damian?

FG Which comedy series features the Beasleys from Bolton?

FF Who received a CBE from the Prime Minister in the 1987 New Year's Honours for playing a prime minister?

IP Which sci-fi series starred Catherine Schell as an alien called Maya?

EH Who hosted the 1989 *Comic Relief* telethon with Smith and Jones?

598

SD Which TV star charted with *Snot Rap*?

SS Who set the Dagmar on fire?

FG Which sergeant was in charge of Corporal Henshaw?

FF Who started, and finished, presenting the BBC's *Chronicle* series?

IP What is the number of the most notorious squad car on New York's 53rd precinct?

EH What sits on a dolly in a TV studio?

599

SD Which Beatles song was performed by a female sextet on the 1989 *Comic Relief* programme?

SS What is the local store called in *Home and Away*?

FG Which part of his body does Mork grasp and twist as he shouts "Nanoo — Nanoo"?

FF Who went from *Carry On* films to become *Coronation Street's* Alma Sedgwick?

IP Which *Mary Tyler Moore Show* character claims that his favourite colour is plaid?

EH What is the full-time occupation of the owners of America's *Eternal World* TV channel?

600

SD What was TV presenter Cilla Black's name when she worked as a cloakroom attendant at the Cavern Club?

SS Which soap is based on the novel *Spender's Mountain*?

FG Which comedian hosted *Big Break*?

FF Which pole vaulter won the television *Superstars* competition?

IP Which Western detective regularly keeps out the New York City chill by donning a sheepskin jacket?

EH Which American comedy series had a spin-off called *Tabatha*?

601

SD Which Dire Straits hit mentions 'colour TV'?

SS Which *Emmerdale* farmer had a secretary called Mrs. Bates?

FG Who left *Man About the House* in 1973 and made a game show comeback as a *Crazy Companions* team captain in 1991?

FF Which newscaster presented a series on tracing family trees?

IP Which spaced-out TV hero has a pal called Twiki?

EH Which TV series was the subject of a book called *A Celebration, Two Decades Through Time and Space*?

602

SD What was TV's next totally-live regular pop show after *Oh Boy*! finished its run in the 1950s?

SS What was Lynne Howard's longest single-handed trip in *Howard's Way*?

FG Who bragged: "Spookily I'd just won Melbourne's Lovely Mother contest"?

FF How does Oprah Winfrey spell her first name?

IP What is the first name of Detective Lacey's husband?

EH Which wildlife series has survived on British Television for more years than any other?

603

SD What name did David Peacock and Charles Hodge use when singing on TV commercials?

SS Who owned the corner shop when *Coronation Street* was first broadcast?

FG What was the name of Dame Edna's bridesmaid?

FF Which newspaper baron was played by Barry Humphries in *Selling Hitler*?

IP Who is being chased across the screen when a fat Mexican shouts: "Lancers, after heeeem!"?

EH What is the real name of American television weather forecaster Storm Field?

604

SD Which night of the week was *Cool For Cats* night?

SS Which soap saw Kim Novak in the role of Skyler Kimble?

FG What is the name of the show if John Goodman plays the husband, Dan?

FF Which *Happy Days* actor became Father Dowling?

IP Which *Miami Vice* character went south to find the drug dealer who murdered his brother?

EH What do the letters ENG mean to a TV journalist?

605

SD Which '60s Doris Day hit re-charted in 1987 after exposure on a TV tights commercial?

SS What is the family relationship between Blake Carrington and Dominique Devereaux?

FG Which game show sees Neil Buchanan inviting youngsters to raid a room full of goodies?

FF Which TV duo was played by Clayton Moore and Jay Silverheels?

IP How old was Kunte Kinte when he was taken to America?

EH Which channel had Britain's first regular hour-long news programme?

606

SD Which TV cartoon duo's name did Simon and Garfunkel perform under, early in their career?

SS Which soap's characters visited the surgery of Dr. Legg?

FG Which game show asked a contestant to equal John Virgo's trick shot?

FF Which all-American super-hero was called: "A capitalist murderer" in Pravda ?

IP What kind of accident left police commissioner McMillan without a wife?

EH Which was the first British news programme to feature two newscasters?

607

SD What was Pearl Carr and Teddy Johnson's 1959 Eurovision entry?

SS Which Last of the Summer Wine star played Coronation Street's Vera Hopkins?

FG What is Tracey and Sharon's family relationship in Birds of a Feather?

FF Which modern pentathlete gets to go away on Holiday?

IP Which show's producer once said: "We soon found out that what the audience wanted was water, water and more water"?

EH Which ship's 1936 docking in Southampton was the subject of the first news item ever filmed specifically for television?

608

SD Which American TV star took over the lead role in the West End production of Time after Cliff Richard?

SS Which soap character had a secretary called Sly?

FG Which game show's segments include Fact or Fib, Star Spin and Crazy Cryptics ?

FF Who had a news bulletin curtailed with the official excuse that he was "Unwell"?

IP Which macho private eye packed a .45 automatic instead of his usual .38 when he appeared on TV in 1984?

EH Which tennis star was the first person to be interviewed in a scheduled British TV programme?

609

SD Which Top of the Pops presenter left the BBC to have a baby in 1987?

SS Which city was the setting for Connie?

FG What's the programme if Gavin, Howard and Kevin are having hysterics over a phallic-shaped carrot?

FF Who went from gardening to presenting Daytime Live?

IP Which cop show do fans refer to as S & H?

EH Which BBC Governor was paid by Granada TV when they used his home, Castle Howard, in Brideshead Revisited?

610

SD Which Eurovision entry included: "You don't want me, come tomorrow you won't want me back again to hold you tightly"?

SS What name is shortened to Sable by The Colbys?

FG What title was given to the 1991 series of Spitting Image repeats?

FF Which former captain of the British Olympic Gymnastics team found a job as a TV presenter?

IP Which Western hero carried a derringer under his belt buckle?

EH Which are the two largest letters when the word Ceefax is seen on TV?

611

SD Which hit single introduced Happy Days until it got its own theme song?

SS What job did Krystle's first husband take at La Mirage in Dynasty?

FG Which comedy series saw Ashley and Elaine involved in a pizza war?

FF Which Tube presenter had white hair and black eyebrows?

IP Which show saw Raymond St. Jacques become the first black actor to be featured regularly in a Western series?

EH Which decade saw the first public demonstration of a television?

612

SD Which 1984 number 1 was banned from Top of the Pops?

SS Which Ramsay Street resident paints pictures?

FG Which Madhouse star presented his own Laughter Show?

FF Which former captain of Australia now reports on cricket for British television?

IP Who did Richie Cunningham use as a stand-in when he married Lori Beth by telephone?

EH How many Monty Python TV series were there?

Photo: Scope Features

613

SD How many years did the legendary *Oh Boy!* last on television?

SS Which *Knots Landing* character divorced his wife after she penned the muckraking novel *Capricorn Crude*?

FG Where is actress Pamela Power seen to work in *Bread*?

FF What is Bill Treacher's *EastEnders* role?

IP What form did these alien's take when they were on Earth?

EH Which production company produces *Dallas*?

614

SD Which British band's 1989 tour of America was partly sponsored by MTV?

SS Which already familiar face became Jenna Wade of Dallas ?

FG What is the name of the Boswells' sister?

FF Which pop singer appeared naked opposite Laurence Olivier in *Ebony Tower*?

IP Which award-winning serial saw detective Ronald Craven avenging the death of his daughter Emma?

EH At what time do ITV and the BBC start to show a range of programmes which may not be suitable for children?

615

SD Which '70s singer/songwriter began legal proceedings in 1990 when a jeans commercial used one of his songs?

SS Which *Dynasty* star met the Queen in 1985?

FG Who, collectively, are Dorothy, Rose, Sophia and Blanche?

FF Which son of a famous actor took over as Robin Hood when Michael Praed left for *Dynasty*?

IP Which mini-series starred John Gielgud in an Indian setting?

EH Which BBC2 series included *Buck Rogers in the 25th Century*?

616

SD Who sang the *No Honestly* theme song?

SS Who were the first residents of *Coronation Street* to have stone cladding stuck onto the front of their house?

FG Who managed the store in *Are You Being Served?*

FF Who went *Around the World in 80 Days* for BBC television?

IP What does the prefix *'U.S.S.'* stand for in the name of *Star Trek's Enterprise?*

EH What epic TV series was based on Paul Scott's *The Raj Quartet?*

Trivial Pursuit

·GAME 1·
TV

1
SD Alan Rothwell
SS *Cerebos Salt's*
FG Jeffrey Holland
FF Richard Burton
IP The Brothers McGregor
EH Popeye

2
SD Chas and Dave's
SS *Gillette*
FG Cook
FF Burt Reynolds
IP Logan (in *Logan's Run*)
EH The computer

3
SD Little and Large's
SS Paris
FG Stephen and Hugh
FF Charlie Chaplin's
IP Circus Boy
EH Politics

4
SD The Wombles
SS Fallon
FG *Brush Strokes*
FF John Cleese
IP *Boys From the Blackstuff*
EH *Fancy Wanders*

5
SD The Rolling Stones
SS *Dynasty*
FG Harry Secombe
FF Simon Dee
IP *Fortunes of War*
EH *Ponderosa*

6
SD "Yab-a-dab-a-doo"
SS Patrick Duffy's
FG The Nag's Head
FF Gene Barry's
IP *The Fall Guy*
EH Edd Byrnes (Kookie)

7
SD Five
SS Denver's
FG Reg Varney
FF David Nixon
IP It was the inspector's call sign
EH *Arrest and Trial*

8
SD The Beatles
SS A Premium Bond win
FG *Sportsmaster*
FF Ian Carmichael
IP 25
EH Adam West

9
SD *Step Inside Love*
SS *Milky Way*
FG Spot
FF Michael
IP Mark Sabre
EH Johnny Craddock

10
SD Herb Alpert
SS Falcon Crest
FG Vanessa Redgrave
FF Roger Moore
IP *The Flying Lady*
EH Starsky

11
SD *Pipes of Peace*
SS *Alka Seltzer*
FG *Marty*
FF Peter Falk
IP Superboy
EH Kate

12
SD *Take My Breath Away*
SS "And all because the lady loves *Milk Tray*"
FG Brothers-in-law
FF Henry Cooper
IP Impossible Missions Force
EH *The Two Ronnies*

13
SD Paul McCartney
SS Polo
FG Kevin Turvey
FF Judy Cornwell
IP A string of pearls
EH Northamptonshire

14
SD Tokyo
SS *Brookside*
FG Stackton Tressle
FF Billie Whitelaw
IP A lighthouse
EH The Mississippi

15
SD ITV
SS Glenda Banks
FG *The Krankies*
FF Robert Blake
IP Starsky and Hutch
EH Baseball

16
SD *Champion the Wonder Horse*
SS The red rec
FG Superted
FF Selina Scott
IP Columbo's
EH Edward Heath

17
SD Casey Kasem
SS Rome
FG Cuddles
FF William Tell
IP Marcus Welby
EH Kiss him

18
SD Perry Como
SS Brian Tilsley
FG "It's *Crackerjack*"
FF David Essex
IP A message
EH None

19
SD Vince Hill
SS Mike Baldwin
FG Yogi Bear's
FF Adam West and Burt Ward
IP *Dallas*
EH Elizabeth II

20
SD Mormon
SS North Yorkshire
FG Trevor
FF Richard Beckinsale
IP *Murder, She Wrote*
EH Spacely Space Sprockets

21
SD Roy Rogers
SS *Dallas's*
FG The Treasure Chest
FF *Gardener's World*
IP *Fantasy Island*
EH *The Goodies*

22
SD Cleo Laine
SS Jack
FG Joan Rivers
FF John Creasey
IP Jersey
EH Julie Walters

23
SD Norman Vaughan
SS Wicksy
FG Adrian
FF *Shane*
IP *Oasis Publishing*
EH Patrick Troughton

24
SD Robin Hood
SS Theresa
FG Scooby Snacks
FF *Floyd on Fish*
IP Hardcastle and McCormick
EH *Undercover Agent*

25
SD *Mr Ed's*
SS *Peyton Place*
FG *The Likely Lads*
FF Alfred the Butler
IP Asta
EH *Burke's Law*

26
SD Ed Sullivan's
SS Eddie Yates
FG *Watching*
FF Himmler's
IP Catering
EH Colonel March

27
SD Mick Jagger
SS Granada
FG Insurance
FF Ross Davidson
IP Arthur
EH They were carpenters

28
SD Joe Brown
SS She was asked to go
FG *The Archers*
FF Thora Hird
IP *Wells Fargo*
EH *Night Gallery*

29
SD Liberace
SS A *Playtex Cross-Your-Heart Bra*
FG "It's the way I tell 'em!"
FF Maureen Lipman
IP Santa Monica
EH Boris Karloff

ANSWERS

30
SD Violet Carson
SS *Opal Fruits*
FG Tommy and Bobby
FF David Attenborough
IP Black
EH Robert Stack

31
SD *No, No, Nannette*
SS Mr Popadopoulos
FG Captain Flack
FF Joan Collins
IP Taxi driver
EH *The Virginian*

32
SD *Wish Me Luck as You Wave Me Goodbye*
SS 40%
FG *Blockbusters*
FF Gwen Taylor
IP *The High Chapparal*
EH The A-Team

33
SD *The Pirates of Penzance*
SS Curly Watts
FG Topo Giggio
FF Peter Purves
IP *The Invisible Man*
EH Librarian

34
SD Eric Coates
SS Kathy Beale
FG Emu's Broadcasting Company
FF Alan Bates
IP *Dennis the Menace*
EH A department store

35
SD A candelabra
SS *Albion Market*
FG *Diff'rent Strokes*
FF Jenny Agutter
IP "Kemo Sabe"
EH Manchester

36
SD 1930s
SS Seth Armstrong
FG Derek
FF Jenny Hanley
IP "Hi ho Silver, awaaaaaay"
EH A bear

37
SD *The Television Toppers*
SS Annie Sugden
FG Ken Goodwin's
FF Charlie Chaplin
IP Florida
EH *From Here to Eternity*

38
SD *Bohemian Rhapsody*
SS Meg Mortimer
FG Jimmy Cricket
FF Eddie Large
IP The Mohicans
EH Stanley Baxter's

39
SD "Early in the morning — Just as day is dawning"
SS Saint Bruno
FG Rodney Bewes'
FF Jimmy Greaves
IP The Bionic Man
EH Office of Strategic Services

40
SD *Johnny Remember Me*
SS Steven Carrington
FG Flintstone
FF Tracey Ullman
IP A balloon
EH *The Pallisers*

41
SD Spike MIlligan
SS Matt Skillbeck
FG Otto
FF Tony Hart
IP Two
EH The Two Ronnies

42
SD The Twist
SS Johnny Briggs
FG Keys
FF Colin Baker
IP Starsky and Hutch
EH A lion

43
SD *Let Your Love Flow*
SS Katherine Wentworth
FG George Burns
FF Cannon and Ball
IP Fleet Street
EH *Public Eye*

44
SD *Nice One Cyril*
SS Jimmy Savile
FG Slowcoach
FF The Queen's
IP *The Dukes of Hazzard*
EH *Sooty*

45
SD Perry Como
SS A boat
FG Elmo's Wine Bar
FF Ray and Allen
IP The RAF
EH *Blakes 7*

46
SD *Z Cars*
SS Violet Carson
FG *I've Got a Secret*
FF Noah Berry
IP In space
EH The *Lady Chatterley's Lover* case

47
SD Pat Boone
SS Ramsay Street
FG Burt Campbell
FF Alec Guinness
IP Gamma Rays
EH *Through the Keyhole*

48
SD Roger Daltrey
SS *The Grove Family*
FG Blue
FF Harry Worth
IP It was sponsored by *Camel* cigarettes
EH Rory Calhoun

49
SD Connie Stevens
SS Mrs. Mangel
FG Wednesday
FF Kenneth Kendall
IP Perry Mason's
EH *University Challenge*

50
SD Eddie Kidd
SS *Coronation Street's*
FG A ghost
FF Ludovic Kennedy
IP Los Angeles'
EH *For Deaf Children*

51
SD German
SS She had a miscarriage
FG *Divided We Stand*
FF Patrick Moore
IP "Who Killed"
EH He had a heart complaint

52
SD *Love Me Tender*
SS That he'd tried to rape her
FG *The Cuckoo Waltz*
FF Prince Charles
IP It was never given
EH *Mission Impossible*

53
SD The Lone Ranger
SS Hilda Ogden
FG Roy Castle
FF Richard Dimbleby
IP His memory
EH Worzel Gummidge

54
SD Russ Abbot
SS Three
FG Brenda
FF Telly Savalas
IP *Hill Street Blues'*
EH *Justice*

55
SD *Banana Rock*
SS *The Bill*
FG Klinger
FF John Stalker
IP Los Angeles
EH Seventy

56
SD Keith Harris and Orville
SS Ernie Bishop
FG Garfield
FF Richard Hearne (Mr Pastry)
IP *The Adventures of Sherlock Holmes*
EH Millicent Martin

57
SD Richard Hearne (Mr. Pastry)
SS *Hofmeister Lager*
FG Ken Dodd
FF Andrew Sachs
IP As a bounty hunter
EH *The Prisoner's*

58
SD Zero
SS One
FG Frankie Howerd
FF Annette Crosby's
IP *First Among Equals*
EH A vintage *Rolls-Royce*

59
SD *Cool For Cats*
SS Nick Cotton
FG The Munsters
FF Johnny Carson's
IP He lost all his money in the Wall Street Crash
EH Peter Sellers

60
- **SD** *The Onedin Line*
- **SS** Larry Hagman
- **FG** Terry Scott
- **FF** Barrister
- **IP** The A-team
- **EH** Barry Norman

61
- **SD** The Kids From Fame
- **SS** *Persil Concentrate*
- **FG** Leopards
- **FF** Eamonn Andrews
- **IP** Six
- **EH** Salt Lake City

62
- **SD** Max Headroom
- **SS** *A Country Practice*
- **FG** *Hogan's Heroes*
- **FF** Michael Wood's
- **IP** Boss Hogg
- **EH** *The Wheeltappers and Shunters Club*

63
- **SD** Russ Abbot
- **SS** *Take the High Road*
- **FG** Gonzo
- **FF** Michael Aspel
- **IP** White
- **EH** Miss World

64
- **SD** Michael Jackson
- **SS** Mike Baldwin
- **FG** Mississippi
- **FF** Hazell
- **IP** *The Dukes of Hazzard*
- **EH** Patty Hearst

Trivial Pursuit™

·GAME 2·

65
- **SD** The Olympics
- **SS** *Dynasty*
- **FG** Sam
- **FF** Dickie Davies
- **IP** Chingachgook
- **EH** Thalidomide

66
- **SD** *Stranger on the Shore*
- **SS** Len Fairclough
- **FG** Lenny Henry
- **FF** John Oaksey's
- **IP** Mr. Hudson
- **EH** Asian immigrants

67
- **SD** *Robin (The Hooded Man)*
- **SS** Ethel
- **FG** Freddie Starr
- **FF** Jimmy Tarbuck's
- **IP** Emma Peel
- **EH** Stanley Holloway

68
- **SD** Cilla Black
- **SS** Stan and Hilda Ogden's
- **FG** Green
- **FF** He was a footballer
- **IP** *The Little Princess*
- **EH** A British butler

69
- **SD** *The Gambler*
- **SS** Home and Away
- **FG** Wimpy
- **FF** David Soul's
- **IP** He was a doctor
- **EH** John Milton

70
- **SD** *Pennies From Heaven*
- **SS** An *Access* card
- **FG** Gunner Graham
- **FF** Michael J. Fox
- **IP** *The Power Game*
- **EH** A moose

71
- **SD** Rupert
- **SS** She'd committed suicide
- **FG** Sarah
- **FF** Evadne Hinge
- **IP** *All Creatures Great and Small*
- **EH** Wile E. Coyote

72
- **SD** Paul Henry
- **SS** Norman
- **FG** *The Fall and Rise of Reginald Perrin*
- **FF** Jack Webb
- **IP** Wonder Woman
- **EH** Boxing

73
- **SD** Tony Blackburn
- **SS** *The Crossroads Motel*
- **FG** Patrick Cargill
- **FF** Wales
- **IP** *V*
- **EH** *Logan's Run*

74
- **SD** 25th
- **SS** Meg Mortimer/Richardson
- **FG** *Whose Line is it Anyway?*
- **FF** Judith Chalmers
- **IP** Father
- **EH** Hugh O'Brien

75
- **SD** *Blue Peter*
- **SS** Coates
- **FG** Nora Batty
- **FF** Cuban
- **IP** *Crimewatch UK*
- **EH** Rock Hudson

76
- **SD** *The Goodies*
- **SS** The hairdressing salon
- **FG** Cassandra
- **FF** New Zealand
- **IP** *All Creatures Great and Small*
- **EH** *Star Trek*

77
- **SD** *Thank Your Lucky Stars*
- **SS** Aspro
- **FG** Jimmy Cricket
- **FF** Paradine
- **IP** San Francisco
- **EH** *SWAT*

78
- **SD** *Paperback Writer*
- **SS** Esso Blue Paraffin
- **FG** Terry Jones
- **FF** Nannette Newman
- **IP** Lou Grant
- **EH** Richie Cunningham

79
- **SD** *Staccato's Theme* from *Johnny Staccato*
- **SS** *Howard's Way*
- **FG** Graham Chapman
- **FF** Gordon Honeycombe
- **IP** Batman's
- **EH** They each had a sting in the tail

80
- **SD** *O.K*
- **SS** It didn't, he died during the ceremony
- **FG** Three
- **FF** Frankie Howerd's
- **IP** Batgirl
- **EH** World War II

81
- **SD** *I Want to Break Free*
- **SS** The Dagmar
- **FG** *Laugh-In*
- **FF** Raymond Baxter
- **IP** *Beauty and the Beast*
- **EH** Red

82
- **SD** *Je T'Aime* by Jane Birkin and Serge Gainsbourg
- **SS** Sarah Louise
- **FG** T.C.
- **FF** John Freeman
- **IP** *First Born*
- **EH** Four

83
- **SD** Teddy Pendergrass
- **SS** Lucky
- **FG** *Happy Days*
- **FF** German
- **IP** *Blind Justice*
- **EH** *Poltergeist*

84
- **SD** Frankie Goes to Hollywood's *Two Tribes*
- **SS** Tomato juice
- **FG** A coffin
- **FF** Oliver Reed
- **IP** Cancer
- **EH** *Black on Black*

85
- **SD** *Top of the Pops*
- **SS** His back
- **FG** Mork
- **FF** Lulu
- **IP** Steve Austin
- **EH** The TV station

86
- **SD** Gene Vincent
- **SS** Kevin Webster
- **FG** "Shootin' at some food"
- **FF** Alan Bennett
- **IP** Sulu
- **EH** The Televisor

87
- **SD** *Part of the Union*
- **SS** Fruit and veg
- **FG** Latka Gravas
- **FF** No relationship at all – they share the same surname "Porter"
- **IP** Kunta Kinte's
- **EH** Thomas the Tank Engine

ANSWERS

(88)
SD *Pipes of Peace*
SS Gardener
FG Beer
FF Garfield Morgan
IP Fonzarelli
EH Greek

(89)
SD The Crowd
SS Divorce papers
FG Mork
FF Roy Rogers
IP *Agatha Christie's Poirot*
EH *Look-In*

(90)
SD Johnny Logan
SS A bill from a restaurant
FG Lucille Ball
FF *The Naked City*
IP *A Tale of Two Cities*
EH Birmingham

(91)
SD Elvis Presley
SS Garrison
FG The attack on Pearl Harbor
FF George Burns
IP New York
EH T-Shirt

(92)
SD Rod Stewart (her husband)
SS Ray Krebbs
FG *And Now for Something Completely Different*
FF Pancho
IP Murder
EH Marineville

(93)
SD Lulu
SS Kate O'Mara
FG Brutus
FF Richard Briers
IP Forensic scientist
EH *Rings on Their Fingers*

(94)
SD Luciano Pavarotti
SS *Home and Away*
FG The actual egg race
FF Yootha Joyce
IP Matt Dillon
EH Newgate

(95)
SD Su Pollard
SS Lynne Perrie (Ivy Brennan)
FG Terry Scott
FF Anna Ford
IP George Dixon
EH *Roots: The New Generation*

(96)
SD Ronnie Barker
SS Adam Chance
FG "My name is"
FF David McCallum
IP Cybermen
EH Somerset Maugham's

(97)
SD Prince Charles and Princess Diana
SS Sally Webster
FG Boxing
FF Her son married his daughter
IP AIDS
EH *Magpie*

(98)
SD Buddy Holly's
SS Leslie Grantham
FG *Rowan and Martin's Laugh-In*
FF David Jason
IP *Virgin of the Secret Service*
EH Ten

(99)
SD Rupert the Bear
SS Twins
FG Wendy Craig
FF Nicholas Witchell
IP Manchester
EH Charged by an elephant

(100)
SD *Snooker Loopy*
SS *Brookside*
FG *The Yob*
FF John Freeman
IP Superman
EH Johnny Speight

(101)
SD *The Maigret Theme*
SS Krystle Carrington
FG Mr. Cromwell
FF Noele Gordon
IP He didn't want to be conspicious
EH Just one

(102)
SD Milli Vanilli
SS Scott
FG Benny Hill
FF Sir Peter Scott
IP *Battlestar Gallactica*
EH New York City

(103)
SD *Captain Beaky*
SS Shingles
FG *After Henry*
FF Jan Leeming
IP Twiggy
EH *Man About the House*

(104)
SD Barcelona
SS He placed an advertisement in the paper
FG Frankie Howerd
FF Angela Rippon
IP Children's nanny
EH *Please Sir*

(105)
SD Musical director
SS *The Practice*
FG Gordon Burns
FF Michael Elphick
IP California Highway Patrol
EH *Great Expectations*

(106)
SD The Steelemen
SS Beattie
FG Edith
FF Jane Wyman
IP Liverpool
EH *The Magic Roundabout*

(107)
SD 30
SS Two
FG Paul Daniels
FF Terry Wogan
IP *The Mistress*
EH *One Man and his Dog*

(108)
SD Gallup
SS Jenny Bradley's
FG Gloria
FF Adam Faith
IP Emma Peel
EH *Just Amazing*

(109)
SD Kent Walton
SS *Smarties*
FG *That Was The Week That Was*
FF Charlie Drake
IP *The Avengers*
EH Prince Philip

(110)
SD Billy Cotton
SS *Persil*
FG Angela Rippon
FF Eric Morecambe
IP DAL-EKS
EH Tex Tucker

(111)
SD Vernons (The Vernons Girls)
SS Dr. Kildare's
FG Terry Hall
FF Underwater natural history
IP Splasher
EH *This Week*

(112)
SD The Rolling Stones
SS 1962
FG Ernest
FF Cliff Michelmore
IP Supercar
EH *The Sky At Night*

(113)
SD A zither
SS Alan Turner
FG Archie Andrews
FF Sgt. Snudge
IP Hercules
EH *Grandstand*

(114)
SD Tommy Trinder
SS The *Esso* sign
FG A juke box
FF Barry Bucknell
IP "I only arsked"
EH David Coleman

(115)
SD *Dixon of Dock Green*
SS *Emergency Ward 10*
FG *Juke Box Jury*
FF *Hawkeye and the Last of the Mohicans*
IP *Highway Patrol*
EH Read the football results

(116)
SD *Come Dancing*
SS *Emergency Ward 10*
FG *Criss Cross Quiz*
FF John Alderton
IP Perry Mason's
EH Patrick Moore

(117)
SD *Opportunity Knocks*
SS Mackeson
FG Knotty Ash
FF Princess Anne
IP General Lee
EH Petra

118
- SD Lord Charles
- SS Christopher Beeny
- FG Mr. Pastry's
- FF Michaela
- IP *The Quatermass Experiment*
- EH *Whirligig*

119
- SD Englebert Humperdinck
- SS Phillip
- FG Mr. Jinks's
- FF Lloyd Bridges
- IP Snowdonia
- EH *Wagon Train*

120
- SD Barbara Castle's
- SS *Fry's Turkish Delight*
- FG Snagglepuss's
- FF John Noakes
- IP Charlie Chan
- EH A tortoise

Trivial Pursuit
· GAME 3 ·
TV

121
- SD The Rolling Stones
- SS *Woodbine*
- FG Ken Dodd's
- FF *Blue Peter's*
- IP Tom Lockhart
- EH Silver paper

122
- SD Jocky Wilson's
- SS *Bucknell's House*
- FG The $64,000 Question
- FF The surname - Colin Baker and Tom Baker
- IP Rin Tin Tin
- EH Video tape

123
- SD BBC
- SS The Ewings
- FG *Birds of a Feather*
- FF They aren't related
- IP *Lost In Space*
- EH The Earthquake

124
- SD It wasn't
- SS Kylie Minogue
- FG *Pebbles and Bam Bam*
- FF Tarzan
- IP Dodge City
- EH The Russian Revolution

125
- SD *19*
- SS Dry rot
- FG Kenny Everett
- FF Ray Brooks
- IP *Bluebell*
- EH *Cinema*

126
- SD Kate Loring (Kate Robins)
- SS Albert
- FG Emu
- FF Roy Rogers'
- IP B.A.Baracus's
- EH The troubles in Northern Ireland

127
- SD Paula Yates
- SS Martha Longhurst
- FG Emu
- FF John Hurt
- IP Wyatt Earp's
- EH *World at War*

128
- SD Stephanie de Sykes
- SS Joan Collins
- FG *Fun House*
- FF Dennis Waterman
- IP San Quentin
- EH *Tonight*

129
- SD *Suddenly*
- SS Albert Tatlock
- FG Cockerel's
- FF Paul Daniels
- IP Buck Rogers
- EH Big Bird

130
- SD George Michael's
- SS *Falcon Crest*
- FG Bill Cosby
- FF Sue Lawley
- IP *Buck Rogers in the 25th Century*
- EH Lord Grade

131
- SD *Donny and Marie*
- SS Milk's
- FG Larry Grayson
- FF Peter Cushing
- IP *A Family at War*
- EH Reading

132
- SD *The Partridge Family*
- SS Tetley
- FG *Mastermind*
- FF Lord Mountbatten
- IP Diana Dors
- EH *On The Move*

133
- SD *The Golden Girls*
- SS Mavis Riley
- FG *Whatever Happened to the Likely Lads*
- FF Keith Michell
- IP The U.S.A.'s
- EH Harold Wilson's

134
- SD Keith Moon
- SS Patrick Allen
- FG Sooty
- FF Michael Palin
- IP *The Avengers*
- EH Mary Whitehouse

135
- SD *Top of the Pops*
- SS Cab driver
- FG Thomas the Tank Engine
- FF Michael Parkinson
- IP Blue
- EH Kenny Everett

136
- SD Frank Ifield
- SS Mike Baldwin
- FG *The Golden Girls*
- FF Dennis Waterman
- IP Anthony
- EH 30th

137
- SD The first manned moon landing
- SS Dolly Skillbeck
- FG Sooty
- FF Mark Hamill
- IP Skin colour
- EH *Peter Pan*

138
- SD Dave Lee Travis
- SS Anne Kirkbride
- FG Robin Tripp
- FF Ray Reardon
- IP Sergeant
- EH *Crossroads*

139
- SD George Michael
- SS Krystle Carrington's
- FG George Layton
- FF Terry Wogan
- IP *The Beiderbecke Affair*
- EH He wasn't

140
- SD Jet Harris
- SS Dirty Den
- FG *A Bit of a Do*
- FF Esther Rantzen
- IP They were firemen
- EH *MTM's*

141
- SD The King Brothers
- SS His brother
- FG Anita Dobson
- FF Norman
- IP Germany
- EH Polo necks instead of shirts

142
- SD *Magical Mystery Tour*
- SS Sally Webster
- FG 1989
- FF Joan Collins
- IP Newspaper industry
- EH The Virginian

143
- SD *The Flowerpot Men*
- SS France
- FG Martin Daniels
- FF Sir John Gielgud
- IP 1984
- EH A brain haemorrhage

144
- SD *Chanel*
- SS The *Crossroads* explosion
- FG *Countdown*
- FF Flesh colour
- IP Antiques
- EH Dr. Smith

145
- SD *Auf Wiedersehen Pet*
- SS He'd broken a strike
- FG A tattoo
- FF Jimmy Hill
- IP *Rumpole of the Bailey*
- EH The Falcons

146
- SD Fab
- SS Eddie Yates
- FG *Through the Keyhole*
- FF Desi Arnaz Junior
- IP *Hold the Dream*
- EH Bill Oddie

ANSWERS

147
- **SD** Kenny Everett
- **SS** Maggie Dunlop
- **FG** Deputy Dawg
- **FF** Andrew Gardner
- **IP** *Planet of the Apes*
- **EH** Jimmy Greaves

148
- **SD** Yes
- **SS** Dot Cotton
- **FG** Lamb Chop
- **FF** Tom Baker
- **IP** Kessler
- **EH** *The Life and Times of Grizzly Adams*

149
- **SD** Michael Groth
- **SS** Eclairs
- **FG** A giant hedgehog
- **FF** Janet Brown
- **IP** *Outer Limits*
- **EH** *The Rag Trade*

150
- **SD** Big Daddy
- **SS** Jack Sugden
- **FG** Quick Draw McGraw
- **FF** Crockett
- **IP** Jack the Ripper's
- **EH** Five

151
- **SD** Dennis Waterman and George Cole
- **SS** A silver rattle engraved with his initials
- **FG** Butler provides the voices for the other two
- **FF** David Jason
- **IP** *Starship Enterprise*
- **EH** Edna O'Brien

152
- **SD** Davy Crockett
- **SS** Dustman
- **FG** Huckleberry Hound
- **FF** Maigret
- **IP** Scotland
- **EH** A Welsh TV channel

153
- **SD** *Opportunity Knocks*
- **SS** J. R. Ewing
- **FG** Mrs Overall
- **FF** Nigel Havers
- **IP** *The Thorn Birds*
- **EH** *Network 7*

154
- **SD** *Whatever Happened to the Likely Lads*
- **SS** Jack Sugden
- **FG** Six
- **FF** Bernie Winters
- **IP** Melonhead
- **EH** Marty

155
- **SD** ITV New Bulletin
- **SS** Dot Colwell
- **FG** Gordon Burns
- **FF** Peter Purves
- **IP** Murdoch
- **EH** The Bloop

156
- **SD** The theme tune for *Coronation Street*
- **SS** Arthur Fowler
- **FG** *Peanuts*
- **FF** John Hurt
- **IP** William Tell
- **EH** Arthur Hailey's

157
- **SD** *Tinker, Tailor, Soldier, Spy*
- **SS** Two thousand pounds
- **FG** Three
- **FF** Caron Keating
- **IP** Arms
- **EH** Jim Rockford

158
- **SD** *Look Through Any Window*
- **SS** *Dallas*
- **FG** Bedrock High
- **FF** Showjumping
- **IP** Corps of Guides
- **EH** Bill Cosby's

159
- **SD** Salvation Army uniform
- **SS** J. R. Ewing
- **FG** Jeremy Beadle
- **FF** Mildred
- **IP** Donna
- **EH** *Captain Zed*

160
- **SD** Hot Gossip
- **SS** Climbing a mountain
- **FG** Spike Milligan
- **FF** Broderick Crawford
- **IP** Tarzan
- **EH** Bill Bixby

161
- **SD** *Joseph and His Amazing Technicolour Dreamcoat*
- **SS** Bobby Ewing
- **FG** Five
- **FF** Anthony Booth
- **IP** "To protect the innocent"
- **EH** A seal

162
- **SD** Nicky Campbell
- **SS** *Knots Landing's*
- **FG** Sabrina
- **FF** Sir Robin Day
- **IP** *The Naked City*
- **EH** Jasper Carrott's

163
- **SD** Mike Reid
- **SS** Michelle
- **FG** Murder
- **FF** Ian McShane
- **IP** Colonel
- **EH** The Coronation of Elizabeth II

164
- **SD** Kylie Minogue
- **SS** Ken Barlow
- **FG** William Tell
- **FF** Harold Pinter
- **IP** *Charlie's Angels*
- **EH** The Eiffel Tower

165
- **SD** The Singing Nun
- **SS** E20
- **FG** Jessica Tate
- **FF** Benny Hill
- **IP** Makepeace
- **EH** Scottish Television

166
- **SD** Richard Clayderman's
- **SS** He died in episode one
- **FG** The Smurfs
- **FF** Jimmy Savile
- **IP** Red
- **EH** *Terrahawks*

167
- **SD** *Love Don't Live Here Anymore*
- **SS** Vera Duckworth
- **FG** Mr Ed
- **FF** *Sea Hunt*
- **IP** Solicitor
- **EH** Diana Spencer

168
- **SD** Robin Hood
- **SS** *The Hotten Courier*
- **FG** Huckleberry Hound
- **FF** *Murder, She Wrote*
- **IP** The Paradise Club
- **EH** White

169
- **SD** Stevie Wonder and Ray Charles
- **SS** Dot Cotton
- **FG** George and Jane Jetson
- **FF** John Gregson
- **IP** Face
- **EH** It's broadcast from LWT's South Bank Studio

170
- **SD** Freddie Mercury
- **SS** Potter
- **FG** White
- **FF** New Zealand
- **IP** One dollar
- **EH** *(Task Force)*

171
- **SD** Tina Turner's
- **SS** Ken Barlow's
- **FG** One
- **FF** *Auf Wiedersehen Pet*
- **IP** Minnesota
- **EH** *Record Breakers*

172
- **SD** Tex Ritter
- **SS** K-A-B-I-N
- **FG** Beer
- **FF** Shaft
- **IP** Hannibal Hayes
- **EH** Oracle

173
- **SD** Mickey Most
- **SS** Ken Barlow
- **FG** Red
- **FF** Nigel Havers
- **IP** One
- **EH** *Blue Peter's*

174
- **SD** *Aztec Gold*
- **SS** He was still a student
- **FG** A pig
- **FF** Hywell Bennett
- **IP** Remington Steele
- **EH** Mel Smith

175
- **SD** *Eight Miles High*
- **SS** Alf Roberts
- **FG** *Mr. and Mrs.*
- **FF** Kathy Staff
- **IP** Ice cubes
- **EH** *Gunsmoke*

176
- **SD** Hot Gossip
- **SS** Sue Ellen
- **FG** *Who Dares Wins*
- **FF** Paul Nicholas
- **IP** Guy Burgess
- **EH** Rupert

(177)
SD Eric Spear
SS A gun
FG *We Love TV*
FF George Peppard
IP *The A-Team*
EH RKO

(178)
SD Howard Keel
SS J.R. Ewing's
FG *Bob's Full House*
FF Charlotte Cornwell
IP *Jemima Shore*
EH Sailing

(179)
SD *Off the Record*
SS Multiple Sclerosis
FG *'Allo 'Allo*
FF Sophia Loren
IP *The Day of the Triffids*
EH Sue Cook

(180)
SD Bruno
SS He was shot
FG Mickey Mouse
FF Robert McKenzie
IP *A Kind of Loving*
EH "Goodnight and sleep well"

(181)
SD Larry Grayson's
SS Frank Bruno
FG Michael Heseltine
FF Coral Browne
IP *Shine On Harvey Moon*
EH *Playschool*

(182)
SD *The Sun Always Shines On TV*
SS *Crossroads*
FG Max Bygraves
FF Kenneth Kendall
IP Sam McCloud's
EH Olive Oyl's

(183)
SD Country and Western
SS A greyhound
FG Liverpool
FF Max Bygraves
IP *Burke's Law*
EH Uganda

(184)
SD Twiggy
SS Bryan Mosley (Alf Roberts)
FG Fort Baxter
FF *The Good Companions*
IP Black
EH Arnold Ridley

Trivial Pursuit

·GAME 4·

(185)
SD Gene Autry
SS Emily Nugent/Bishop
FG Tickle
FF Ronnie Barker
IP Africa
EH The Vietnam War

(186)
SD Danny La Rue
SS Rita Littlewood
FG "Bye bye everyone, bye bye."
FF Jim Davidson
IP Sri Lanka
EH Vanessa

(187)
SD Bonnie Langford
SS Fiona Fullerton
FG Prince Edward
FF Liza Goddard
IP Eton
EH Buzz Aldrin

(188)
SD *When A Man Loves A Woman* (Percy Sledge)
SS Maureen Lipman
FG Frankie Howerd
FF David Frost
IP *Elizabeth R*
EH Beryl Reid

(189)
SD BBC1
SS Kate O'Mara
FG *Blockbusters*
FF Harry H. Corbett
IP Taffy
EH Ken Russell

(190)
SD The Bedrocks
SS Annie Walker's
FG David Frost
FF Astronomy
IP Los Angeles
EH Troy Tempest

(191)
SD *The Cosmos's*
SS Peyton Place
FG *The Monster*
FF Bob Monkhouse's
IP *Petrocelli*
EH Liverpool

(192)
SD *Get Fresh*
SS Ivy Brennan
FG Wood and Walters
FF Barry Norman
IP Rockliffe's Babies
EH The Royal Family

(193)
SD The Beatles
SS Gold
FG Great Dane
FF Alexei Sayle
IP Detective Inspector
EH The Cisco Kid

(194)
SD Joan Collins
SS He changed his trilby for a flat cap
FG *'Allo 'Allo*
FF Rowan Atkinson
IP Tyne Daley's
EH *The Wombles*

(195)
SD *Butlins Holidays*
SS The Henderson Kids
FG Gladys Pugh
FF Craig Charles
IP F Troop
EH East End of London

(196)
SD Les Dawson
SS *P.G. Tips*
FG *Double Your Money*
FF The Queen
IP Eric
EH The Queen's and Winston Churchill's

(197)
SD Nicky Horne
SS *Coronation Street*
FG Flash
FF Bill Fraser
IP A radio station
EH *Batman*

(198)
SD *Hold Me Now*
SS She had blue eyes
FG Canada
FF Eric Morecambe
IP Question marks
EH Superboy

(199)
SD David McCallum
SS Claudia
FG *'Allo 'Allo*
FF Barbara Woodhouse
IP Peggetty
EH The Flowerpot Men

(200)
SD *No Hiding Place*
SS Steven
FG She died
FF Bacon and Fish
IP Magnus Pym
EH The Suntots

(201)
SD The Beverley Sisters
SS Footballer
FG Father and son
FF Anthony Valentine
IP Dentist
EH Humpty

(202)
SD None
SS *Crossroads*
FG *Candid Camera*
FF Appeared on the test card
IP He was blind
EH David Attenborough

(203)
SD Adam Ant
SS Sue Ellen
FG Pamela Stephenson
FF *Wagon Train*
IP *The Fall of Eagles*
EH Rugby Union

(204)
SD The Archies
SS The *Milky Bar* Kid
FG *Bewitched*
FF Dennis Waterman
IP Chisholm
EH Snooker

(205)
SD The Bangles
SS *Avon* cosmetics
FG Groutie
FF A Christmas tree
IP Quincy
EH In *Fraggle Rock*

206
- **SD** Bryan Adams
- **SS** George Brown
- **FG** Beryl Reid
- **FF** Laurence Olivier
- **IP** Quincy
- **EH** Waitress

207
- **SD** *Jake the Peg*
- **SS** Peggy
- **FG** *Me Mammy*
- **FF** William Conrad
- **IP** Treasury Dept
- **EH** Alan Lake

208
- **SD** *Juke Box Jury*
- **SS** *The Bill*
- **FG** The Krankies
- **FF** William Shatner
- **IP** Jane Asher
- **EH** Dandy Nichols

209
- **SD** *Holiday Rock*
- **SS** Jackie Merrick
- **FG** A bear
- **FF** Razzamatazz
- **IP** Brideshead Castle
- **EH** Mr T

210
- **SD** *Beat the Clock*
- **SS** Spain
- **FG** Gomez in *The Addams Family*
- **FF** Bette Midler
- **IP** The Klingons
- **EH** Waldorf

211
- **SD** Duane Eddy
- **SS** Miss Ellie
- **FG** *Up Pompeii*
- **FF** Sue Cook
- **IP** Greek
- **EH** *This Is Your Life*

212
- **SD** *Supergran*
- **SS** Manchester
- **FG** Victoria Wood's
- **FF** Bob Wilson
- **IP** Lieutenant
- **EH** Wrinkles

213
- **SD** *Puddle Lane*
- **SS** Hilda Ogden
- **FG** *The Sun's*
- **FF** Robert Wagner
- **IP** Yorkshire
- **EH** *The Doctor*

214
- **SD** Simon le Bon
- **SS** Hilda Ogden
- **FG** *The Price is Right*
- **FF** Christopher Beeny
- **IP** *Lou Grant*
- **EH** Stoneway

215
- **SD** Legs and Co
- **SS** Dot Cotton
- **FG** *Going for Gold*
- **FF** The Galapagos Islands
- **IP** *A Very Peculiar Practice*
- **EH** Skeletor

216
- **SD** Cliff Richard
- **SS** Alexis Carrington
- **FG** Ted Bovis
- **FF** John Betjeman
- **IP** Antiques
- **EH** New York

217
- **SD** "The Six-Five Special right on time."
- **SS** *Crossroads'*
- **FG** Cheers Bar
- **FF** David Steel
- **IP** The Batlab
- **EH** Twentieth

218
- **SD** *Peter Gunn*
- **SS** Albert Square (They are both *EastEnders* dogs)
- **FG** *Double or Drop*
- **FF** Adolf Hitler
- **IP** *Going Straight*
- **EH** Belgium's

219
- **SD** She didn't wear shoes
- **SS** The Costa Del Sol
- **FG** Prince Charles
- **FF** Nick Owen
- **IP** 1940s
- **EH** Roy Castle

220
- **SD** *The Funky Gibbon*
- **SS** Crossroads, Kings Oak
- **FG** *Brass*
- **FF** Adrian Edmondson
- **IP** *The Borgias*
- **EH** On Mount Everest

221
- **SD** *Monty Python's Flying Circus*
- **SS** Charlton Heston
- **FG** Annabel Croft
- **FF** *Where There's Life*
- **IP** California
- **EH** Sir Winston Churchill's

222
- **SD** Richard Williams
- **SS** Michael Elphick
- **FG** *Name That Tune*
- **FF** Judi Dench
- **IP** Bulman
- **EH** *News at Ten*

223
- **SD** Roger Daltrey
- **SS** British Gas
- **FG** Erics
- **FF** Norman Wisdom
- **IP** *The Gentle Touch*
- **EH** *On The Braden Beat*

224
- **SD** Lionel Richie
- **SS** Rover
- **FG** Al
- **FF** Jimmy Greaves
- **IP** *Scoop*
- **EH** Charles and Diana's wedding

225
- **SD** Johnny Logan
- **SS** It was adopted
- **FG** A tie
- **FF** Austin Mitchell
- **IP** Customs and Excise Officers
- **EH** St. Paul's Cathedral

226
- **SD** Natalie Cole
- **SS** Vera Duckworth
- **FG** Rik Wakeman
- **FF** Alan Whicker
- **IP** George
- **EH** ITV were on strike

227
- **SD** *Gloria*
- **SS** Hilda Ogden
- **FG** *Criss Cross Quiz*
- **FF** Virgil Tibbs
- **IP** *The Charmer*
- **EH** Horse racing

228
- **SD** The Vernons Girls
- **SS** *Coronation Street's*
- **FG** Bernie the Bolt
- **FF** Trevor Eve
- **IP** *Rockliffe's Follies*
- **EH** Magic

229
- **SD** *The Monkees*
- **SS** Bettie Turpin
- **FG** Jack Klugman's
- **FF** Sabrina
- **IP** The Pope
- **EH** TVam's

230
- **SD** Lord Rockingham's XI.
- **SS** Ali McGraw
- **FG** Potsie
- **FF** John Noakes
- **IP** *A Very British Coup*
- **EH** Television

231
- **SD** Brighton
- **SS** Dirty Den Watts's
- **FG** One
- **FF** Marilyn Monroe
- **IP** *Hill Street Blues's*
- **EH** Tennessee Williams's

232
- **SD** Don Lang's
- **SS** *Falcon Crest*
- **FG** Jim Davidson
- **FF** *Fresh Fields*
- **IP** Miss Marple
- **EH** *The Fosdyke Saga*

233
- **SD** Elvis Presley
- **SS** *Dallas*
- **FG** Noel Edmonds
- **FF** Leonard Rossiter
- **IP** Mike Hammer
- **EH** None

234
- **SD** Nelson Mandela
- **SS** Jamie Ewing
- **FG** Three
- **FF** John Thaw
- **IP** Amy Johnson
- **EH** Arthur Hailey's

235
- **SD** Gloria Estefan
- **SS** Jeff
- **FG** Joey Boswell
- **FF** David Suchet
- **IP** *V*
- **EH** *Coronation Street*

(236)
SD Piano
SS Terry Duckworth
FG Ben Elton
FF Rock Hudson
IP *Rebecca*
EH Channel 4's

(237)
SD M.C.Hammer
SS Jane Wyman
FG Three
FF Michael Palin
IP Trampas
EH His rifle

(238)
SD Eamonn Andrews
SS Sue Ellen
FG *The Clangers*
FF Pip
IP *Shady Tales*
EH *Tenderfoot*

(239)
SD Doc Cox
SS Run a marathon
FG He usually
   appeared as
   Margaret Thatcher
FF Deborah Kerr
IP The Marcie Blaine
   School for Girls
EH Magnus
   Magnusson

(240)
SD Tintin (Stephen
   'Tintin' Duffy)
SS Alma Sedgwick
FG Ralph Malph
FF David Frost
IP Face
EH *Shelley*

(241)
SD Kylie Minogue
SS Seth Armstrong
FG The bottle capping
   section
FF David Frost's
IP *M*A*S*H*
EH Steptoe and Son

(242)
SD Kid Creole
SS Sharon
FG *Crackerjack*
FF *Hooperman*
IP London
EH Jack Ruby's

(243)
SD Placido Domingo
SS The Merricks
FG Terry Jones
FF David McCallum
IP Falkland Islands
EH Petra's

(244)
SD Jonathan King
SS For assaulting a
   policeman
FG Ivy
FF Billy Boswell
IP She was deaf
EH Lynn

(245)
SD Gloria Hunniford
SS Alf Roberts
FG Fred
FF Judith Chalmers
IP *CHiPs*
EH *Randall and Hopkirk
   (Deceased)*

(246)
SD Una Stubbs
SS Jane Wyman
FG "Miss Jones"
FF Muriel Gray
IP Adam
EH A hotel

(247)
SD Adrian Boswell
SS *Brookside*
FG Presented *Candid
   Camera*
FF Noel Edmonds
IP To help him stop
   smoking
EH Ginger Rogers

(248)
SD Lulu
SS *Soapdish*
FG The cartoonerator
FF Uncle and nephew
IP The *Starship
   Enterprise*
EH Jean-Paul Sartre's

Trivial Pursuit
· G A M E   5 ·
TV

(249)
SD *Pop Quest*
SS *Should I Stay or
   Should I Go?*
FG That's All Folks!
FF Paul Shane
IP *Police Surgeon*
EH She's Penelope's
   voice

(250)
SD *Razzamatazz*
SS *Love's Unkind*
FG *Marty*
FF Cannon and Ball
IP Ford Prefect
EH Bette Davis

(251)
SD Phillip Schofield
SS Annie Walker
FG Kenneth Williams
FF Nobby
IP Boston's
EH 100

(252)
SD *Ready Steady Go*
SS Noele Gordon
FG Garage mechanic
FF Larry Hagman
IP Dr Who
EH Florida

(253)
SD Danny La Rue
SS Kevin Webster
FG Jim Davidson
FF Bobby Davro
IP A psychiatrist's
   surgery
EH India

(254)
SD Bonnie Langford
SS *Dynasty*
FG Billy Bean
FF Gideon in *Gideon's
   Way*
IP The bombing of
   Hiroshima
EH Larry Hagman

(255)
SD *Oxygene Part IV*
SS Mastectomy
FG *All Clued Up*
FF John Wayne
IP *Les Miserables*
EH *Roadrunner*

(256)
SD *Holiday 80*
SS Ewing Oil
FG David Hamilton
FF Robin Day
IP Dame Peggy
   Ashcroft
EH Stig

(257)
SD Edward Woodward
SS *Albion Market*
FG Italian
FF David Nixon
IP Sullivan
EH Macbeth

(258)
SD Ralph McTell
SS Bet Gilroy
FG Seven
FF Phillip Schofield
IP The Southern Cross
EH The Lone Ranger

(259)
SD Donovan
SS Area Manager of
   the Queen Victoria
   in Albert Square
FG Beryl
FF Jancis Robinson
IP Max
EH James Thurber's

(260)
SD *Top of the Pops*
SS Ken Barlow
FG Vivian Vance's
FF Bryan Forbes
IP *A Perfect Spy*
EH It was changed to
   give better TV
   contrast

(261)
SD "They're creepy and
   they're cooky"
SS Beckindale
FG Sign their name
FF David Coleman
IP Magnum
EH A swimming pool

(262)
SD *Coca-Cola*
SS *Neighbours*
FG 101
FF James Randi
IP Test pilot/
   astronaut
EH Harold Wilson's

(263)
SD *Spot the Tune*
SS Electrician
FG Six
FF Princess Anne
IP Japan's
EH *Bonanza*

(264)
SD Davy Crockett
SS *Wall's Pork
   Sausages*
FG Sgt. Bilko
FF Terry Wogan
IP LAPD
EH *The Sweeney*

ANSWERS

265
SD Anne Nightingale
SS Caviar
FG Stuart Hall
FF Prince Philip
IP *Big Deal*
EH Sid James

266
SD Jonathan Ross
SS Steven
FG Von Klinkerhoffen
FF *Lou Grant*
IP Robin Hood
EH It's a ZIP Code
   (Post Code)

267
SD Tom Jones
SS Martha Longhurst
FG *A Bit of a Do*
FF John Suchet
IP The Texas Rangers
EH *Columbo*

268
SD *Bohemian Rhapsody*
SS Derbyshire
FG Benson
FF Alfred Hitchcock
IP *Batman*
EH *Antiques Roadshow*

269
SD Simon
SS Walter
FG Angela Rippon
FF Blake Edwards
IP His mask
EH *Have Gun Will
   Travel*

270
SD It didn't enter
SS Fluffy dice
FG Little Weed in *The
   Flowerpot Men*
FF Tony Robinson
IP 12th
EH *Very Big Very Soon*

271
SD Seventh
SS Pauline Fowler
FG Red, Green and
   Yellow
FF Kenneth Cranham
IP Utterthwaite
EH *Hart to Hart*

272
SD *Eye Level*
   (Van der Valk)
SS *Cat and Mouse*
FG Hawthorne
FF Peter Alliss
IP Holly
EH Leo Tolstoy's

273
SD *God Save the Queen*
SS Cafe Osman
FG Barry Cryer
FF Mr. T.
IP San Francisco's
EH Dying

274
SD Alexei Sayle
SS Phyllis
FG Fort Baxter
FF Michael Caine
IP Banker
EH *Route 66*

275
SD Shakin' Stevens
SS Three
FG Bullfighting
FF Julie Walters
IP *Ferrari*
EH Jim Fixed It For Me

276
SD *Spitting Image*
SS Pauline Fowler
FG Nanu
FF Michael Parkinson
IP Angus
EH *The Prime of Miss
   Jean Brodie*

277
SD Su Pollard
SS Ken Barlow
FG Leonard Rossiter
FF The Queen
IP Hollywood
EH Felicity Kendal

278
SD Magnus Pyke
SS He was a GI
FG Captain
   Mainwaring
FF Dickie Davis
IP As debt collectors
EH *Young Krypton*

279
SD *Watching*
SS Stan Harvey
FG A dictionary
FF Mary
IP John Mannering
EH John

280
SD Millicent Martin
SS The Mermaid
   Boatyard
FG Kenny Everett's
FF Gene Barry
IP *Lace*
EH Richard Whiteley

281
SD Honor Blackman
SS Moldavia
FG Jim Backus
FF Muriel Young
IP Diamante Lil
EH Oliver Tobias

282
SD *Who Pays the
   Ferryman*
SS Miles Colby
FG Winston
FF Alan Bates
IP The mail
EH Harry Lime

283
SD *The Thorn Birds'*
SS PET
FG A duffel coat
FF *F Troop*
IP Richard Hannay
EH Leonard Nimoy

284
SD *Love Is Blue*
SS On religious
   grounds, she's a
   Roman Catholic
FG Delbert Wilkins
FF A beard
IP A chimpanzee
EH Sir Robin Day

285
SD Kylie Minogue
SS At a gay disco
FG None
FF Moira Stuart
IP Billy Liar
EH His memory

286
SD *The Army Game*
SS Alan Partridge
FG "Sausages"
FF Angela Rippon
IP *Lovejoy*
EH Georges Simenon

287
SD *Juke Box Jury's*
SS Dolly Skillbeck
FG Nooky Bear
FF Keith Harris
IP *Worzel Gummidge*
EH A hotel

288
SD Shakin' Stevens
SS She said she was
   his wife
FG *Whose Baby?*
FF Sue Lawley
IP "Have Gun Will
   Travel"
EH *The Outer Limits*

289
SD *Chariots of Fire*
SS Green
FG *Me and My Girl*
FF *Don't Wait Up*
IP A Russian doll
EH Joan Hickson

290
SD Cilla Black
SS Hitchhiking
FG The moon
FF Bruce Forsyth
IP *Hill Street Blues*
EH Liverpool

291
SD Baccara
SS Miss Diane
FG Endora
FF Joan Collins
IP He won a power
   boat race
EH Kenny Everett

292
SD 1987
SS Steve Davis
FG Darren
FF Terry Wogan
IP Cambridge
EH Fulchester

293
SD Three
SS Mike Baldwin
FG *The Phil Silvers
   Show*
FF Terry Wogan
IP Parkinson
EH His father

294
SD Chubby Checker
SS Lucy Ewing
FG Gloria Hunniford
FF Hughie Green
IP *First Among Equals*
EH Farrah Fawcett-
   Majors

295
- **SD** *Whistle Test*
- **SS** Mike Baldwin
- **FG** *The Flintstones*
- **FF** Lee Majors
- **IP** A telephone answering machine
- **EH** Sergeant

296
- **SD** *Dee Time*
- **SS** *Pal* meat for dogs
- **FG** John Inman
- **FF** The Mock Turtle and the Gryphon
- **IP** A crown
- **EH** Inside Westminster Abbey

297
- **SD** Jess Yates
- **SS** *Coronation Street*
- **FG** *Bootsie and Snudge*
- **FF** *All Gas and Gaiters*
- **IP** Lewis Carroll
- **EH** Richard Dimbleby

298
- **SD** Irene Handl
- **SS** *Crossroads*
- **FG** *Ask The Family*
- **FF** Patrick Allen
- **IP** Alf Garnett
- **EH** *The Flowerpot Men*

299
- **SD** *The Old Grey Whistle Test*
- **SS** Meg Richardson
- **FG** Secret Squirrel
- **FF** Looby Loo
- **IP** Australia
- **EH** *Watch with Mother*

300
- **SD** Little Jimmy Osmond
- **SS** *Crossroads*
- **FG** *What's My Line?*
- **FF** Arthur Negus
- **IP** *Are You Being Served?*
- **EH** President Kennedy's assassination

301
- **SD** "It's Now or Never"
- **SS** *The Sullivans*
- **FG** Lloyd Grossman's
- **IP** John Steed
- **EH** Ebony

302
- **SD** Adam Faith
- **SS** Holloway
- **FG** *Happy Days*
- **FF** Mickey Spillane
- **IP** *Dragnet*
- **EH** J.F. Kennedy's assassination

303
- **SD** He died
- **SS** Saturday
- **FG** Nick Tortelli
- **FF** Sally
- **IP** Sonny Crockett
- **EH** Blue

304
- **SD** Benny Hill
- **SS** Henry Wilks
- **FG** Miss Cathcart
- **FF** Johnny Weissmuller
- **IP** Pug
- **EH** Go-karts

305
- **SD** Wayne Sleep
- **SS** Rum
- **FG** Motley Hall
- **FF** Richard O'Sullivan
- **IP** *CHiPs*
- **EH** Daleks

306
- **SD** Wendy Richards
- **SS** *Dallas*
- **FG** Fred Flintstone
- **FF** Lloyd Grossman's
- **IP** Grizzly Adams's
- **EH** *Armchair Theatre*

307
- **SD** *Great Expectations*
- **SS** Emily Bishop's
- **FG** Faked suicide by leaving their clothes on a beach
- **FF** Brian Rix
- **IP** *M*A*S*H*
- **EH** HMS Ark Royal

308
- **SD** Jason Donovan
- **SS** Larry Hagman
- **FG** *TISWAS*
- **FF** Ronnie Barker
- **IP** Elizabeth II
- **EH** Sunday

309
- **SD** Hot Gossip
- **SS** Bobby Ewing
- **FG** Bob Monkhouse
- **FF** Anthea Redfern
- **IP** Road haulage
- **EH** *Telford's Change*

310
- **SD** Bonnie Langford
- **SS** Victor Borge
- **FG** Reginald Perrin's
- **FF** Richard Chamberlain
- **IP** *M*A*S*H*
- **EH** He was a steeplejack

311
- **SD** *May Each Day of Your Life*
- **SS** Sir Robert Mark
- **FG** Frank Oz
- **FF** *The Protectors*
- **IP** Frank Spencer
- **EH** Homosexuality

312
- **SD** *The Mary Tyler Moore Show*
- **SS** The Alps
- **FG** A pink hippopotamus
- **FF** Reg Varney
- **IP** *Upstairs Downstairs*
- **EH** *Roots*

Trivial Pursuit

·GAME 6·

313
- **SD** *77 Sunset Strip's*
- **SS** St.Angela's
- **FG** Taxi driver
- **FF** Graeme Garden
- **IP** Pauline Collins
- **EH** *Jesus of Nazareth*

314
- **SD** Cars
- **SS** Meg Richardson
- **FG** Magnus Magnusson's
- **FF** Michael
- **IP** Bruce
- **EH** Streaked across the pitch

315
- **SD** *The Multi-Coloured Swap Shop*
- **SS** Alec Gilroy
- **FG** *The Golden Shot*
- **FF** Sylvia Peters
- **IP** *Mogul*
- **EH** *Stingray*

316
- **SD** Cocaine
- **SS** British Rail *Intercity*
- **FG** *The Sky's the Limit*
- **FF** Patrick Moore
- **IP** Wilfred Pickles
- **EH** Thirteen

317
- **SD** Glen Frey
- **SS** *Pepsi*
- **FG** Spike Milligan
- **FF** John Nettles
- **IP** Six
- **EH** Water

318
- **SD** John Lennon's
- **SS** *Yellow Pages*
- **FG** Larry Grayson
- **FF** Germaine Greer
- **IP** Sulu
- **EH** *Don't Ask Me*

319
- **SD** Ukelele
- **SS** *Cadbury's*
- **FG** *My Wife Next Door*
- **FF** Alan Whicker
- **IP** Yorkshire
- **EH** 1974

320
- **SD** *Wheels*
- **SS** General Hospital
- **FG** *The Goodies*
- **FF** Harry H.Corbett
- **IP** A train
- **EH** John Craven

321
- **SD** *The Mary Tyler Moore Show*
- **SS** Sandy Richardson
- **FG** *The Lovers*
- **FF** Goldie Hawn
- **IP** *The Strange Report*
- **EH** Russell Harty

322
- **SD** Jack Jones
- **SS** Stan Ogden
- **FG** Henry Cooper
- **FF** Ian Lavender
- **IP** The Mysterons
- **EH** *John Craven's Newsround*

323
- **SD** The Monkees
- **SS** Ken Barlow
- **FG** *The Generation Game*
- **FF** Patrick Cargill
- **IP** *Hawaii Five-O*
- **EH** *Are You Being Served*

ANSWERS

324
SD *Miami Vice*
SS *Cointreau*
FG Emu (and Rod Hull)
FF John Alderton
IP *Take Three Women*
EH Dylan

325
SD Jazz
SS Bet Lynch's
FG *Clapperboard*
FF Susan Stranks
IP James Hadleigh
EH Princess Anne's

326
SD *Rawhide's*
SS *The Waltons*
FG *The Fenn Street Gang*
FF John Alderton
IP *Big Breadwinner Hog*
EH A guitar

327
SD "Welcome Back"
SS Wonderful World (Sam Cooke)
FG A cuddly toy
FF Hylda Baker
IP *Take Three Girls*
EH BBC2

328
SD *It's a Long Way to Tipperary*
SS Dunlop
FG Dylan
FF *The Braden Beat*
IP Paul Temple
EH Laurence Olivier

329
SD *Miami Vice*
SS *Coronation Street*
FG Princess Anne
FF Judy Carne
IP *The Champions*
EH *Rainbow*

330
SD Bert Weedon
SS Mavis
FG Inspector Blakey's
FF Simon Dee
IP *The High Chapparal*
EH *Pebble Mill at One*

331
SD *Crackerjack*
SS *Emmerdale Farm*
FG *Curry and Chips*
FF Nyree Dawn Porter
IP London
EH Colditz

332
SD Tony Hatch
SS Minnie Caldwell
FG John Cleese
FF *The Magic Roundabout*
IP Sunday
EH Skippy

333
SD Samantha Fox
SS An electric shock from a hairdryer
FG Spike Milligan
FF *The Frost Report*
IP 6
EH Harold Wilson

334
SD Robin Hall and Jimmie Macgregor
SS Beckindale
FG Bernard Cribbins
FF The Riddler
IP Callan
EH The Woolpack

335
SD *The White Heather Club*
SS Matt
FG Frankie Howerd
FF Susan Hampshire
IP Kenneth More
EH *Colditz*

336
SD Russ Conway
SS Brooke Bond
FG Mutley
FF Stuart Hall
IP Lonely
EH Barry Norman

337
SD *Like a Prayer*
SS Stan and Hilda Ogden
FG Rodney Bewes
FF Julie Felix
IP Number 2
EH Eight

338
SD Charlene
SS Tanner, the same as her first!
FG *Monty Python*
FF Warren Mitchell
IP *The Prisoner*
EH He'd injured his right hand in a motoring accident

339
SD Cheryl Baker
SS Bobbie
FG Basil Brush
FF Illya Kuryakin
IP *The War Game*
EH He died

340
SD *Blind Date*
SS *Trebor Mints*
FG David Nixon's
FF Peter Cooke and Dudley Moore
IP *Daktari*
EH *Holiday 69*

341
SD Billy Conolly
SS *Golden Wonder*
FG Basil Brush's
FF Eamonn Andrews
IP *Daktari*
EH *Pot Black*

342
SD *Tutti Frutti*
SS Cyril
FG *Monty Python's Flying Circus*
FF *Sherlock Holmes*
IP *The Baron*
EH Trekkies

343
SD Robbins
SS Jack Walker
FG *Monty Python's Flying Circus*
FF Parker
IP *The Forsyte Saga*
EH Keith Michell

344
SD Raw Sex
SS *Martini*
FG David Jason
FF Jeeves and Wooster
IP *Mrs Thursday*
EH Became the first topless Page Three Girl

345
SD Mike Smith
SS *The Doctors*
FG "Boom! Boom!"
FF Robert Robinson
IP *Softly, Softly, Task Force*
EH Mr. Spock's ears

346
SD Lulu
SS Harold Wilson's
FG Caretaker
FF Churchill's funeral
IP *The Girl from Uncle*
EH *Civilisation*

347
SD Helen Shapiro
SS *Cadbury's Smash*
FG Pickles
FF Anna Ford
IP *The War Game*
EH Kenneth Clark

348
SD Jan Leeming
SS Gretchen Franklin
FG Jackie Rae
FF Patrick McGoohan
IP The Pacific
EH Portmeirion

349
SD Paula Yates
SS *Lifebuoy*
FG Anne Aston
FF Johnny Morris
IP The first five American astronauts
EH *News at Ten*

350
SD Over The Top
SS William Franklin
FG Charlie Williams
FF Tom Baker
IP FAB 1
EH Alastair Burnet

351
SD *Six-Fifty-Five Special*
SS Ena Sharples
FG *Never Mind the Quality, Feel the Width*
FF Steve Zodiac
IP Docker
EH Reginald Bosanquet

352
SD *Courage*
SS Arthur
FG Captain Mainwaring
FF Patrick Moore
IP Alf Garnett
EH *Omnibus*

353
SD *Live Aid*
SS *Cadbury's Dairy Milk*
FG Richard Nixon
FF Richard Dimbleby
IP Mary Whitehouse's
EH *Magpie*

354
- SD Elvis
- SS Ena Sharples
- FG Morecambe and Wise
- FF Ronald Allen
- IP *In Sickness and in Health*
- EH The first manned moon landing

355
- SD Sheena Easton
- SS *Crossroads*
- FG Glenda Jackson
- FF *Tomorrow's World*
- IP *Cathy Come Home*
- EH The Prince of Wales' investiture

356
- SD Wham!
- SS Mary Hopkin
- FG Tony Hancock
- FF Anna Ford
- IP *Cathy Come Home*
- EH 1969

357
- SD *Miami Vice*
- SS Len Faiclough's
- FG Ernie Wise
- FF Raymond Baxter
- IP Edward Heath
- EH ITV

358
- SD *Live Aid*
- SS *Captain Birdseye*
- FG John Wayne
- FF Frank Sinatra
- IP *Till Death Us Do Part*
- EH *Hector's House*

359
- SD Cilla Black
- SS "Beanz meanz Heinz"
- FG Dan Rowan and Dick Martin
- FF Gene Barry
- IP The Virgin Mary
- EH *Please Sir*

360
- SD *Blockbusters*
- SS Stan Ogden
- FG *Dad's Army*
- FF Joan Bakewell
- IP Mary Whitehouse
- EH Reginald Bosanquet

361
- SD B.A.Robertson
- SS George Lazenby
- FG Ronnie Corbett
- FF Robert Maxwell
- IP *Till Death Us Do Part*
- EH Reginald Bosanquet

362
- SD Jools Holland
- SS Egg-shaped
- FG Bob Monkhouse
- FF Ian Ogilvy
- IP Brains
- EH Big Ben

363
- SD Rod Stewart (*Sailing*)
- SS *Peyton Place*
- FG Blue and white
- FF Gilbert Harding
- IP Daleks
- EH The world's first news programme for the deaf

364
- SD Roxy Music
- SS Brentwich United
- FG *Billy Bunter (of Greyfriars School)*
- FF A hedgehog
- IP *The Plane Makers*
- EH *Tonight*

365
- SD David Soul
- SS *The Newcomers*
- FG Tingha and Tucker
- FF *See-Saw*
- IP *Our Man At St. Mark's*
- EH Thursday

366
- SD Dr. Teeth and the Electric Mayhem
- SS Wendy Richards
- FG Bernie Winters
- FF McDonald Hobley
- IP Beer
- EH *World of Sport*

367
- SD Donny Osmond appeared on the *Andy Williams Show*
- SS Norman Vaughan
- FG *That Was The Week That Was*
- FF Billy Bunter
- IP Frank Marker
- EH Harold Wilson

368
- SD Bruce Forsyth's
- SS *Fairy Liquid*
- FG The Clampetts
- FF Shaw Taylor
- IP Mr. Waverly
- EH Stuart Hall

Trivial Pursuit
·GAME 7·

369
- SD Windsor Davies and Don Estelle
- SS Cigarette commercials
- FG Billy
- FF A mouse
- IP Queen Victoria
- EH Winston Churchill

370
- SD The Little Ladies
- SS *United*
- FG Andy Pandy
- FF One
- IP *The Fugitive*
- EH *Up the Junction*

371
- SD Q
- SS *Peyton Place*
- FG *Andy Pandy*
- FF Richard Dimbleby
- IP The Tardis
- EH *Vision On*

372
- SD Isla St.Clair
- SS Peter Sellers
- FG *The Magic Roundabout*
- FF To distinguish himself from Sooty's dad
- IP THRUSH
- EH Wimbledon

373
- SD Bruce Forsyth's
- SS *Esso*
- FG Freddie Frinton
- FF *Brideshead Revisited*
- IP The United Network Command for Law Enforcement
- EH *Jeux Sans Frontieres*

374
- SD *Grange Hill*
- SS Finer flour
- FG Mandy
- FF 29
- IP *Public Eye*
- EH Pinky and Perky

375
- SD The Sex Pistols
- SS Pat Phoenix
- FG *The Telegoons*
- FF Mary Malcolm
- IP Yorkshire
- EH *Jackanory*

376
- SD Rowlf
- SS *The Newcomers*
- FG Mr. Ed
- FF Friday
- IP *The Likely Lads*
- EH Ian Fleming

377
- SD *Stars on Sunday*
- SS Flash
- FG *The Army Game*
- FF Pete Duel
- IP *Alias Smith and Jones*
- EH Winston Churchill

378
- SD *Chirpy Chirpy Cheep Cheep*
- SS Jill Richardson of *Crossroads*
- FG Aimi Macdonald
- FF Andy Pandy
- IP *And Mother Makes Five*
- EH Hawkins was all of their voices

379
- SD *The Wombles*
- SS *Crossroads*
- FG Michael Aspel
- FF Dave Allen
- IP *All Creatures Great and Small*
- EH *Panorama*

380
- SD *I'd Like to Teach the World to Sing*
- SS Jill Richardson (Chance)
- FG Eamonn Andrews
- FF Yul Brynner
- IP Football Association
- EH The Steptoes' horse

381
- SD Abba, with *Waterloo*
- SS Katie Boyle
- FG Lady Isobel Barnett
- FF Lucille Ball
- IP Sunday
- EH *That Was The Week That Was*

382
- SD He was ignoring her
- SS *Dulux*
- FG Harry Corbett
- FF Dame Peggy Ashcroft
- IP "Crikey"
- EH *Steptoe and Son*

383
SD *Suicide is Painless*
SS Emily Nugent
FG Ramsbottom
FF *Champion the Wonder Horse*
IP *Bouquet of Barbed Wire*
EH BBC2

384
SD The Bay City Rollers
SS Martha Longhurst
FG Andy Pandy
FF *Muffin the Mule*
IP Tannochbrae
EH Valerie Singleton

385
SD Bob Harris
SS Michael Caine
FG Potter
FF Matthew Parris
IP By shooting himself
EH Steve Jones

386
SD *M*A*S*H*
SS Dulux
FG "Izzy Wizzy Let's Get Busy"
FF David Attenborough
IP Billy Bunter's
EH BBC2

387
SD *Isadora*
SS Gordon Collins
FG *Happy Days*
FF David Coleman
IP *Edward the Seventh*
EH Yeah! Yeah! Yeah!

388
SD *Oh Boy!*
SS *M and M's*
FG *Whack-O*
FF Geoffrey Hayes
IP *The Rag Trade*
EH Party political broadcasts

389
SD *Batman*
SS Ray Langton
FG *I Dream of Jeannie*
FF *All Your Own*
IP Nelson's
EH *Hine*

390
SD Kathy Kirby
SS *Coronation Street*
FG Denis Healey
FF Michael Heseltine
IP Labour
EH Leicester's

391
SD John Gorman
SS Jason Donovan
FG Alastair Burnet
FF Frank Bough
IP *We'll Meet Again*
EH BBC2's

392
SD Apple Films
SS Denver
FG *A Question of Entertainment*
FF Nicholas Lyndhurst
IP *Inside Story*
EH 1950s

393
SD *Maverick*
SS Den and Michelle
FG Train-driver
FF Bryan Mosley
IP A cruise on the *Titanic*
EH The Pope's

394
SD *The Flintstones*
SS *Yorkie*
FG Richard O'Sullivan
FF Glenda Jackson
IP Sid James
EH *Hospital*

395
SD Kim Wilde's
SS *Coronation Street*
FG Miss Ewell
FF Graham Kerr
IP Kojak
EH *Wagon Train*

396
SD Gene Kelly
SS *Harmony*
FG Bonnie Langford
FF Radar O'Reilly
IP *Bergerac*
EH Ferret

397
SD Wayne Sleep
SS Lorraine Chase
FG *Sunshine Desserts*
FF Patricia Hayes
IP *M*A*S*H*
EH *Life on Earth*

398
SD Scott and Charlene's
SS Six
FG *TISWAS*
FF Nicholas Parsons
IP *Skippy*
EH *The Antiques Roadshow*

399
SD Henry Mancini
SS The Ewings
FG Sybil
FF Adam Faith
IP *The Adventures of Black Beauty*
EH John le Carre

400
SD *Anyone Can Fall In Love*
SS *Empire Road*
FG Bernard Manning
FF Ronnie Barker
IP *Van Der Valk*
EH John le Carre's

401
SD Mike Nesmith
SS Yes
FG *Mastermind*
FF Frankie Howerd
IP *Catweazle*
EH Fishing

402
SD The Beach Boys
SS April was shot dead
FG Duncan Norvelle
FF Jane Asher
IP Inspector Lockhart
EH Robert McKenzie

403
SD The Chipmunks
SS A toothbrush
FG Larry Grayson's
FF Colin Welland
IP Robbie Box
EH Orville's

404
SD *Is This the Way to Amarillo*
SS Katie Holland
FG *On the Buses*
FF Angela Rippon
IP Geneva
EH Two

405
SD *Layla*
SS The *PG Tips* chimps
FG Captain Kremmen
FF Anna Ford
IP Jack Daniels
EH *Hill Street Blues*

406
SD See You Later Alligator
SS J.R.Ewing's
FG Jim Davidson
FF *Ever Decreasing Circles*
IP *The Bill*
EH Atlanta

407
SD *Hound Dog*
SS Gary
FG Julian Pettifer
FF Stacy Keach
IP Robin Hood
EH *Kipperbang*

408
SD Buddy Holly
SS *Idris*
FG Golf
FF David Attenborugh (Cocky was his pet cockatoo)
IP Jamie
EH Corporal

409
SD *Hazell*
SS Bernard Cribbins
FG John Inman
FF Paula Yates
IP A still
EH *Just Good Friends*

410
SD *Cutty Sark*
SS Five
FG Paula Wilcox
FF David Frost
IP Just good friends
EH The city of domes

411
SD Luciano Pavarotti
SS *Kleenex Tissues*
FG Rhoda
FF *The Untouchables*
IP Australia
EH *The Six Million Dollar Man*

412
SD Saxaphone
SS *Omo*
FG Psychiatrist
FF Ruth Madoc
IP *Manimal*
EH Northumberland

413
- SD Clarinet
- SS Henry
- FG A bow-tie
- IP *Dragnet*
- EH Derek

414
- SD Johnny Cash
- SS Hilda Ogden
- FG Herman
- FF Susan Dey
- IP Solicitor
- EH The General Election

415
- SD Coopers Crossing
- SS Sunny Jim
- FG *The Wide-Awake Club*
- FF Fraser Hines
- IP Thomas Magnum
- EH Children's or Youth programmes

416
- SD *Sealed With A Kiss*
- SS Dry her hair
- FG Dennis Norden
- FF Ludovic Kennedy
- IP Captain James
- EH *Starship Enterprise*

417
- SD *Boy Meets Girl*
- SS Ryan O'Neal
- FG Stalag 13
- FF Michael Douglas
- IP Ironside's
- EH Martin Luther King

418
- SD Elton John
- SS *Brylcreme's*
- FG Jennifer Saunders
- FF Muhammad Ali
- IP Oscar Wilde
- EH Gordon Jackson

419
- SD Eric Spear
- SS John Le Mesurier
- FG Dustin Gee
- FF Andrew Faulds
- IP Edward VII's
- EH *The Los Angeles Tribune*

420
- SD Mike Reid
- SS Cyril Lord's
- FG *One Foot in the Grave*
- FF Torvill and Dean
- IP *Blake's Seven*
- EH Peter Gunn

421
- SD *The Last Resort*
- SS Alan Freeman
- FG RAF
- FF His father
- IP Mrs. Thursday
- EH Laurel and Hardy's

422
- SD *The Comic Strip Presents*
- SS Laurence Olivier
- FG *Meet the Wife*
- FF Rula Lenska
- IP Simon Templar — *The Saint*
- EH David Jason

423
- SD Roy Castle
- SS A block of ice
- FG Spotty Dog
- FF Coral Browne
- IP Ross
- EH Robert Powell

424
- SD Tracy Chapman's
- SS Denver-Carrington
- FG Schoolteacher
- FF *Miami Vice*
- IP Oscar Wilde
- EH Its nose

425
- SD The Escape Club
- SS Sue Ellen
- FG Roy Walker
- FF Omar Sharif
- IP *Hold the Back Page*
- EH *The Multi-Coloured Swap Shop*

426
- SD Jimmy Savile
- SS Ray Krebbs
- FG Nigel Planer
- FF Nerys Hughes
- IP *The Jewel in the Crown*
- EH *Def II*

427
- SD Anthony Newley
- SS Fallon Carrington's
- FG Alan B'Stard
- FF Deborah Kerr
- IP *Hollywood Wives*
- EH *The Stars*

428
- SD Janice Long
- SS Alexis Carrington
- FG Dawn and Jennifer
- FF Tom Baker
- IP Cars and rally driving
- EH "Nuts! Who-ole ha-a-zelnuts!"

429
- SD Abba
- SS Larry Hagman
- FG Condoms
- FF Alastair Burnet
- IP Tam-o'-shanter
- EH Chuck

430
- SD *Ready Steady Go!*
- SS Cliff Barnes
- FG Cambridge
- FF Prince Charles
- IP Supergran's
- EH Robbie

431
- SD The Beverly Sisters
- SS Seventeen
- FG Rory Bremner
- FF Vincent
- IP Brains
- EH Paul Gascoigne

432
- SD *Waterloo*
- SS The Rovers Return
- FG Dennis Waterman
- FF Alan Bennett
- IP Glasgow
- EH 20th

Trivial Pursuit

·GAME 8·

433
- SD Jan Hammer
- SS New York
- FG 3-2-1
- FF *Go with Noakes*
- IP *Fawlty Towers*
- EH In the *TV Times*

434
- SD Steve Race
- SS Mike Baldwin
- FG Griff Rhys Jones
- FF Queen Victoria
- IP *Moses*
- EH The Duchess of York

435
- SD Julia McKenzie
- SS *King's Royal*
- FG *Blankety Blank*
- FF *The Pallisers*
- IP *A Bouquet of Barbed Wire*
- EH *Casualty*

436
- SD Mr.Pickwick
- SS Paul Hogan
- FG *Give Us A Clue*
- FF "She knows ya know"
- IP Jumbo
- EH *Life on Earth*

437
- SD Petula Clark
- SS Seb Coe
- FG The Queen Mother
- FF Kenneth More
- IP Pepper Anderson
- EH A nuclear attack

438
- SD Red
- SS *Brookside*
- FG *Going Straight*
- FF Leonard Rossiter
- IP Huggy Bear
- EH Fawn

439
- SD Ed Sullivan's
- SS *Brookside's*
- FG Bruce Forsyth
- FF Bob Hoskins
- IP Quentin Crisp
- EH Red

440
- SD Valerie Singleton
- SS *Triangle*
- FG A ceramic Dusty Bin
- FF Richard Burton and Elizabeth Taylor
- IP Fawlty Towers
- EH Gerald Seymour

441
- SD Harry H.Corbett and Wilfred Brambell
- SS A close
- FG 3-2-1's
- FF David Carradine
- IP Rhyming slang, Sweeney Todd- Flying Squad
- EH Frank Bough

442
- **SD** Alma Cogan
- **SS** John Forsythe
- **FG** Haltenprice
- **FF** John Thaw
- **IP** He was an art school model
- **EH** Russel Grant

443
- **SD** Cher
- **SS** Two
- **FG** *Soap*
- **FF** Miss Jones
- **IP** *The Streets of San Francisco*
- **EH** Channel 4

444
- **SD** Geoff Love
- **SS** Seb Coe
- **FG** Lionel Blair
- **FF** *Don't Ask Me*
- **IP** *The Duchess of Duke Street*
- **EH** Norman Tebbit

445
- **SD** The George Mitchell Singers
- **SS** Whisky
- **FG** *Blankety Blank*
- **FF** *When the Boat Comes In*
- **IP** *I, Claudius*
- **EH** Dennis Taylor

446
- **SD** Joe Cooper
- **SS** Wine
- **FG** Six
- **FF** Disraeli
- **IP** *A Bouquet of Barbed Wire*
- **EH** Kate Adie

447
- **SD** Ian Wallace
- **SS** Deirdre Barlow had an affair with Mike Baldwin
- **FG** Mel Smith and Pamela Stephenson
- **FF** Connie Booth
- **IP** *Clayhanger*
- **EH** Prince Edward's

448
- **SD** Julian and Andrew Lloyd Webber
- **SS** *Cinzano*
- **FG** Three
- **FF** Dennis Waterman
- **IP** Gladys Emmanuel
- **EH** Prince Philip

449
- **SD** *Eye Level*
- **SS** *Crossroads*
- **FG** *In Loving Memory*
- **FF** John Hurt
- **IP** Robert Powell
- **EH** Princess Michael of Kent

450
- **SD** Kids from Fame's
- **SS** Cecil Colby
- **FG** 1920s
- **FF** John Hurt
- **IP** *Roots*
- **EH** Alan Bennett

451
- **SD** Nina and Frederick
- **SS** *The Bill*
- **FG** *Pig in the Middle*
- **FF** Ronnie Barker
- **IP** George Cowley
- **EH** Wrestling

452
- **SD** Roger Daltrey
- **SS** Portugal
- **FG** *Yes, Minister*
- **FF** Laurence Olivier
- **IP** *Spend, Spend, Spend*
- **EH** Mary Whitehouse

453
- **SD** *Magical Mystery Tour*
- **SS** Their *Renault*
- **FG** Margaret Thatcher
- **FF** *Jesus of Nazareth*
- **IP** *Who Pays the Ferryman*
- **EH** Sky

454
- **SD** Jonathan King
- **SS** *Shredded Wheat*
- **FG** *Play Your Cards Right*
- **FF** Nixon
- **IP** *Hard Times*
- **EH** BSB

455
- **SD** Johnny Logan
- **SS** *Shredded Wheat*
- **FG** *Family Fortunes*
- **FF** Lorne Greene
- **IP** Robin Tripp
- **EH** Sky

456
- **SD** The Monkees
- **SS** Miss Ellie
- **FG** Jim Hacker
- **FF** Olivia Hussey
- **IP** *All Creatures Great and Small*
- **EH** Hillsborough's

457
- **SD** Roland Rat
- **SS** Mavis and Derek
- **FG** Magnus Magnusson
- **FF** Gambit
- **IP** *The Professionals*
- **EH** Sumo wrestling

458
- **SD** *Halfway Up the Stairs*
- **SS** *The Bill*
- **FG** Aunt and nephew
- **FF** Moses
- **IP** *Love for Lydia*
- **EH** *Tumbledown*

459
- **SD** *Benny's Theme*
- **SS** Making love to Alexis
- **FG** Yorkshire
- **FF** Morecambe and Wise
- **IP** Palm Sunday and Easter Sunday
- **EH** His Batman mask

460
- **SD** *Revolver*
- **SS** *Hertz*
- **FG** *Metal Mickey*
- **FF** Stephanie Turner
- **IP** *The Glittering Prizes*
- **EH** The Queen Mother

461
- **SD** New York City
- **SS** The *Oxo* family's
- **FG** Pamela Stephenson
- **FF** Prunella Scales
- **IP** Granville
- **EH** Prince Edward

462
- **SD** *Stars In Their Eyes*
- **SS** *EastEnders*
- **FG** Evens
- **FF** Melvyn Bragg
- **IP** Worzel Gummidge
- **EH** Felix Unger

463
- **SD** *John Kettley is a Weatherman*
- **SS** 'Dirty' Den Watts
- **FG** *Russ Abbot's Madhouse*
- **FF** *The Prime of Miss Jean Brodie*
- **IP** *Laramie*
- **EH** Kermit the Frog

464
- **SD** Tracey Ullman
- **SS** *EastEnders*
- **FG** Arthur Lowe's
- **FF** Leo McKern
- **IP** James Hazell
- **EH** Cheyenne Bodie's

465
- **SD** Bananarama
- **SS** *EastEnders*
- **FG** Cartoonist
- **FF** Victoria Principal
- **IP** *Edward and Mrs.Simpson*
- **EH** Toledo

466
- **SD** Piano
- **SS** Walford
- **FG** *Play Your Cards Right*
- **FF** *All Creatures Great and Small*
- **IP** Horace Rumpole's
- **EH** None

467
- **SD** *I Could Be So Good For You*
- **SS** *Typhoo*
- **FG** Max Bygraves
- **FF** John Forsythe
- **IP** Horace Rumpole
- **EH** *Picture Book*

468
- **SD** David Kid Jensen
- **SS** Victor Kiam
- **FG** Five
- **FF** Gordon Jackson
- **IP** *Will Shakespeare*
- **EH** Birth control

469
- **SD** Andre Previn
- **SS** *Carling Black Label*
- **FG** *Family Fortunes*
- **FF** Nixon
- **IP** Grange Hill's
- **EH** *Flying Squad*

470
- **SD** *The Ugly Duckling*
- **SS** *Powergen*
- **FG** Max Bygraves
- **FF** Martin Shaw
- **IP** Horace Rumpole
- **EH** 1989

471
- **SD** Paul McCartney's
- **SS** *Coca-Cola*
- **FG** Les Dennis
- **FF** James Herriot
- **IP** Horace Rumpole
- **EH** J.R.Ewing

ANSWERS

472
- **D** *My Way*
- **S** Hercules the Bear
- **G** *Citizen Smith*
- **F** Brian Wilde
- **P** *When the Boat Comes In*
- **H** Janitor/caretaker

473
- **SD** Edith Piaf
- **SS** A chimpanzee
- **FG** He only had one arm
- **FF** Alan Alda
- **IP** Columbo
- **EH** Prince Charles and Lady Diana's wedding

474
- **SD** Tom Jones
- **SS** Twiggy
- **FG** Roper
- **FF** Russell Harty
- **IP** *Within These Walls*
- **EH** Malta

475
- **SD** Dave Lee Travis
- **SS** "A cigar called Hamlet"
- **FG** *The Cuckoo Waltz*
- **FF** Blue
- **IP** Grace Brothers
- **EH** A choke chain

476
- **SD** Manchester
- **SS** Benny
- **FG** *Yus My Dear*
- **FF** Oliver Tobias
- **IP** Sid's Cafe
- **EH** TSW

477
- **SD** Kylie Minogue
- **SS** *Goodyear*
- **FG** Bill Maynard
- **FF** *Weekend World*
- **IP** Honor Blackman
- **EH** Barbara Woodhouse

478
- **D** *The Last Resort's*
- **S** Embassy
- **G** Roland Rat
- **F** Wendy Craig
- **P** *Death of a Princess*
- **H** Aviation

479
- **SD** Max Bygraves
- **SS** Pat Butcher
- **FG** Noel Edmonds
- **FF** Robbie Coltrane
- **IP** Labour
- **EH** France (*Floyd on France*)

480
- **SD** Payola
- **SS** Sue Ellen
- **FG** Andy Capp
- **FF** John Thaw
- **IP** Paradise (*Paradise Postponed*)
- **EH** *The Victorian Kitchen Garden*

481
- **SD** *Another Brick in the Wall — Pink Floyd*
- **SS** A nun
- **FG** Frances De La Tour
- **FF** Stratford Johns
- **IP** V.D.
- **EH** Drive a car

482
- **SD** Jimi Hendrix
- **SS** Jack Duckworth
- **FG** Linda Lusardi
- **FF** Derek Jameson
- **IP** *Batman*
- **EH** The Magic Garden

483
- **SD** *Tell Laura I Love Her*
- **SS** Dirty Den Watts
- **FG** Fred Flintstone
- **FF** Richard Burton
- **IP** Australia
- **EH** Ted Lowe

484
- **D** *Vincent*
- **S** Pet rabbits
- **G** Grandma
- **F** Norman Tebbit
- **P** Anthony Blunt
- **H** The *Mary Rose*

485
- **SD** Perry Como
- **SS** Joan Collins
- **FG** Dusty Bin
- **FF** Richard Burton
- **IP** *Fawlty Towers*
- **EH** *In at the Deep End*

486
- **SD** Peter Cook
- **SS** 23
- **FG** Dick Van Dyke
- **FF** Anne Diamond
- **IP** Petrocelli
- **EH** Jilly Cooper

487
- **SD** Showaddywaddy
- **SS** A window at the Queen Vic
- **FG** Motorcycle couriers
- **FF** Tony Hancock
- **IP** The *Starship Enterprise*
- **EH** Goldie Hawn

488
- **SD** Number One
- **SS** Lou Beale
- **FG** Mafia
- **FF** Morecambe and Wise
- **IP** AIDS
- **EH** Dame Edna Everage's

489
- **SD** His ears
- **SS** Ray Langton
- **FG** Rhoda
- **FF** Tim Brooke-Taylor
- **IP** It made people tell the truth
- **EH** Malcolm Muggeridge

490
- **D** Harry Secombe
- **S** Beckindale
- **G** *Do Not Adjust Your Set*
- **F** Nero Wolfe
- **P** *The Sweeney*
- **H** Miss Piggy

491
- **SD** Alexei Sayle
- **SS** Seth's donkey
- **FG** Tommy Cooper
- **FF** Fred Astaire
- **IP** Space Intruder Detector
- **EH** David Jason

492
- **SD** Kate Bush
- **SS** Kevin Webster
- **FG** Bullwinkle
- **FF** Keith Floyd
- **IP** Garage mechanic
- **EH** Yellow and green

493
- **SD** Clannad
- **SS** Alexis Colby's
- **FG** Elaine's
- **FF** Peter O'Toole
- **IP** Jack the Ripper's
- **EH** The rocking chair

494
- **SD** Drums
- **SS** The Fowlers
- **FG** *The Price is Right*
- **FF** Leslie Grantham
- **IP** *Game, Set and Match*
- **EH** *Telstar*

495
- **SD** *Livin' Doll*
- **SS** Bet Lynch
- **FG** *May to December*
- **FF** Donald Campbell
- **IP** Oxford's
- **EH** Winston Churchill

496
- **D** The Partridge Family
- **S** Steven Carrington
- **G** Eric Sykes
- **F** Dame Edna
- **P** A cream cracker
- **H** Ian Fleming

Trivial Pursuit
GAME 9
TV

497
- **SD** Zero
- **SS** *Bird's Eye* frozen peas
- **FG** Terry
- **FF** Robin Hood's
- **IP** *Gulliver In Lilliput*
- **EH** Count Duckula

498
- **SD** Barry McGuigan
- **SS** Smith
- **FG** Colonel Hall
- **FF** Felicity Kendal
- **IP** *Rolls-Royce*
- **EH** Max

499
- **SD** Liverpool's
- **SS** By taking an overdose
- **FG** Rutland Weekend TV
- **FF** Roy Marsden
- **IP** Mrs. Bridges
- **EH** Mailman

500
- **SD** Channel 4
- **SS** Bet Lynch
- **FG** Blue
- **FF** Faye Dunaway
- **IP** A baby
- **EH** Starr and Harrison

501
- **SD** They weren't related
- **SS** Vera Duckworth
- **FG** Freddie Davis
- **FF** David Attenborough
- **IP** Birmingham
- **EH** The Theme from *Cheers*

502
- **SD** Ron Grainger
- **SS** She was too old
- **FG** *Hector's House*
- **FF** David Vine
- **IP** *The Terrahawks*
- **EH** The Manson Murders

503
- **SD** *News At Ten*
- **SS** Pauline Fowler
- **FG** Tessa Wyatt
- **FF** Peter Duncan
- **IP** Amy
- **EH** Robert McCall

504
- **SD** *Halfway Down the Stairs* (by Kermit's nephew Robin)
- **SS** Jane Harris
- **FG** Minister of Administrative Affairs
- **FF** David Bellamy
- **IP** New Mexico
- **EH** Reporter

505
- **SD** The Krankies
- **SS** *The New Globe*
- **FG** Gomez
- **FF** John Oaksey
- **IP** Ali McGraw
- **EH** Clive James

506
- **SD** *Prisoner: Cell Block H*
- **SS** The Crossroads Motel
- **FG** A *Jaguar*
- **FF** Leo McKern
- **IP** Flying
- **EH** Eric the Viking

507
- **SD** *Crockett's Theme*
- **SS** The Malt Shovel
- **FG** "Greetings"
- **FF** *Mission Impossible*
- **IP** Alan B'Stard
- **EH** Lilo Lill

508
- **SD** The World Cup
- **SS** Jack
- **FG** Jasper Carrott
- **FF** Marlon Brando
- **IP** Journalist
- **EH** Nick Owen

509
- **SD** Zero - it was a charity record
- **SS** She was a prostitute
- **FG** *All In Good Faith*
- **FF** Shaw Taylor
- **IP** Lord Brett Sinclair
- **EH** Caterpillar

510
- **SD** *The Grand Ole Opry*
- **SS** J. R. Ewing
- **FG** *The Secret Diary of Adrian Mole, Aged 13³/₄*
- **FF** D. I. Burnside's
- **IP** Welsh
- **EH** *The Far Pavilions*

511
- **SD** *Rodent*
- **SS** *Volvo*
- **FG** Tommy Cooper
- **FF** Sharon Gless
- **IP** The 1950s
- **EH** The Crucible

512
- **SD** Harry (Loadsamoney) Enfield
- **SS** Flinker
- **FG** Kenny Everett
- **FF** Ted Dexter
- **IP** Two
- **EH** Hastings

513
- **SD** David Jacobs'
- **SS** Violet Carson
- **FG** On the ceiling
- **FF** Larry Grayson
- **IP** Chester
- **EH** Cat and dog

514
- **SD** Bruno Brookes
- **SS** Orchids
- **FG** *Singles*
- **FF** Michael Parkinson
- **IP** Poland
- **EH** The *Blue Peter* dog and cat

515
- **SD** Telly Savalas
- **SS** Beckindale
- **FG** *Mastermind*
- **FF** Ian Botham
- **IP** The Korean War
- **EH** Roger Moore

516
- **SD** *Postman Pat*
- **SS** Eddie Yates
- **FG** Bananaman
- **FF** Gary Wilmot
- **IP** *Crime of Passion*
- **EH** The Osmonds'

517
- **SD** Sheena Easton
- **SS** Alf Robert's
- **FG** Antiques
- **FF** *Brass*
- **IP** Glasgow
- **EH** *Connections*

518
- **SD** Dolly Parton
- **SS** Booth
- **FG** Jenny
- **FF** Petra
- **IP** Kojak's
- **EH** *Match of the Day*

519
- **SD** *All Right Now*
- **SS** The Crossroads Motel
- **FG** Sixty
- **FF** Peter Jay
- **IP** Three
- **EH** Alastair Burnet

520
- **SD** *Guys and Dolls*
- **SS** *Dulux* paint
- **FG** Stu Francis's
- **FF** Eric Morley
- **IP** *The Duchess of Duke Street*
- **EH** Ian Lavender

521
- **SD** Gary Davies
- **SS** *Bandit*
- **FG** Emlyn Hughes
- **FF** Brian Walden
- **IP** Adam Adamant
- **EH** *Give Us A Clue*

522
- **SD** Gracie Fields
- **SS** Joe Sugden
- **FG** Bernard Breslaw
- **FF** Gyles Brandreth
- **IP** James
- **EH** Kenya

523
- **SD** Waylon Jennings
- **SS** N.Y.Estates
- **FG** Four
- **FF** Honor Blackman
- **IP** Snooker
- **EH** Jeffrey Archer

524
- **SD** Suzi Quatro
- **SS** *Flamingo Road*
- **FG** The Army Game
- **FF** Cybill Shepherd
- **IP** California
- **EH** Aristotle

525
- **SD** Boxing Day
- **SS** "Princess"
- **FG** Stavros
- **FF** Jonathan Ross's
- **IP** Psoriasis
- **EH** *Blue Peter*

526
- **SD** "One, two, three, four, five, six, seven, eight."
- **SS** Kenneth Williams
- **FG** *New Faces*
- **FF** Keith Michell
- **IP** *The Onedin Line* (Charlotte was the ship)
- **EH** Harold Wilson

527
- **SD** David Hamilton
- **SS** Mr Kipling
- **FG** *Black Adder*
- **FF** Barbara Woodhouse
- **IP** Boss Hogg
- **EH** *Panorama*

528
- **SD** Henry Winkler
- **SS** *Crossroads*
- **FG** Lew Grade
- **FF** Lord Peter Wimsey
- **IP** *Last of the Summer Wine*
- **EH** Strangeways

529
- **SD** Alan Freeman
- **SS** The *Milky Bar Kid*
- **FG** *Duty Free*
- **FF** Laurence Olivier
- **IP** *Reilly, Ace of Spies*
- **EH** Hullabaloo and Custard

530
- **SD** Elton John
- **SS** Sue Ellen
- **FG** *Alas Smith and Jones*
- **FF** William Shatner
- **IP** Vietnam
- **EH** Yellow and black

ANSWERS

531
- **D** Noel Edmonds
- **S** *Bettabuy*
- **G** Barbara Kelly
- **F** John and Jacqueline Kennedy
- **P** *The Irish R.M.*
- **H** Two

532
- **SD** *Mission: Impossible*
- **SS** Sixty
- **FG** *Acorn Antiques*
- **FF** Charlotte Cornwell
- **IP** Tennis
- **EH** *Get Fresh*

533
- **SD** Angela Rippon
- **SS** French and Italian
- **FG** *Girls on Top*
- **FF** Oliver Reed
- **IP** *The Jewel in the Crown*
- **EH** *Kilroy*

534
- **SD** Cliff Richard
- **SS** White
- **FG** Victoria Wood
- **FF** *The Jewel in the Crown*
- **IP** *The Jewel in the Crown*
- **EH** *The Match*

535
- **SD** Tom Jones
- **SS** The corner shop
- **FG** "We're wide awake"
- **FF** Tony Hancock
- **IP** As snuff
- **EH** Yorkshire

536
- **SD** Jack Jones
- **SS** Bert Tilsley
- **FG** Kenny Everett
- **FF** John Thaw
- **IP** Steve McGarrett's
- **EH** She was a folk singer

537
- **D** *Ready Steady Go*
- **S** Noele Gordon
- **G** *Clapperboard*
- **F** Gareth
- **P** *Elephant Boy*
- **H** Horace Rumpole

538
- **SD** The Beatles
- **SS** Joan Collins'
- **FG** Hanna Barbera's
- **FF** Keith Chegwin
- **IP** Three
- **EH** Their jobs

539
- **SD** Sir Thomas Beecham
- **SS** Hawaii
- **FG** Freddie
- **FF** Mary Tyler Moore
- **IP** He grew a beard
- **EH** Pink

540
- **SD** *It's Now or Never*
- **SS** *Dynasty*
- **FG** Evil Edna
- **FF** Hannah Gordon
- **IP** 10%
- **EH** *Round the Horne*

541
- **SD** The First Night of the Proms
- **SS** Sue Ellen
- **FG** Hot spots
- **FF** Vincent Hanna
- **IP** *After Henry*
- **EH** *Down Your Way*

542
- **SD** The BBC Television Orchestra
- **SS** J.R.Ewing
- **FG** Dr.Thorpe
- **FF** Brian Blessed
- **IP** *Family Affair*
- **EH** *Jaguar*

543
- **D** *Tea for Two*
- **S** Wine bar
- **G** *Trumpton's*
- **F** Russell Harty's
- **P** Nelson
- **H** *Here's Lucy*

544
- **SD** Napoleon
- **SS** Dot Cotton
- **FG** Tim Brooke-Taylor
- **FF** Michael Barratt
- **IP** Glasgow
- **EH** In the heel of his shoe

545
- **SD** *Riders on the Storm*
- **SS** Jane Harris
- **FG** *The Fame Game*
- **FF** David Jason
- **IP** Professor Quatermass
- **EH** Peter Ustinov

546
- **SD** Johnny Kidd
- **SS** The Salvation Army
- **FG** "Very interesting — but stupid"
- **FF** Sarah Kennedy
- **IP** Sicily
- **EH** Chris Tarrant

547
- **SD** Duane Eddy
- **SS** Christopher
- **FG** *Laugh-In*
- **FF** Michael Bentine
- **IP** *UFO*
- **EH** James T. Kirk

548
- **SD** Andre Previn's
- **SS** Number 6
- **FG** David Copperfield
- **FF** Peter Bowles
- **IP** Spiderman's (Peter Parker)
- **EH** Claire Rayner

549
- **D** Billy Cotton
- **S** Katherine Wentworth
- **G** *The Brains Trust*
- **F** John Le Mesurier
- **P** *The Time Tunnel*
- **H** Peter Sallis

550
- **SD** Roy Castle
- **SS** Rock Hudson
- **FG** Morecambe and Wise
- **FF** Shirley MacLaine
- **IP** *Star Trek*
- **EH** William Shatner

551
- **SD** Catwoman
- **SS** Daphne
- **FG** A showcase
- **FF** Buddy Ebsen
- **IP** A virus
- **EH** Donald Sinden

552
- **SD** They were all joint winners in 1969
- **SS** Brigit Forsyth
- **FG** Moggie
- **FF** Richard Chamberlain
- **IP** Photographer
- **EH** Bill Pertwee

553
- **SD** Richard Stilgoe
- **SS** *Howard's Way*
- **FG** A dog
- **FF** David Bellamy
- **IP** Tim
- **EH** Michael Parkinson

554
- **SD** *Dragnet*
- **SS** Rosalyn Landor
- **FG** Roland Rat
- **FF** Sandra Dickinson
- **IP** Spiderman
- **EH** Ron Pickering

555
- **D** Charlie Drake
- **S** She was his sister
- **G** Trapper
- **F** Robert Robinson
- **P** *Pacific Princess*
- **H** William Rushton

556
- **SD** Millie
- **SS** *Howard's Way*
- **FG** Jonathan Ross
- **FF** John Ritter
- **IP** He was the solicitor for her divorce
- **EH** Prunella Scales

557
- **SD** "And take it away"
- **SS** Carmen Silvera
- **FG** Nelson Mandela House
- **FF** School teacher
- **IP** The *Orient Express*
- **EH** Pamela Stephenson

558
- **SD** *Back Home*
- **SS** Mrs. Mangel
- **FG** Bernie Winters
- **FF** James Mason
- **IP** *Hitchhiker's Guide to the Galaxy*
- **EH** Donald Sinden

559
- **SD** Bert Weedon
- **SS** *Falcon Crest*
- **FG** Blonde
- **FF** Jimmy Greaves
- **IP** Bowler hat
- **EH** Eric Sykes

560
- **SD** *The Old Grey Whistle Test*
- **SS** Norwich
- **FG** Walter
- **FF** *Callan*
- **IP** T-negative
- **EH** Peter Ustinov

ANSWERS

Trivial Pursuit

·GAME 10·

TV

561
SD Tony Blackburn
SS *Murray Mints*
FG Liza Goddard
FF Robert Shaw
IP London
EH Phil Silvers

562
SD *We All Stand*
    Together
SS Mike Baldwin
FG *Gilligan's Isle's*
FF Joss Ackland
IP Three
EH Two

563
SD Alma Cogan
SS *Brookside*
FG Pink
FF Patrick Campbell
IP *The Ruth Rendell*
    Mysteries
EH *Star Wars*

564
SD The Royal
    Philharmonic
    Orchestra
SS Bunny Girl
FG Phil Cool
FF Richard Nixon
IP "In the village"
EH The Monkees

565
SD *Crown Paint*
SS His drums
FG *The Daily Slate*
FF Robert Dougall
IP 23rd
EH Factory foreman

566
SD Madonna
SS Mike Baldwin
FG *Huckleberry Hound's*
FF Spiderman's
IP Chicken George
EH Foster parents

567
SD The Playboys
SS Driving whilst
    under the influence
FG Top Cat's
FF Brian Blessed
IP *Miami Vice*
EH George VI's

568
SD Marti Webb's
SS The Graffiti Club
FG Eamonn Andrews
FF David Icke
IP Texas
EH 25th December

569
SD *Owen M.D.*
SS Ken Barlow
FG Emu hasn't got a
    voice
FF Ronnie Barker
IP Makepeace
EH Buckingham
    Palace's

570
SD *Alice's*
SS The Weatherfield
    Recorder
FG The Phantom Flan
    Flinger
FF *Hale and Pace*
IP Fantasy Island's
EH 10 Downing Street

571
SD Black
SS A birthmark
    removed
FG Rosco P. Coltrane
FF Denis Norden
IP Richard Kimble
EH *Yes, Minister*

572
SD David Essex
SS *Crossroads*
FG Rodney Bewes
FF *Just a Nimmo*
IP *Shogun*
EH *Grandstand*

573
SD *Give Me Sunshine*
SS For drinking and
    driving
FG *Steptoe and Son*
FF Ed Murrow
IP The St.Gregory
EH *Starsky and Hutch*

574
SD Perry Como's
SS Lou Beale
FG Nicky Campbell
FF Weatherman
IP Mexican
EH Rio de Janeiro

575
SD Israel
SS Sinbad
FG Hinge and Brackett
FF Omar Sharif
IP *Public Eye*
EH Juliet Bravo

576
SD Hot Gossip
SS San Francisco
FG Bruno Brookes
FF Ian Lavender
IP *How Green Was My*
    Valley
EH Green

577
SD A rude Valentine
    card
SS *Brookside's*
FG The Salvation
    Army
FF Nehru
IP "Mind how you go
EH Anderson

578
SD Gary Numan
SS Andrew
FG *Fawlty Towers*
FF William Shatner
IP Wormwood Scrubs
EH The Bermuda
    Triangle

579
SD Arthur Daley
SS Gail Tilsley (Platt)
FG *Les Girls*
FF A leg
IP *Prisoner:*
    Cell Block H
EH *Space 1999's*

580
SD *Games Without*
    Frontiers (Jeux Sans
    Frontieres)
SS *Crossroads Motel*
FG *Blankety Blank*
FF *The Human Jungle*
IP The Ponderosa
EH McArdle

581
SD The Fraggles
SS Brian Tilsley
FG *The Generation Game*
FF David Jacobs
IP Two legs, one arm
    and one eye
EH Hugh Lloyd

582
SD *Take My Breath Away*
SS Terry Duckworth
FG 100
FF Ned Sherrin
IP They couldn't do
    anything if
    someone hadn't
    done it before
EH Charlton

583
SD *Star Trekkin'*
SS Tracy Barlow
FG Mr.Mott
FF Lenny Henry
IP *Gunsmoke's*
EH Trigger

584
SD *T.V.*
SS Brian Tilsley
FG Perry Mason
FF Esther Rantzen
IP A tennis star and
    his coach
EH Brothers

585
SD *The Simpsons*
SS To claim his
    inheritance after his
    father's death
FG Larry Grayson
FF Susannah York
IP Kookie
EH Scally

586
SD *Worzel's Song*
SS Ross
FG *Bullseye*
FF James Garner
IP Coal miner
EH Roy Kinnear

587
SD Dance band music
SS *EastEnders'*
FG Corky
FF James Garner
IP 2000
EH *Hammer*

588
SD *Come Dancing*
SS *Brookside's*
FG A bloodhound
FF Nyree Dawn Porter
IP *Grange Hill*
EH The RAF

589
SD Neil Sedaka
SS J.R. Ewing
FG *The Liver Birds*
FF Edward Asner
IP Cab driver
EH A computer

ANSWERS

590
- SD Dean Martin
- SS A prostitute
- FG The President's
- FF Sue Lawley
- IP McKay
- EH *Private Benjamin*

591
- SD *The Stylistics*
- SS Hawaii
- FG Basil Brush
- FF Magnus Magnusson
- IP Daisy
- EH The dog section

592
- SD *Because of You* (the theme from *Brush Strokes*)
- SS The Viaduct Sporting Club
- FG Terry
- FF Richard Dimbleby
- IP Harry
- EH Greendale

593
- SD Anita Dobson
- SS The Poison Dwarf
- FG Librarian
- FF P.C. 49
- IP *Shogun*
- EH John Alderton and Pauline Collins

594
- SD *Profoundly In Love With Pandora*
- SS The wages
- FG Four
- FF Nyree Dawn Porter
- IP *Danger Man*
- EH *Winds of War*

595
- SD *Roll Over Beethoven*
- SS Fred Gee
- FG Ray Allan
- FF Sue Lawley
- IP Alison
- EH Great Uncle Bulgaria

596
- SD *Step Inside Love*
- SS Mavis Riley
- FG *Cross Wits*
- FF Carroll Levis
- IP Stavros
- EH *The Snoop Sisters*

597
- SD M.C. Parker
- SS Stan and Hilda Ogden's
- FG *A Kind of Living*
- FF Paul Eddington
- IP *Space 1999*
- EH Jonathan Ross

598
- SD Kenny Everett
- SS 'Dirty' Den Watts
- FG Sergeant Bilko
- FF Magnus Magnusson
- IP Fifty-four
- EH A camera

599
- SD *Help!*
- SS Alf's Store
- FG His ears
- FF Amanda Barrie
- IP Ted Baxter
- EH Nuns

600
- SD Priscilla White
- SS *The Waltons*
- FG Jim Davidson
- FF Brian Hooper
- IP Sam McCloud
- EH *Bewitched*

601
- SD *Money for Nothing*
- SS Alan Turner
- FG Paula Wilcox
- FF Gordon Honeycombe
- IP Buck Rogers
- EH *Dr. Who*

602
- SD *The Tube*
- SS Trans-Atlantic
- FG Dame Edna Everage
- FF O-P-R-A-H
- IP Harvey
- EH *Survival*

603
- SD Chas and Dave
- SS Florrie Lindley
- FG Madge Allsop
- FF Rupert Murdoch
- IP Zorro
- EH Storm Field

604
- SD Friday
- SS *Falcon Crest*
- FG Roseanne
- FF Tom Bosley
- IP Ricardo Tubbs
- EH Electronic News Gathering

605
- SD *Move Over Darling*
- SS She's his half sister
- FG *Finders Keepers*
- FF The Lone Ranger and Tonto
- IP Seventeen
- EH Channel 4

606
- SD Tom and Jerry
- SS *EastEnders*
- FG *Big Break*
- FF Superman
- IP A plane crash
- EH *News at Ten*

607
- SD *Sing Little Birdie*
- SS Kathy Staff
- FG Sisters
- FF Kathy Taylor
- IP *Sea Hunt's*
- EH The *Queen Mary's*

608
- SD David Cassidy
- SS J.R. Ewing
- FG *Takeover Bid's*
- FF Peter Woods
- IP Mike Hammer
- EH Fred Perry

609
- SD Janice Long
- SS Nottingham
- FG *That's Life*
- FF Alan Titchmarsh
- IP *Starsky and Hutch*
- EH George Howard

610
- SD *Are You Sure* (The Alisons)
- SS Sabella
- FG *Spitting Back*
- FF Suzanne Dando
- IP Paladin
- EH C and F

611
- SD *Rock Around The Clock*
- SS Tennis coach
- FG *The Two of Us*
- FF Muriel Gray
- IP *Rawhide*
- EH 1920s

612
- SD *Relax* — Frankie Goes to Hollywood
- SS Helen Daniels
- FG Les Dennis
- FF Richie Benaud
- IP Fonzarelli
- EH Four

613
- SD One
- SS Gary Ewing
- FG The DHSS
- FF Arthur Fowler
- IP Human
- EH Lorimar

614
- SD The Rolling Stones'
- SS Priscilla Presley
- FG Aveline
- FF Toyah Wilcox
- IP *Edge of Darkness*
- EH 9.00pm

615
- SD Neil Young
- SS Joan Collins
- FG *The Golden Girls*
- FF Jason Connery
- IP *The Far Pavilions*
- EH Def II

616
- SD Lynsey de Paul
- SS The Duckworths
- FG The Grace Brothers
- FF Michael Palin
- IP United Star Ship
- EH *The Jewel in the Crown*

· O R D E R   F O R M ·

HOW TO ORDER YOUR BOXTREE QUIZ BOOKS

TV 242 8	15–1 QUIZ	£2.99
TV 135 9	15–1 SUPERCHALLENGE QUIZ	£2.99
TV 695 4	$64,000 QUESTION BOOK	£2.99
TV 298 3	CATCHPHRASE QUIZ	£2.99
291 6	CORONATION STREET QUIZ	£2.99
TV 072 7	COUNTDOWN PUZZLE BOOK	£2.99
TV 694 6	CROSS WITS QUIZ	£2.99
TV 708 X	DICKIE DAVIS' SPORTS QUIZ	£2.99
TV 266 5	KRYPTON FACTOR QUIZ	£2.99
729 2	MOVIE SUPERCHALLENGE QUIZ	£2.99
TV 735 7	STRIKE IT LUCKY QUIZ	£2.99
028 X	SUPERSOAPS QUIZ NO.1	£2.99
279 9	SUPERSOAPS QUIZ NO.2	£2.99
604 0	SUPERSOAPS QUIZ NO.3	£2.99
261 4	TV'S GREATEST HITS QUIZ	£2.99
767 5	WILLIAM HILL HORSE RACING QUIZ	£2.99
TV 588 5	TRIVIAL PURSUIT – GENUS™ EDITION	£7.99

All these books are available at your local bookshop or newsagent, or can be ordered direct from the publisher. Just tick the titles you want and fill in the form below.

Prices and availability subject to change without notice.

Boxtree Cash Sales, P.O. Box 11, Falmouth, Cornwall TR10 9EN

Please send cheque or postal order for the value of the book, and add the following for postage and packing:

U.K. including B.F.P.O. – £1.00 for one book, plus 50p for the second book, and 30p for each additional book ordered up to a £3.00 maximum.

Overseas including Eire – £2.00 for the first book, plus £1.00 for the second book, and 50p for each additional book ordered

OR please debit this amount from my Access/Visa Card (delete as appropriate).

Card No. _____

Amount £ _____ Exp. Date _____

Signed _____

Name _____

Address _____

_____

_____